Performing Hybridity

Performing Hybridity

May Joseph
Jennifer Natalya Fink
Editors

University of Minnesota Press
Minneapolis • London

Published by the University of Minnesota Press
111 Third Avenue South, Suite 290
Minneapolis, MN 55401-2520
http://www.upress.umn.edu

Printed in the United States of America on acid-free paper

Library of Congress Cataloging-in-Publication Data

Performing hybridity / May Joseph and Jennifer Natalya Fink, editors.
    p.   cm.
    ISBN 0-8166-3010-0 (hc : alk. paper). — ISBN 0-8166-3011-9 (pbk. : alk. paper)
    1. Hybridity (Social sciences) and the arts.   I. Joseph, May.
II. Fink, Jennifer.
NX180.H93P47   1999
700'.1'03—dc21   98-43817

The University of Minnesota is an equal-opportunity educator and employer.

10 09 08 07 06 05 04 03 02 01 00 99   10 9 8 7 6 5 4 3 2 1

Contents

Acknowledgments

This project began as a special issue of *Women & Performance: A Journal of Feminist Theory* titled "New Hybrid Identities: Performing Race/Gender/Nation/Sexuality." The work of the Board of *Women & Performance* was essential to this project. We thank all involved for their help and support.

The Department of Performance Studies at New York University, under the direction of the former chair, Peggy Phelan, and the current chair, Diana Taylor, also generously provided intellectual and material help in the completion of this book.

Our editor at the University of Minnesota Press, Micah Kleit, was instrumental in the conception, editing, and realization of our book. We are indebted to him for his astute editorial suggestions, insightful comments, and continual support. His assistant, Jennifer Moore, also provided significant good-humored encouragement and technical advice.

We especially thank our contributors for the time and effort they put into this project. Their generous contributions made this book a more complete one.

Finally, we would like to thank Jon Keith Brunelle and Geoffrey Rogers for their love and support.

Introduction:
New Hybrid Identities and Performance

May Joseph

Hybridity, Sovereignty, and Pan-Identities

The discourse of hybridity has numerous international points of emergence. It emerges in the twentieth century alongside autochthonous nationalisms in the struggles for territorial and cultural sovereignty across Francophone, Lusophone, Iberian, Dutch, German, and Anglophone colonies. Although the foundational discourses of hybridity lie in the anthropological and biological discourses of conquest and colonization, the modern move to deploy hybridity as a disruptive democratic discourse of cultural citizenship is a distinctly anti-imperial and antiauthoritarian development. The antecedents for this discourse lie in an intricate negotiation between colonial abjectness and modernity's new historic subjects, who are both colonizer and colonized. Always framing the struggles for democratic rights and sovereignty in the twentieth century is the language of internationalism, shaping global colonial policies as well as international solidarity movements.

The internationalism embedded in contemporary discourses of hybridity and its mobilizing political energy open up new ways of perceiving cultural and political practices. Through historical excavation, cultural reclamation, and aesthetic appropriations across different national contexts, new forms of internationalism are articulated. However, these discourses are embedded in older tensions between nationalist sentiments and articulations of world citizenship that have operated globally through one of the earliest ideologies of internationalism, that of empire. Other influential international discourses that underlie twentieth-century critiques of autochthonous identities are the mercantilist, commercial, and maritime narratives of travel and colonization through which particularistic identities and universalist philosophies of belonging have struggled to realize modern ideas of the citizen.

The idea that strategies of democratic hybrid citizenship were already shaping in relation to international power struggles, local hegemonies, and transnational allegiances over the last five hundred years is central to the notion of "new hybrid identities" as it is developed in our collection. Such an understanding of "new hybrid identities" locates this project in a diachronic conversation with previous junctures between internationalist movements and particularisms.[1] By "new hybrid identities," we mean a nexus of affiliations that self-consciously perform contemporary acts of citizenship through which modern social and political alliances are formed. It is the intersection between transforming global capital and postcolonial conditions.

"New hybrid identities" stress the contemporaneity of these affiliations as *political* gestures, as opposed to the historical conditions of plurality, travel, miscegenation, nomadism, displacement, conquest, and exile that have informed ideas of hybridization globally. Hybridity in these writings is an expression of everyday life. It continuously alters what we mean by both the national and the international. Hybridity draws on local and transnational identifications, including primordial as well as postidentitarian conceptions of the nation. It generates historically new mediations. They are "new" because they are located outside the official practices of citizenship, situated in the interstices of numerous legal and cultural borders, while being increasingly self-conscious of an international political economy of subjectivities. The proliferations of syncretic cultures has exploded the boundaries of aesthetic hybridity to the terrain of lived and performed spaces of cultural citizenship.

The history of Pan-Africanism over the last five hundred years in the struggle for international Black citizenship and self-determination provides one compelling example of the tensions at work in new hybrid identities. Pan-Africanism is a richly evocative site of contestation between contemporary citizenship, emerging pan-identities, and the claims for sovereignties. In the case of the development of a Pan-African identity in the twentieth century, its manifestation as an international project for Black self-determination, spearheaded by an "Africa for Africans" committed to addressing questions of Black modernity in its full range of experiences, marked a new conception of modern citizenship. It produced an idea of modern citizenship that was simultaneously national and international, bound by broader historical movements, and interlocked in its future transnational commitments toward progressive emancipation.[2]

The emergence, impact, and consolidation of Pan-Africanism through colonial, postindependence, and postnational phases are important instances of the intricacies of transhistorical and intralocal commitments. Pan-Africanism forged a particular transnational conception of a pan-identity that was distinctly shaped through its international histories of subjugation and interconnected struggles for modern forms of statehood. The particular transformation of Pan-Africanism from local mobilizations within various empires from the sixteenth century onward, to an international idea circulated across colonial and emerging national contexts, encapsulates the surreptitious and explicit international economies through which social movements and subjectivities have been constituted in the articulation of modern citizenship.

Continental developments of Pan-Africanism defied the boundaries of both the French and British states by necessity. The efflorescence of metropolitan Black cultural movements alongside repressed indigenous movements during the expansion of Europe's own cultural boundaries produced a complex transoceanic exchange in bodies and ideas. Such a three-sided discursive framework provided the ground from which to depart, in a search for a new kind of aesthetics that could make vocal the emerging sphere of transforming diasporic migrant culture. Struggles to historicize postcolonial cultural expressions through the ideologies of Eurocentrism, whose tentacles enveloped the globalizing machines of knowledge, formed the crux of these hybrid identities.

Anglophone Caribbean writings from the 1920s to the 1950s expressly address the complexities of new, postcolonial identities across the national configurations of Jamaica, Barbados, and Trinidad and Tobago. As Gordon K. Lewis points out:

> Cultural imperialism . . . by seeking through education to convert the West Indian person into a coloured English gentleman produced the contemporary spectacle of the West Indian as a culturally disinherited individual, an Anglicized colonial set within an Afro-Asian cultural environment, caught between the dying Anglophile world and the new world of Caribbean democracy and nationalism seeking to be born.[3]

Lewis foregrounds the emergence of national societies from under the yoke of colonial rule in Jamaica, Barbados, Guyana, British Honduras, and Trinidad and Tobago. But, he cautions, the struggles that followed the emergence of territorial sovereignty in the forging of participatory democracy often metamorphosed into a struggle between peasant individualism, international finance capital, and the new anxieties of establishing national culture. Lewis remarks:

Independence—which, unlike Emancipation, is merely a redefinition of the legal status of the society not necessarily bringing in its wake a profound social metamorphosis such as characterized post-Emancipation society—inherits those problems created by the slave and Creole societies. It is true to say, in essence, that the central reality of independence is the need to convert the patterns set by those earlier social systems into an independent national society run primarily in the interests of its independent citizens.[4]

In the interests of these new emerging citizens in nascent postcolonial states, pan-identities such as West Indian, Anglophone, and Afro-Asian generated a political "third space." Pan-identities offered a space between legal categories of national identities and the informal as well as cumulative affiliations across national borders: the space of new hybrid identities. Lewis's analysis of the emergence of West Indian nations presents the central contradiction that is embodied by the concept of new hybrid identities. It is the reiteration of the conceptions of the state and nationness, while simultaneously catalyzing movements within the state against the consolidation of a singular ethnicity as a national culture.

Consequently, cultural pan-identities such as Afro-Arab, Asian/Pacific/American, Afro-Asian, and South Asian gesture to larger organizing rubrics that exceed the geographic boundaries of any one state in the interests of a broader international alliance. Such rubrics have made it possible to conceptualize a postnational realm of identifications, of which some of the more recent influential manifestations were the 1956 Bandung Conference, the Pan-African conferences, and the nonaligned movement. These strategically deployed hybrid political identities have simultaneously operated from within national and international pressures to galvanize coalitions across geographic and political divides. Such identities have always drawn on notions of world citizenship to foreground the claims of peripheral states to universalist causes for sovereignty, autonomy, development, and modernization.

Many of these political identities were expressions of anticolonial and anti-imperial strategies against a reductive humanization in response to the empire's dehumanizing of the colonized subject, whether of African or of Asian descent. Although the particular moves toward building national consciousness differed across colonial histories, the implicit understanding of the ordering of power aligned peoples across empires in international expressions of solidarity against foreign yoke. These expressions of solidarity and the fomenting of insurgencies against the colonial presence drew on colonial notions of state and nation in order to conceptualize sovereignty. Their historical particularities distinguished these twentieth-century movements from those of eighteenth-century European nationalisms. In response to the inter-nationalist logics of the civilizing mission to Christianize and Islamicize the globe, twentieth-century decolonizing movements proliferated through secu-lar demands for individual rights and territorial autonomy. These nationalist movements and sovereign states contain local histories of tensions between national identities, multicultural democracy, and new hybrid identities that move beyond ethnic and national lines.

In the post–civil rights era, hybridity emerges as a democratic expres-sion of multiple affiliations of cultural citizenship in the United States. It announces its visibility through the self-conscious, free, and participatory performance of personhood in the formal and informal spheres of the state. Drawing on the histories of struggles for cultural sovereignty across Third World locations, the claims of hybridity in the United States persist as a per-formative space of enunciatory social practices with disruptive political con-sequences. The various social movements mobilized around race and state, such as the Chicano/a cultural movements, Asian-American claims for politi-cal representation, Native American battles for territorial and cultural recla-mations, and African-American demands for equal rights, have often been framed in the language of nationalism, a strategic reduction of hybridity in the interests of sovereignty. Framing many of these battles against disenfran-chisement in the international rhetoric of cultural rights as human rights, minority communities in the United States have contested the particularist interests of dominant power (read as white privilege) to demand a democra-tic and heterogeneous polity.[5]

Cultural sovereignty, the exercise of particularistic interests in keeping with the larger public good, has been a particularly powerful enunciatory site for the performance of hybridity. Deployed by minority social move-ments, it has drawn on the contradicting tensions between hybrid cultural pasts, national belonging, and international citizenship. Minority perfor-mance artists such as Guillermo Gómez-Peña, the Colorado Sisters, Patricia Hoffbauer, George Emilio Sanchez, Roger Guenvere Smith, Shishir Kurup, Jessica Hagedorn, Anna Deveare Smith, Page Leong, and Urban Bush Women are just a few of the many who have addressed concerns of cultural sover-eignty in the United States. Los-Angeles-based Asian-American performer Dan Kwong's autobiographical one-person shows, performed at Highways in Los Angeles during the early 1990s, complicate the elaborate connections between Asian-American subject formation and the psychic realms of identi-fication with an ancestral past located in China. They are illustrative exam-ples of this contradictory struggle.

Although cultural sovereignty is expressed as a monolithic construct for particularism, it produces itself as a pan-identity between local ethnicities and internationally articulated political identities such as feminists, Third World women, minorities, refugees, migrants, illegal workers, immigrants, and exiles. Guillermo Gómez-Peña's hybridized border performances are notable for the range of links they make to some of these identities.[6] Embedded within these tensions between cultural sovereignty and hybridity are the constantly changing formulations of citizenship materially inhabited by New World subjects. They are caught between legal categories, historical legacies, the changing political landscape, and the increasingly diminishing conception of the international in the face of the elusive but seductive language of globalization.

Performing Hybridities: Writing History

"This journey is a narrative of loss," writes Meena Alexander. "History comes / without cost . . . / Our poverty is in the nerves, / the stubble of migrancy." Alexander's words echo the dramatic implosion of possible political internationals with the cataclysmic collapse of the East European Communist states in 1989 and the celebratory announcements of the globalization of capitalism. "I saw the sari that bound her / dropping her free, feet cut at the ankles, / severed from her thighs, slicked with red earth." Alexander offers her poem as one possible response to the question of what possible conceptions of a political international can be raised out of the hybrid identities spawned by the ashes of history. How do these new identities, "feet cut at the ankles," affect the political climate of global citizenship?

Antecedents to this question lie ensconced in former twentieth-century internationalisms such as philosophies of socialism and international law, as well as in mercantilist and nationalist sentiments of blood and roots. In the wake of a narrowed sense of contemporary political possibilities in the United States symbolized by Alexander's "feet cut at the ankles," fueled by the gloating and uncritical relief that socialism failed because state socialisms proved untenable as ideologies of governance, the question of a changing international that takes into account the implications of global capital and consumption impacts contemporary concerns of hybridity within local citizenship, particularly for Third World states.

Twentieth-century notions of hybridity and creolization cross colonial and national boundaries. The resurgence of narrow nationalisms, minor ethnic regionalisms, and new postnational identifications, however, has foregrounded the fragility and pertinence of hybridity as a critique of autochthonous identities. Although the prominence of hybridity as a literary, aesthetic, and identitarian project has restrained its impact in contaminating other discourses of global interventionism, the implications of a politics of hybridity far exceed the boundaries of the aesthetic. Its history lies embedded in an older Enlightenment discourse of nationalism and internationalism.

The focus on cultural performance found in this collection locates it in the arena of cultural internationalism, an area of inquiry that emerged out of an engagement with and across cultures. Cultural internationalism bears the baggage of its nineteenth-century assumptions, with origins in nineteenth-century natural law, anthropology, and colonial history.[7] Its impact in the humanities and the arts as cultural critique reproduces its colonial categories, much in the way that earlier ethnographic and folkloristic accounts of Third World cultures as bastions of tradition and primordial identities assume a neatly divided world with a unilinear trajectory of travel of ethnographer to the ethnographed, of First World anthropologist to Third World native.

Cultural theory inherits the paradigms and conflicts of its concerns from a cultural internationalism shaped by the Cold War. A product of an earlier cultural internationalism, it has had to engage with its ethnologically inscribed interest in Third World sites as cultural arbiters of both tradition and modernity. Although there are many genealogies that could illustrate this point, the contribution of early British social anthropology such as Max Gluckman's work in the 1940s on workers in Zululand, Godfrey Wilson's work on labor migration in central Africa, Victor Turner's notion of social drama developed in his study of the Ndembu of central Africa in 1957, Clyde Mitchell's 1956 study of the Kalela dance, and Abner Cohen's concept of microhistory among Hausa migrants of Yoruba towns developed in the late 1960s all suggest the inextricable connections between British colonial legacies and the production of knowledges underlying theories of cultural performance.

The postcolonial period saw the rising influence of American conceptions of cultural performance that drew on theater, dance, ritual, folklore, religious and linguistic practices, foregrounded by the work of Dell Hymes, Richard Bauman, James Fernandez, and Richard Schechner, among others. These theorists pursued the idea of performance as a liminal, negotiating arena of social efficaciousness.[8] In many of these pioneering ethnographic studies, conventional categories of tradition are destabilized through readings of modern transformative practices, interrogating the transitioning places of cultural exchange in non-Western societies. These important contributions explored the tensions between methodology and site, theoretical models and context, shaping changing notions of tradition and modernity within cultural paradigms.

Influenced by these different approaches and insights, while drawing on other historical trajectories, postcolonial scholarship has stressed the growing relevance of hybridization in understanding contemporary cultural practices. It offers an interdependent critique of the influence of international forces in the production of knowledge about cultures in the global periphery. Drawing on anthropology, ethnology, folklore, sociology, cultural studies, and critical theory since the 1960s, it has opened up avenues of interrogation between lived practice, embodiment, and performance, while moving between the systemic logic of a three-world system.

Ethnographic, neocolonial, and dependency relationships between Western and non-Western states have been central to postcolonial cultural critiques. The move to complicate the relations of center and periphery, by renegotiating theoretical categories of First World/Third World and ethnographer/native, has foregrounded questions of modernity, and forced a conception of the transnational relations of power on concerns of cultural performance.

Consequently, many postcolonial scholars propose a complex transnational network of relations that goes beyond a three-world system theory. The focus on transnational and intralocal, rather than intercultural, is a crucial shift in this intellectual formation. Situating new emergent ethnicities in relation to global migrations of people has generated a more nuanced "third space" of political change. The work of Arjun Appadurai on cultural commodities, Samir Amin's critique of delinking, Rathna Kapur and Brenda Cossman's work on gender and women's rights in India, Néstor García Canclini's study of Latin American modernity, and Mahmood Mamdani's study of democratization in East and South Africa are cases in point. By foregrounding modernization and development, the impact and growing complexity of the resultant new secular identities that are spawned by the globalizing tendencies through which they are mediated can now be read as new hybrid identities.[9]

By foregrounding the idea of hybrid identities in the context of shifting global tendencies, this collection draws attention to the invisible pressures within internationalism that have historically inflected the kind of research done around cultural performance. It disrupts easy notions of identities in formation. In juxtaposing these writers to the kinds of knowledges they are producing about hybrid political identities in both the North and the South, these essays complicate the three-world approach. They blur the obvious boundaries of the state and instead present a more interdependent network of hybrid identifications in a transnational context.[10]

Aesthetic Hybridities, Performed Syncretisms

In response to the neocolonial relations of knowledge, emerging postcolonial states generated new conceptions of the citizen, language, and ways of being in the world. Issues of *métissage* and *creolite* in the Francophone Caribbean; ideas of anthropophagy and the carnivalesque in Brazilian discourses about modernization during the 1920s and 1930s; phenomenologies of Negritude and Negrissimo influenced by the writings of Aimé Césaire, Frantz Fanon, Leon Damas, Birago Diop, and Léopold Sédar Senghor; and notions of indigenous national consciousness being promoted by Kwame Nkrumah, Jomo Kenyatta, and Sékou Touré, among others, contaminated other nascent ideologies of nationness with long-term repercussions in the struggles for heterogeneous citizenship within the fictionalized, sovereign, monolithic postcolonial state.

Since the 1930s, various conceptual frameworks for galvanizing ideas of plurality and multicultural citizenship against monocultural national identities within the state have been pursued, by positing notions of a "third" space politically, geographically, and historically. The idea of a third space in aesthetics, political affiliations, and the international political economy keeps interrupting the seamless narrative of oppressed and oppressor, colonized and colonizer, First World and Third World, dominant and subaltern. Such absolutist, binary terms are problematized by the notion of a third space.[11]

From the debates on Third Cinema and Third World aesthetics that inspired the Third Cinema conference in Edinburgh in 1986; to the idea of Third Theater explored by Eugenio Barba; to Augusto Boal's theater of the oppressed and various street-theater forms; to Paulo Freire's pedagogy of the oppressed; to Rustum Bharucha's experiments in a third space for postcolonial theater; to Vijay Tendulkar's protest theater and Jerzy Grotowski's poor theater to Guillermo Gómez-Peña's Border Brujo and the Border Arts Workshop's border activism; to Ngugi Wa' Thiongo's notion of "orature" and Penina Mhando's conception of theater for development, cultural practitioners have struggled to destabilize economic reductionism in the interests of new cultural hybridities.[12]

In many postcolonial states, alternative art movements have privileged a retro-nationalist move toward indigenization in the search for native roots in disrupted postcolonial cultural forms. By merging vernacular languages, folk forms, European avant-garde forms, and secular concerns, these postcolonial playwrights, directors, visual artists, and performers offer a variety of interpretations of contemporary aesthetics across national borders. For instance, the work of Utpal Dutt in India, through his incorporation of *Jatra* in Calcutta, and Girish Karnad's blending of Sanskrit folk mythologies into Indian theater in English in Bangalore share various hybridizing influences with Jatinder Varma's experimental work with the Tara Arts Group in London. All three directors employ Indian mythology, use English as well as Indian languages as vehicles of performance, and explore Indian dramatic forms for presenting contemporary life in London, Calcutta, or Bangalore.[13]

Other concepts of hybridity such as Oswald de Andrade's "anthropophagy," Homi Bhabha's "mimicry," Kobena Mercer's "creolizing practices," Stuart Hall's "new ethnicities," Paul Gilroy's "syncretism," Manthia Diawara's "Afro-kitsch," Edouard Glissant's "transversality," Marlene Nourbese Philip's "babu english," Roberto Fernández Retamar's "Caliban," Antonio Benítez-Rojo's "super-syncretism," Assia Djebar's "nomad memory," Arjun Appadurai's "global ethnoscapes," Lisa Lowe's "heterogeneity," José Martí's "Our America," Nicolás Guillén's and Françoise Lionnet's uses of *métissage,* Néstor García Canclini's "cultural reconversion," Celeste Olalquiaga's "Tupinicopolitan aesthetic," Robert Stam's "carnivalesque," and Michelle Cliff's "ruination," to name a few, have specifically addressed issues of contemporary hybridities in relation to state sovereignty and transnational movements of peoples.[14]

Many of these conceptual hybridities move beyond the idea of the nation to reveal the interdependent ways in which transnational circulations of commodities operate. As a result of the increasingly mediated globalizing economy, such conceptions of hybridity destabilize authoritarian forms of control, while interrogating the parameters and limits of the democratic state. Instead of working within the narrow boundaries of the state, these theories of hybridity pose a challenge to the limits of its sovereignty. By proposing alternative economies of aesthetic and political viability through ideas of a "third" space, these theorists of hybridity offer ways out of narrowly defined ideas of artistic possibility. Instead, they pose broader syncretic identities, such as "international feminist" (Assia Djebar, Michelle Cliff, Nourbese Philip), "Third World," "Asian-American" (Lisa Lowe), "postcolonial," and "socialist" as a means of creating alternative international communities through which to create social, aesthetic, and political communities.

Hybrid Knowledges, Secular Assumptions, and the Liberal Democratic Model

Globalizing tendencies in the language of cultural internationalism, and its uneasy relationship to the international political economy, are crucial in understanding their interdependent histories of disciplinary production.

The development of cultural internationalism in the context of empire, emerging European nationalisms, and the civilizing mission locates ideas of the international at the heart of modernity itself. Its agendas through the centuries shift from its Eurocentric recognitions of sovereignty to twentieth-century struggles against slavery, indentured labor, and colonial rule.

Autochthonous nationalisms, alternative modernities, and customary practices forced a reconsideration of what cultural internationalism might be. Through the collision of the international legal process with contemporary postcolonial political formations, its Eurocentric logic was exposed. Under colonial rule, the dictates of international law created alternative structures for indigenous rule, generating spheres of subjectivity between colonial law, civil law, and native authority, called customary law. The emergence of hybrid identities in the interstices of these interpretative boundaries provides the backdrop for contemporary identifications that extend beyond the confines of territorial borders. Instead, these hybrid identities forged new conceptions of the state, of sovereignty, and of ideas about the international, thereby exposing the indeterminacies of legal internationalism.[15]

The history of customary practice in postcolonial states such as Kenya, India, Nigeria, and South Africa highlights the connections between the development of the international legal process and shifting postcolonial identities. It foregrounds the juridical practices that forcefully produced a whole realm of social and legal experiences between the colonial state and native authority, between the colonizer and the colonized. These juridical practices were created to protect mercantilist interests in the negotiation of territorial claims. Therefore, the colonized had to operate within both these codes of law, as native and as colonial subject. This double movement within colonial juridical practices shaped a whole sphere of practices that were simultaneous local and international, tribal and modern, indigenous and hybrid. Such a mediated production of modern African identities through the lens of its hybrid juridical practices, operating between African customary law and contemporary political movements, establishes one instance of the historical and ongoing mechanisms through which postcolonial subjectivity is constituted. It presents for us the long-term task of unpacking hybrid knowledges.[16]

As the example of customary law suggests, the indeterminacies of legal and cultural internationalism frame the tensions between hybrid identities and their national histories. Early international law suggests that until decolonization, independent states were responsible only for their own wealth and welfare. For these states, international law merely acknowledged their own freedom to promote their self-interests without external hindrance from the resulting indeterminacies of legal internationalism. But with decolonization, this relationship was no longer possible. The relationship between sovereignty and development had to be reconfigured. The inequities of modernization demanded new approaches to dependency theory, as development became an international expectation. Sovereign Third World states found themselves in new relations of financial and technical aid, and debt relief with Western states. The evolving General Agreement on Tariffs and Trade (GATT) inaugurated in 1948 had to recognize that all members are not economically equal, as unequal development between states raised questions about the capability of economic reciprocity.[17]

Such indeterminacies reveal the underestimation of the international legal process in ushering in the new world order. As B. S. Chimni, Mahmood Mamdani, Jean-François Bayart, Will Kymlicka, and others suggest, the international legal process does not fully account for the kinds of modern identities that have emerged in the twentieth century. Instead, a prescriptive approach toward development and international political economy has disregarded the radical indeterminacies generated by the international legal process on postcolonial migrancy across states. Such erasure of the indeterminacies of citizenship assailing many postcolonial states had extensive repercussions for contemporary identities. Political identities such as migrants, refugees, tourists, part-time laborers, Third World migrants abroad, and Third World immigrants to other Third World sites encompass some of these arenas of new hybrid identities that often fail to be of direct concern either to Third World states or to the international legal process. The resistance to adequately addressing these new political identities seriously by considering culture affects the impact that international law can exercise on marginal and nomadic communities today.[18]

Instead, a number of assumptions lie behind the approach of the international legal community to postcolonial states. For example, one legacy of earlier international laws that carved up colonial territories to create what would become postcolonial states was the assumption that an acultural approach would be the only approach with regard to Third World states. Such an acultural approach privileged discourses of the state over culture, and was unwilling to consider the importance and limits of cultural differences. It was largely interest-driven, with the objective being to continue older mercantile relationships under new economic markets. This assumption of disregarding the cultural specificity of the states in question was motivated by the long-term goal of protecting foreign interests by maintaining a comprador class within the new state, in alliance with its neocolonial relationships. Consequently, the assumption that the liberal democratic model is the only model for the Third World state was not interest-free.[19]

The belief in the liberal democratic model as the only model for the Third World state, a notion shared by international legal scholars, social theorists, and cultural theorists, was disengaged from the critique of the liberal democratic model launched by postcolonial legal scholars from the Third World. During the 1970s, critiques of modernity by Samir Amin, Tariq Banhuri, Ashis Nandy, and other subaltern intellectuals developed alongside the Marxist/structuralist approaches to international law, but were never seriously engaged with by international legal scholars. By disregarding the intersections between civil society and international law, through which Third World approaches to the international legal process critiqued the developmental model, earlier international legal scholars ignored a crucial move on the part of Third World scholars such as Amin, Banhuri, and Nandy to produce alternatives to Western notions of the liberal democratic state.[20]

What emerged was a parallel movement of dominant universalist methodological approaches, on the one hand, and alternative political structures, on the other, which did not translate in nuanced ways under the extant lens of structuralist theory. As in other spheres of the social sciences, culture was confined to the private domain. Consequently, a dual, interlocking system of hybridization and reduction emerged, where Third World sites are reduced by international law to structuralist categories, while subaltern intellectuals, in a move away from development theories of modernization in the Third World, complicate the three-worlds theory to incorporate hybrid identities in the struggle for social justice.

Opposed to the overarching narrative of the liberal democratic model is the proposition that each Third World state is a closed system.[21] The historical particularities that created individual Third World states demand that each state be dealt with in specific ways. Such a move foregrounds culture, and has far-reaching implications for conceptions of what a democratic state might look like. It underscores the epistemological tensions that underlie notions of individual rights, civil society, ideas of the self, and the importance of consumption in determining rights, which shape ideas of participatory democracy in the United States.

For a cultural critic of performance art in the United States, this debate is of significant import when one undertakes a comparative analysis. The performance work of feminist, gay, and lesbian performers such as Carolee Schneeman, Holly Hughes, Tim Miller, Bina Sharif, and Jessica Hagedorn is forged out of a distinctly U.S. notion of rights and a space to claim those rights as a historic subject. The claims of subjectivity found in this work cannot unilaterally be transferred onto the national context of, for example, contemporary Indian cultural politics; nor can this work be seen to make easy connections with other political contexts. These performative acts of individual subjectivity are historically situated in a particular political culture, within which these performances are read as gestures of the right to individual expression as much as they are interventions into a discursive history of individuated notions of race, sexuality, and community. To transfer the codes of such culturally specific acts of prohibition and transgression onto a framework where the separation between church and state is less clear, as in the case of states in the Indian subcontinent, the Middle East, and Muslim countries in African and Asia, would reproduce the reductive methodologies of earlier international legal theories. These theories assume that most Third World states are failed states because they do not resemble the liberal democratic state.

Transnational Hybridities

The mise-en-scène of this project is hybridity in performance. By situating the production of hybrid identities in the context of a changing cultural internationalism, these writings dramatize the paradoxes, dangers, and possibilities embedded in such an elusive idea. They draw attention to the tensions between cultural hybridities and the international political economy that structures sovereign states. Ensconced at the thresholds of various disciplinary boundaries, they express shifts in ideas of hybridization and its implications for the production of knowledges. Through their particular interrogations of the meanings and paradoxes of hybrid identities, they offer a critical appraisal of the strategies and options for internationally engaged cultural work.

The diverse genres, geographies, and theories of hybridity laid out in these pages juxtapose arguments for hybridity in local contexts, while also making broader linkages across national and regional discourses. Bringing together critical theorists, visual artists, poets, curators, anthropologists, performers, and writers, this anthology accentuates the connections between these context-specific readings on the condition of hybridity. These essays are in conversation with one another, and interlock across theoretical and aesthetic languages that are nuanced in their political insight. Their heterogeneous styles, national contexts, and mediums of inquiry stage the paradoxical pleasures of hybrid identities within and beyond the state.

Toby Miller underscores in his essay how the new international division of cultural labor demands that cultural practitioners grapple with the economic, textual, and distributional aspects of culture. Miller urges that a more integrative methodology, one that merges concerns about performance with issues of context, economy, and globalizing tendencies, be considered. It is this interdependent, hybrid strategy in the analysis of syncretic material culture that this volume stages. As Miller points out, the implications of the new cultural division of labor are far-reaching for cultural workers, as American universities, research institutes, and international organizations aid the international spread of capitalist production. Consequently, the legal, economic, and political implications of hybridity embedded in the new cultural division of labor have drawn together concerns about migrating populations across national and regional contexts. These issues continuously interrogate the meaning of the state, and gesture toward the invisible legal and economic processes that have historically molded the terrain of the cultural.

Whereas the market and the cultural division of labor dissolve traditional boundaries of the state and sovereignty through deregulation and transnational capital flows, other kinds of borders and local claims to sovereignty are raised in relation to the state. Fiona Foley points out that diasporic displacements and minority or hybrid identities, such as those of the Australian Aboriginal peoples, have been invasively generated, and now remain to haunt modernity. For these communities, the coerced hybridities of place and language have returned as a demand for cultural sovereignty, despite globalization's dispersals. Foley situates the struggles for Aboriginal, specifically Badtjala, land rights in the historical context of imperial internationalism and the contemporary international circuit of symposiums. Through a feminist rereading of the disappeared colonial archive, she visually inscribes the repressed history of indigenous woman into the Australian national imaginary. Foley reconstitutes the heroic indigenous woman as a forgotten myth. Merging personal and public memory, she locates the history of the Badtjala people within an international history of the struggles for sovereignty and rights of indigenous peoples in Australia. She draws out the tensions between international forces, native rights, and the violences that led to the hybridizing of specific local economies. Violent hybridization and creolization shape the concerns of Aboriginal peoples, specifically Aboriginal women, Foley argues. Consequently, the strategic reduction of hybridity in the interests of sovereignty informs Aboriginal peoples' policy strategies.

Laying out another transnational archive of dispossession—that of Arab-Jews—Ella Shohat addresses the invisible regional histories embedded in Miller's international division of cultural labor. Disentangling the intertwined histories of Zionism, colonial historiography, and Arab-Jewish identity, Shohat offers a methodology of reading a minor history "in relation" to contingent communities and genealogies. Her intricate remapping of epistemological and tectonic shifts demonstrates the contradictory ways in which the postcolonial nation-state functions. Against the backdrop of mass movements of peoples across oceans, continents, and seas, Shohat fore-grounds a moving visual history of the interlocked trajectories of Jews and Muslims in the violent swirl of diasporic modernity. She demarcates the elaborate machinations of the international legal process that have produced modern states in the Middle East, often in conflict with their hybrid geogra-phies and ethnicities. But through the surreptitious consumption and cir-culation of video music performances, the attempts to suppress Sephardi-Mizrahi cultural identity are disrupted.

Whereas Miller, Foley, and Shohat address the tensions between sover-eignty and hybridity that shape globalizing influences, Robert Stam, Barbara Browning, Awam Amkpa, Shani Mootoo, and José Esteban Muñoz offer aesthetic hybridities as self-conscious and critical performances of political dystopias. Drawing on Mikhail Bakhtin's notion of the "chronotope," the relation between time and space in the novel, Stam develops the concept of the cinematic chronotope. Cinema embodies this compression of time and space in conceptually important ways, Stam argues. Stam plays with the neologisms of Latin American discourse, and proposes the Brazilian "aes-thetics of garbage" as a convergence of chronotopic multiplicity. Through a gargantuan archive of Latin American hybridities, Stam provocatively argues for a redemption of detritus. His scrambled, fast-forward, montage-like play with space-time compression presents a palimpsestic model of cultural glob-alization. Radically disrupting temporal hybridity for a multichronotopic conception of duration, Stam's theory of garbage aesthetics challenges post-modern indifference with the possibility for a relational politics of the social. Instead of postmodern excess, transnational scarcity looms ahead in the trash can of history.

Against the gluttony of hybrid excess in Stam's pantheon of detritus, Browning offers a lyrical but no less ferocious glimpse into the taxonomies of identity in Bahian carnival. Through an analysis of the *candomblé* dance, Browning portrays the intricacies of sexuality and gender that inform these carnivalesque performances. By looking at cross-dressing, transvestism, homosexual negotiations, and Pan-African resonances in the *candomblé*, Browning layers her theory of syncretism with a transhistorical resonance, reflecting the interconnected histories of the region. Gandhi, Apaches, and African religions are brought together in anthropophagic ecstasy. Browning's reading resists fixed notions of Brazilianness, while gesturing toward the embedded class ambivalences of these secular and spiritual carnivalesque performances.

For Amkpa, carnival is a powerfully evocative "theatre of memory," to use Meena Alexander's phrase. Expressions of hybridity, "calypso, reggae, raggamuffin, jungle, hip-hop, ska . . ." perform an interruptive "presencing." It is the corporeality of the carnival that remembers unofficial identities, through the performance of presencing—"pidginizing," "creolizing," and the production of enforced hybridities. The potential and possibilities for affiliatory politics in front of and because of the state's repressive apparatus fuel the carnival's performance strategies. Carnival opens up the transgressive enunciations of self and community, an interactive performance of desire in spaces allocated by the state. For Amkpa, the repressive regimes of the multicultural state (in this case, Britain) have to be actively contested through the very laws and practices that limit the minority citizen's access to the state.

Whereas Amkpa's essay addresses black British communities with connections to the Caribbean, Mootoo and Muñoz present the hybridity of Trinidadian identities in the diaspora. Mootoo accentuates the creolization and pidginizing of language through which she can recuperate her place in diaspora. India, Nepal, Trinidad, Canada, Ireland, and Britain cumulatively shape Mootoo's lexicon of hybridity, struggling between a search for locational moorings and linguistic coherence. Her language embodies Stam's anthropophagic distortions, recycling the detritus of history to produce a Caribbean hybridity. Embedded in Mootoo's rendering of hybridity is the surreptitious inscription of lesbian identity ("brown as I am / other as I am") onto this new evolving landscape between Trinidad, Hindu gods, and North America.

Muñoz foregrounds Richard Fung's queer hybridity by linking the structuring pleasures of ethnography with pornography in Fung's videos. For Muñoz, Fung's performances are autoethnographic, intertwining postcolonial mimicry with a combative performative presence. Linking issues of place and displacement, Muñoz unpacks the social realms of queer hybrid self-fashioning. Through Trinidad and Canada, Fung produces a visual ambivalence connecting queerness and hybridity in his visual lexicon, disrupting mainstream gay pornography as well as disidentifying with Asian representations of sexuality. In the process, the possibility for antiracist political positions is explored by Muñoz.

Urban Hybridities

Discourses of urban hybridity have been most effective in opening up the realms of possibility for imagining new kinds of citizenship through cultural production. Graffiti, street performances, urban fashion, body piercing, hair culture, clubs, sex work, style politics, freeways, galleries, music, malls, and the marketplace are some of the popular locations for expressing urban culture in the United States. As the United States is a major exporter of popular culture, its own contradictions in terms of the global circulation of commodities and local struggles for rights and sovereignty brush up against each other. Often, the claims of minority communities in the United States get lost in the seductive proclamations of globalization. In the process of cultural reclamation, the transnational links to other countries and histories get flattened out.

This motivating conundrum is the disjunction between the hybrid individualism of distinctly U.S. identities and the growing ethnocentric, anti-international tendency toward cultural consolidation and expansionism deployed by the United States. This disjunction—the heterogeneity of identities and lifestyles in the increasingly homogenizing sphere of U.S. public discourse, and its exacerbated sense of a reduced heterogeneity in the international public domain—delineates the paradox of First World writings about hybrid identities within the United States, as well as in Third World states. This double movement is a crucial reconfiguration of postmodern plurality through unequal economies of exchange and circulation. It is this double movement toward the heterogenization within the national in the United States, and the homogenization of the international, particularly of the new economic configuration called the South, that gives the idea of hybridity its disconcerting valence as a prism of inquiry into the production of the social.

Tony Birch's chilling poem works to disrupt the geographic relations of North-South discourse by presenting the concerns of Aboriginal peoples in an allegorical tale of imperial cannibalism. Birch begins with the archive of the disappeared body. Colonial names, university anatomy collections of aboriginal body parts, and the meticulous taxonomy of species and type jar against unnamed remains: "so I imagine her face / about to surface / in a shallow rock pool /on a Bunnarong coastline." In conjunction with Fiona Foley's piece, Birch's haunting reminder of the colonial history of collecting aboriginal bones and the contemporary international trade in organs within the medical industry accentuates the painful history of violent traffic in native bodies. Birch's writing eloquently performs itself as an enunciative act of reclamation.

Celeste Olalquiaga's syncretic writing of Imán reverses the claims to sovereignty by privileging hybridity and its labyrinthine avenues of self-fashioning. Imán's gay Latino-American subjectivity violates all the borders of affiliation in creating a new identity, as he joins the House of Xtravaganza. Merging cosmopolitanism with baroque glossolalia, Spanglish with urban polyvalence, Imán emerges similarly to Stam's chronotopic multiplicity: a palimpsestic native of urban New York subculture. Imán combines androgynous pastiche visuality with a macaronic verbality. For Olalquiaga, Imán's polyglotism unravels his urban persona through cityspeak. Olalquiaga, like Stam, plays with neologisms as she performs hybridity through her own writing of Imán.

In an elaboration of Miller's international division of cultural labor, Manthia Diawara offers a tale of hybrid identities in the formation of transnational urban culture. Diawara describes how, through the export of African-American culture, the cultural arm of the United States Information Agency partook in the hybridization of local Third World cultures in Mali during the 1960s. Diawara argues for the pertinence of "Afro-kitsch" in considering alternative cultural capital. African-American culture, symbolized by James Brown, offered new structures of feeling, new ways of experiencing hybridity for a young person from Bamako.

In opposition to Olalquiaga's Imán, who produces identity through self-fashioning, Chon A. Noriega offers a spatial rethinking of hybridity through U.S. Latino identity and Latino installation art. Foregrounding a pan-national "American" project initiated by José Martí in 1891, Noriega explores the contradictions of pan-identities through the practice of hybrid genres such as installation art. Like Stam, Noriega proposes the layered simultaneity of time-space compressions. Through Martí and U.S. Latino cultural work, Noriega depicts communities-in-relation. Drawing on Martí's genealogy of *mestizo* (mixed race), *indio* (indigenous), *negro* (black), *criollo* (Creole), and *mestizaje* (mixed race), Noriega elaborates on the arguments regarding particularisms versus universalisms in the formation of hybrid states of the New World, Martí's "Our America."

Opening out the city by privileging its most ephemeral site, the highway, Sikivu Hutchinson writes of transiting culture. Unlike the mass movements of people across nations narrativized in Shohat's, Mootoo's, and Amkpa's readings of hybridity, Hutchinson focuses on the migration of people within the nation. An imaginary urban history of black women migrants from the South to the North during the early part of the twentieth century, Hutchinson's essay fills out the absent spaces of the early modern American city. Between the interstate highway development and the inner city, Hutchinson locates the bodies of black women. This history of migration is also a quest for democratic rights and cultural sovereignty. Hutchinson's essay offers a powerfully evocative connection between the limits of hybridity allowed in a racist hybrid state and the repressive economies that have resulted in the forced migrations of African-American people from the South to the North.

Whereas junctions and interstate highways form the hybrid spaces of Hutchinson's genealogy, the marketplace allows Deborah A. Kapchan to explore the hybrid genres of public oration. By sketching the performed identities of women vendors, Kapchan draws a feminist history of the Moroccan marketplace Beni Mellal. Bargaining, hawking, swearing, and divining are some of the intertextual strategies through which vendor women self-fashion new identities in the public space of the market. As a performative and hybrid genre, Kapchan describes these innovations in oration as a revoicing of women in the social arena of selling and buying. The theatricality of this local performance encapsulates the globalizing influences of transnational markets.

In contrast to the grounded performance space of the market, Fred Moten presents the sonic urban space of hybridity, the space of James Brown, and the "ensemblic one." Moten's seductive excursions into what he calls new models of reality in search of a liberatory politics of form suggest urban hybridity as an unheard scream. Playing on ideas of interruption, innovation, and transference, Moten fashions hybridity through the practice of writing. As with Alexander, Stam, Browning, Mootoo, Olalquiaga, Hutchinson, and Diawara, hybridity for Moten is found in the performative act of writing. It is an incommensurability that is uncontainable. Located between the pages, it is unworded sound.

Hybridity and Global Citizenship

As this collection of essays cautions us, hybrid subjectivities have always been, and continue to be, mediated through censoring modes such as religious, political, legal, and psychic regulatory regimes. The pretense at democratization and participatory politics has led to the public disavowal of the state by its underrepresented citizens. Instead, the increased delegitimation of governance across national contexts, and the consolidation of neoliberal economics globally, have accentuated the emptiness of hybridity as a serious political intervention in the light of a narrowing international.[22]

With the rise of voluntary and involuntary migrations of peoples across the globe with dizzying rapidity, so the laws and regimes that try to contain the movement of peoples are being enforced with greater vigilance. In conjunction with the globalizing influences of the international division of cultural labor that Miller has pointed to, the resultant concerns around hybrid identities, hybrid aesthetics, and hybrid states will only proliferate internationally.

This collection of writings offers compelling aesthetic and political arguments about the implications of hybridity for world citizenship. Its gestures of hybridity accentuate the nationally specific contexts that make such enactments possible or even meaningful, drawing home the limits of a transhistorical tendency to assume that concerns and practices of hybridity might indeed bear equivocal resonances across national contexts. At the same time, it makes links across historical, geographic, and linguistic contexts, and demonstrates the overarching concerns, claims, and hopes that lie embedded in the idea of hybridity and continue to impinge upon everyday life.

As Part I of this book, "Transnational Hybridities," demonstrates, the different regional discourses of hybridity—whether British, Australian, Brazilian, Trinidadian, Canadian, Israeli, Arab, or South Asian—still hold on to a possible liberatory politics, despite the onslaught of neoliberal economics. Part II, "Urban Hybridities," looks at the local ways in which hybridity operates as an arena for personal and communal self-fashioning. Through coalitions around feminism, sexuality, race, class, and nation, these urban hybrid experiences gain a mobility and a power that are potentially transformative, even in their ephemerality.

The disenchantment exacerbated by the increased rapidity of movement and the inundation of information is leading to more local discussions of politics and meaning. For this group of writers, the call for intralocal exchanges, a South-South dialogue, and a move away from statist or corporate intervention into urban life are indicated. Instead of framing discussions of hybridity in terms of a North-South dialogue, or a First World–Third World relationship, these writers make us consider Glissant's transversality in new, contingent ways. Hybridity here is configured in local terms, from the inside out, from the micro to the macro, across local contexts. The increasingly seductive alienation inflicted through global penetration of consumer capital demands that we reconsider strategies of cultural survival. It is crucial to address the kinds of violence imposed by transnational processes onto local cultures, and take seriously the seduction and resistance of communities to these changes. We hope that this anthology offers insights into such an understanding.

Notes

I thank Jennifer Fink for the spirit and energy that drove this project. Thanks also to Jayati Lal, Micah Kleit, Geoffrey Rogers, Robert Stam, and Toby Miller for editorial suggestions and illuminating conversations. James Gathii, Celestine Nyamu, Nathaniel Berman, Ibrahim Gassama, and Tayyab Mahmud generously shared ideas that have informed this paper.

1. Micheline R. Ishay, *Internationalism and Its Betrayal* (Minneapolis: University of Minnesota Press, 1995).

2. W. E. B. Du Bois, "The Pan-African Movement," in *The 1945 Manchester Pan-African Congress,* ed. George Padmore, rev. Hakim Adi and Marika Sherwood (London: New Beacon Books, 1995), 63.

3. Gordon K. Lewis, "The West Indian Scene," in *The Growth of the Modern West Indies* (New York: Monthly Review Press, 1968), 19.

4. Gordon K. Lewis, "The Challenge of Independence," in ibid., 387.

5. See Lisa Lowe, *Immigrant Acts: On Asian American Cultural Politics* (Durham, N.C., and London: Duke University Press, 1996), 18–24. Also see Will Kymlicka, *Multicultural Citizenship* (Oxford: Oxford University Press, 1995); Gotanda Crenshaw and Thomas Peller, *Critical Race Theory* (New York: New Press, 1995); and Cedric J. Robinson, *Black Movements in America* (New York and London: Routledge, 1997).

6. See Guillermo Gómez-Peña, "The Multicultural Paradigm: An Open Letter to the National Arts Community," in *Negotiating Performance: Gender, Sexuality, and Theatricality in Latino/a America,* ed. Diana Taylor and Juan Villegas (Durham, N.C., and London: Duke University Press, 1994).

7. For a broad history of natural law and the social contract, see Ishay, *Internationalism and Its Betrayal.*

8. David Parkin, Lionel Caplan, and Humphrey Fisher, eds., *The Politics of Cultural Performance* (Oxford: Berghahn Books, 1996), xvii. See also Richard Bauman, *Story, Performance and Event: Contextual Studies of Oral Narrative* (New York: Cambridge University Press, 1986); Abner Cohen, *Custom and Politics in Urban Africa* (Berkeley and Los Angeles: University of California Press, 1969); James Fernandez, *Persuasions and Performances: The Play of Tropes in Culture* (Bloomington: Indiana University Press, 1986); Max Gluckman, "Analysis of a Social Situation in Modern Zululand," *Rhodes-Livingstone Papers* no. 28 (Manchester: Manchester University Press, 1958); Dell Hymes, "Breakthrough into Performance," in *Folklore: Performance and Communication,* ed. Dan Ben-Amos and Kenneth S. Goldstein (The Hague: Mouton, 1975); Richard Schechner, *The Future of Ritual: Writings on Culture and Performance* (New York: Routledge, 1993); and Victor Turner, *Schism and Continuity in an African Society* (Manchester: Manchester University Press, 1957).

9. Arjun Appadurai, *Modernity at Large: Cultural Dimensions of Globalization* (Minneapolis: University of Minnesota Press, 1996); Samir Amin, *Delinking* (London: Zed Books, 1990); Rathna Kapur and Brenda Cossman, *Subversive Sites: Feminist Engagements with Law in India* (London: Thousand Oaks, 1996); Néstor García Canclini, *Hybrid Cultures: Strategies for Entering and Leaving Modernity,* trans. Christopher L. Chiappari and Silvia L. López (Minneapolis: University of Minnesota Press, 1995); Mahmood Mamdani, *Citizen and Subject: Contemporary African and the Legacy of Late Colonialism* (Princeton, N.J.: Princeton University Press, 1996).

10. See Ann Cvetkovich and Douglas Kellner, eds., "Introduction: Thinking Global and Local," in *Articulating the Global and the Local* (Boulder, Colo.: Westview Press: 1997). See also Inderpal Grewal and Caren Kaplan, eds., *Scattered Hegemonies: Postmodernity and Transnational Feminist Practices* (Minneapolis: University of Minnesota Press, 1994), 11–15; Rob Wilson and Wimal Dissanayake, eds., *Global/Local: Cultural*

Production and the Transnational Imaginary (Durham, N.C.: Duke University Press, 1996).

11. Edward Soja, *Thirdspace: Journeys to Los Angeles and other Real-and-Imagined Places* (Oxford: Blackwell, 1996). See also David Harvey, *The Condition of Postmodernity* (Oxford: Blackwell, 1990), and Henri Lefebvre, *The Production of Space* (Oxford: Blackwell, 1991), for extensive discussions on postmodernity and space.

12. Jim Pines and Paul Willemen, *Questions of Third Cinema* (London: British Film Institute, 1989).

13. Jatinder Varma, personal interview, London, summer 1990. See Kirtinath Kutkoti, "Introduction," in *Hayavadana: New Drama in India,* ed. Girish Karnad (Calcutta: Oxford University Press, 1975). I am referring here to the production of *The Little Clay Cart,* directed by Jatinder Varma, Tara Arts Group, in London in the late 1980s.

14. See Ella Shohat and Robert Stam, *Unthinking Eurocentrism: Multiculturalism and the Media* (London: Routledge, 1994), 309; Homi K. Bhabha, *The Location of Culture* (New York and London: Routledge, 1994), 87; Kobena Mercer, *Welcome to the Jungle: New Positions in Black Cultural Studies* (New York and London: Routledge, 1994), 63; Stuart Hall, "New Ethnicities," in *Stuart Hall: Critical Dialogues in Cultural Studies,* ed. David Morley and Kuan-Hsing Chen (London and New York: Routledge, 1996), 441; Paul Gilroy, *There Ain't No Black in the Union Jack* (London: Hutchinson Education, 1987), 217; Édouard Glissant, *Caribbean Discourse* (Charlottesville: University Press of Virginia, 1992), 66; Marlene Nourbese Philip, *she tries her tongue, her silence softly breaks* (London: Women's Press, 1993), 47; Antonio Benítez-Rojo, *The Repeating Island* (Durham, N.C., and London: Duke University Press, 1992), 12; Assia Djebar, *Fantasia: An Algerian Cavalcade* (Portsmouth, N.H.: Heinemann, 1993), 226; Appadurai, *Modernity at Large,* 48; Lowe, *Immigrant Acts,* 60; Françoise Lionnet, *Autobiographical Voices: Race, Gender, Self-Portraiture* (Ithaca, N.Y. and London: Cornell University Press, 1989), 9–10, 15; Néstor García Canclini, "Cultural Reconversion," in *On Edge: The Crisis of Contemporary Latin American Culture,* ed. George Yúdice, Jean Franco, and Juan Flores (Minneapolis: University of Minnesota Press, 1992); Celeste Olalquiaga, *Megalopolis: Contemporary Cultural Sensibilities* (Minneapolis: University of Minnesota Press, 1992), 83; Michelle Cliff, *No Telephone to Heaven* (New York: Vintage International), 1.

15. See Mahmood Mamdani, *Citizen and Subject: Contemporary Africa and the Legacy of Late Colonialism* (Princeton, N.J.: Princeton University Press, 1996), chapters 4 and 5, for debates around customary law and contemporary cultural practices.

16. See Mamdani, ibid., for a historical analysis of customary practice and its relation to colonial rule and contemporary social formations in South Africa.

17. Robert H. Jackson, "The Destitute Image of the Third World," in *Quasi States: Sovereignty, International Relations and the Third World* (Cambridge: Cambridge University Press, 1990).

18. The numerous unpublicized incidents of Indians in the United Arab Emirates and Saudi Arabia being detained without trial and deported without legal recourse are a case in point. The diplomatic silence on the part of the Indian government when such cases arise is striking.

19. B. S. Chimni, talk at Harvard University, March 7, 1997. Chimni's concept of the acultural approach holds interesting implications for theories of cultural performance. It draws out the tensions between supposedly objective approaches to the development of states and the subjective practices that sustain states through culture. See B. S. Chimni, *International Law and World Order: A Critique of Contemporary Approaches* (New Delhi: Sage Publications, 1993).

20. For further postcolonial critiques of the liberal democratic model of the state, see Samir Amin, *Re-Reading the Postwar Period: An Intellectual History* (New York: Monthly Review Press, 1994); Tariq Banuri, "Development and the Politics of Knowledge: A Critical Interpretation of the Social Role of Modernization Theories in the Development of the Third World," in *Dominating Knowledge: Development, Culture, and Resistance,* ed. Frederique Apfel Marglin and Stephen A. Marglin (Oxford: Clarendon, 1990), 29–72; and Ashis Nandy, *The Savage Freud* (Princeton, N.J.: Princeton University Press, 1995).

21. Chimni, talk at Harvard University, March 7, 1997.

22. See Kymlicka, *Multicultural Citizenship,* and Lowe, *Immigrant Acts,* for arguments on the delegitimated state.

Part I   Transnational Hybridities

Three Poems on the Poverty of History

Meena Alexander

Gold Horizon

I

She waited where the river ran
that summer as the floods began
stones sinking, fireflies murmuring
in paddy fields, herons on stumps of trees
the axe planted where little else would work
and everywhere the mess of water.

"So you have entered a new world"
her voice was low, growling even.
There was nothing humble in her voice.
Sometimes the dead behave in that know-all-way
ploughing the ruts of disaster,
their unease part of our very pith—
what the axe discovers marrow and meat to us.

"So what's it like there?" she asked.

I replied: "As the Hudson pours
the river wall clings tight with glinting stones.
Yet what's so bright makes for odd imaginings.
Sometimes I feel as if a metal bowl had split
dented by blows from a woman's fist
and bits of spelling lessons, shards of script
struck from a past locked into privacy,

—this is the immigrant's fury, no?
Who understands my speech, further what is my speech?—
dropped, pounding as rice grains might."

"You think that bowl's your head
your words a crypt! Look at your feet!
How can you stand addressing me?"
I heard her laughing bitterly.

"What's with you?" I shot back
"What's with the dead, sheer jealousy?"

Her fingers waved a whitened scrap
paper or cloth I could not tell.
She held it out to me: "Take! Eat!"

I saw the sari that bound her
dropping free, feet cut at the ankles,
severed from her thighs, slicked with red earth.
Water poured in short streams
over her mutilated parts.
She stood, shored by a single elbow
against a mango branch.

II

Place-names splinter
on my tongue and flee:
Allahabad, Tiruvella, Kozhencheri, Khartoum,
Nottingham, New Delhi, Hyderabad, New York
—the piecework of sanity,
stitching them into a coruscating geography,
why a single long drawn breath
in an infant's dream might do,
—ruined by black water in a paddy field.

We wrestle on wet ground,
she and I, living and dead,
stripped to our skins,
naked, shining free in
the gold of a torn horizon.

Our thrashing is not nice.
Her ankle stumps shove against my eyes.

Words bolt, syllables rasp
an altered script

theatre of memory I could never have wished.
Breathless I search for a scene
mile-long city blocks,
iron bridges scraping back short hills,
asphalt pierced with neon plots,
the rage of sense:
bodegas in the barrio, Billy's topless bar,
Vineeta's Video Store crammed with cartoons
of Nutan and Madhuri
—"Kya, kya hum kon hai? Idher hum kon hai"
"Namal ivide ara? Ivide namal ara?"—

The mixed up speech of newness,
flashing as a kite might,
pale paper on a mango branch.

III

She waited where the river ran,
that summer as the floods began.

Is this mere repetition,
or the warm sprawl of time,
inscribed in limestone?
Who can cry back into a first world
a barefoot child on a mud forking path,
fields gold with monsoon water,
haunt of the snail and dragonfly?
What makes the narrative whole?

Beneath my cheek I feel her belly's bowl
thick with blood, the woman who waits for me.
Are these her lips or mine?
Whose tongue is this
melting to the quick of migrancy?
I touch raw bones, the skull's precise asymmetry.

As rivers north and rivers south soar
into tongues of mist parting our ribs
I hear voices of children whisper from red hills:
'An angel, you have caught an angel!'

June 29–August 20, 1996

She Speaks to a Man in a Red Shirt

> *Quick! Are there other lives?*
> *—Rimbaud*

1

"We are poor people,
a people without history."

She saw his shirt
red cotton, open at the throat

Hair on his chest
taut as the wind blew.

She could not tell
which people he meant

His shirt open in that way,
his flesh hard under coarse cloth.

2

If she were to write a poem
it would start like this:

"A woman stood at the edge of a terrace
saw white letters someone scrawled

FROM THURSDAY ON TILL NEVER
THIS JOURNEY IS A NARRATIVE OF LOSS."

Beyond the terrace
is a river few boats cross.

3

Call out the phoenix, let it shake
its wings, soar over water.

What burns is loss. History comes
without cost, in dreams alone.

Our poverty is in the nerves,
the stubble of migrancy, tied up with hope

Stacked in a wooden boat,
the sails lie flat.

4

She hears his words:
"Let us be one people."

Man in a red shirt,
why move me so?

Touching you,
will I know how the wind blows?

Translated Lives

The past that we make, presumes us as pure invention might—
our being here compels it: an eye cries out for an eye
a throat for a throat, we muse on Rimbaud's lips caked with soil,
his Parisian whites stiffening: Quick! are there other lives?

Who shall fit her self for translation—word for word, line
for line, eyes flashing at squat gulls on this mid-Atlantic
shore, sailboats rudderless, the horizon scrawled in indigo?
What water here, or air? A terrible heat comes on, birds scurry,
swallowing their own shadows and lovers coupling on hard rock
turn grotesque, forced to grope at the sea's edge.

Neon mirages mock the world Columbus sought. In Times Square,
selling the National Debt, electronic numbers triple on the light
strip—and where the digits run, pure ciphers—000
mark heaven's haven. Into that nothingness, a poverty of flesh
track tanpura and oudh, the torn ligaments of a goat's throat,
still bloodied, strummed against sand.

As boats set sail through our migrant worlds, faxes splutter
their texts into the crumpled spaces in our skin, and the
academies bow low, white shirts, threadbare elbows scraped
into arcane incandescence, shall we touch each other
stiffened with sense, bodies set as if in Egyptian perspective,
full frontal, necks craned to the glint of the horizon?
Will a nervous knowledge, a millennial sense be kindled?
Must the past we make consume us?

Psychic Graffiti: A Poet's Note

These three poems were composed roughly about the same time: "Translated Lives" and "Gold Horizon" side by side in the summer of 1996; "She Speaks to a Man in a Red Shirt" a few months earlier. As I worked my way through the drafts of each poem, crossing out, adding, fixing a line or image, allowing the breath to flow better, I felt I was inching through a palimpsest of paper, battling with shadow selves, discarded lives, dealing with psychic graffiti. Edgy, jagged characters scrawled on a ready surface, eruptions from hand and fist, from lives forced to make up history.

At that time too I was finishing "Manhattan Music." Sandhya R. feels angelic wings sweep time back: "a velocity, a swift corrosive motion." Street signs in English, "bright and jittery," start to spin in the "wild incandescence" of Malayalam. She is transfixed by these illegible "hybrid syllables."

Who is she? Where is she? When is she?

On a draft of the poem "Translated Lives" I scribbled a note: "Rimbaud's 'Saison en Enfer' is much in my mind and also the condition of these immigrant lives we lead and what it means to write (= to translate) across a border—a trip wire. How to summon this up and say, 'this is my past, our past: the great challenge as I see it.'" I initialed and dated the note as if wanting to fix it in the unstable realm of poetic composition: "MA July 15, 1996."

And now I want to ask: what does it mean to stumble on that trip wire, the migratory border? How is it bound to the metamorphosis European sailors feared so much? Traveling east on the waters of the Atlantic, some dreamed of an invisible line not far from the Cape of Good Hope daring which their bodies would grow dark, sprout horns, oddments of hair, a rare bestiality reserved for those who cross borders.

Spatial transgressions work differently for us now, migrants westwards. The poems we compose spin themselves out in a cocoon of cold air, inventions born of unvoiced need and our layerings of self making up a dark soil that we can recall best in dreams. It is a kind of imaginative difficulty for which ordinarily we have few words, a condition of spiritual poverty, lives lived in a world without a readily available history.

So fragmenting the self into two, three, ever so many, we invent what we need: a raw theater of sense.

We carry the fear of those white sailors within us: but changed beyond recognition. What we are in our bodies becomes fierce, raw, fragmented. Our skin becomes a shield. We tremble to touch.

When Rimbaud mused "Je est un autre" or scribbled thoughts on the *dérèglement* of the senses, little did he know the power his lines would exert on us, we who understand, however fitfully, that desire is always for the other, the other who forces us into history. And it is precisely this entry into history that lets us see the condition of our migrancy, our days lived out in the vivid air, cut from the dream of a steadfast home.

Culture and the Global Economy

Toby Miller

I want to do two things in this essay: first, propose a means of theorizing the global cultural economy based on what I call the new international division of cultural labor; and second, look at the implications of that understanding of the economy for cultural intellectuals. Throughout, my stress will be on the need to connect the distributional and the textual aspects of culture. Rather than splitting off questions of performance from context or economy, my intention is to intricate them, and to do so in the light of a geopolitics that is necessarily hybrid.

In June 1965, a conference titled "Conditions of World Order" was convened in Italy. Henry Kissinger, Hans-Georg Gadamer, Raymond Aron, and others planned the future of the world. The proceedings were published in *Daedalus,* the journal of the American Academy of Arts and Sciences. The conference's chief rapporteur, Stanley Hoffmann, began his summary as follows:

> The twenty-one men who met at Bellagio . . . in order to define conditions of World Order participated in a double experiment. One was intellectual—the attempt to discuss both the chances for and obstacles to world order as they appear in 1965. . . . The other experiment was really an enterprise in collective psychology—a psychodrama of sorts. How would men coming from different countries, from different cultural and ideological backgrounds, from different professions and disciplines interpret the subject, lock horns, join issues, and reach conclusions? (Hoffman 1996, 455)

How, indeed? Life has often been tough for Western men as we have locked horns together, but we have been prepared to keep doing it, to keep performing, and I will do my bit by reengaging *Daedalus* later.

Of course, in the 1960s, modernity was set up as an actionable condition, to be striven for via the implementation of policies and programs by government and capital in what were variously named "developing countries," the "Third World," and other teleological marks. Modernity was designated as a complex imbrication of industrial, economic, social, cultural, and political development. The founders and husbanders of this discourse were First World political scientists and economists, mostly associated with American universities, research institutes, and corporations, or with international organizations. Among the foundational premises of this version of modernity were the formation of nationalism and state sovereignty as habits of thought. The "modern individual" would not be prey to the temptations of Marxism-Leninism. Development necessitated the displacement of the "particularistic norms" of tradition by "more universalistic" blends of the modern, as part of the creation of an "achievement-oriented" society (Pye 1965, 19). The successful importation of Western media technologies would be a critical component in this replicant figure, as elite sectors of society were trained to be exemplars for a wider populace mired in backward, folkloric forms of thought that lacked the trust in national organizations required for modernization.

This model was inflected with assumptions from evolutionary thought in its search for hidden unanimities that would bind humanity in singular directions and forms of development. That enabled the owners of the discourse to investigate life in the Southern Hemisphere and police what they found there as part of a drive toward uniformity of human definition, achievement, and organization (Axtmann 1993, 64–65). These precepts ignored the way in which the very life of the modern had been defined in colonial and international experience, both by differentiating the metropole from the periphery and by importing ideas, fashions, and people back to the core (T. Miller 1995). Rather implausibly solipsistic as a policy model, modernization was criticized from within by calls for a more subtle, locally sensitive acknowledgment of conflicts over wealth, influence, and status, and challenged from without by theories of dependent development, underdevelopment, unequal exchange, world-systems history, center-periphery relations, and cultural or media imperialism. Although these latter positions had disagreements and differences, they shared the view that the transfer of technology, politics, and economics was not taking place in a desirable way. The emergence of multinational corporations had produced a unified interest between business and government at the center in search of cheap labor, new markets, and pliant regimes (Reeves 1993, 24–25, 30).

There is particular concern today about the traffic in meaning generated by this inequality, as textual trade has been so one-sided. The contemporary ur-term, *globalization,* is a floating signifier. As Elizabeth Jacka notes, its meanings vary between an American-dominated cultural flow, the international spread of capitalist production, and the chaotic, splintered circulation of signs across cultures (Jacka 1992, 5, 2). Capital moves in a state of high velocity, lighting on areas and countries promiscuously. Materials and people are exchanged simultaneously across the globe, but in an asymmetrical way. The United States has a boundless taste for such activity. Therefore, when Thomas Krens marks his arrival as director of the Guggenheim Museum by declaring that he will transform it into a multinational, or Peter Sellars announces an expansion of the LA Festival, one needs to question whether this involves a relationship of equal exchange with the rest of the world. It is hard to deny the adjacent fact that Hollywood produced eighty-eight of the world's one hundred top-grossing films in 1993 (Frow 1992, 14–15; Sankowski 1992, 6; Rockwell 1994, H1).

Of course, when cultural commodities have lengthy careers, they undergo retraining to suit new circumstances. Culture is simultaneously the key to international textual trade and one of its limiting factors. Ethics, affect, custom, and other forms of knowledge both enable commodification and restrict it (Frow 1992, 18–20). As Liberace once said: "If I play Tchaikovsky I play his melodies and skip his spiritual struggles. . . . I have to know just how many notes my audience will stand for" (quoted in Hall and Whannell 1965, 70). Thus, General Motors, which own Australia's General Motors Holden, translates its "hot dogs, baseball, apple pie, and Chevrolet" jingle into "meat pies, football, kangaroos, and Holden cars" for the Australian market. This can be read either as an indication of the paradigmatic nature of the national in an era of global companies or as the requirement to reference the local in a form that is obliged to do something with cultural-economic meeting grounds. The *Economist's* 1994 TV survey remarked that politics is always so localized in its first and last instances, through production and audience uptake, that the "electronic bonds" of exported TV are "threadbare" (Heilemann 1994, 4). One might think of this as the point where audiences themselves produce meaning, either through their own connotative customization of texts to suit particular circumstances or because companies endeavor to denote standardized, international performances as impeccably domestic at each site: "randomness, if viewed from a postmodern aesthetics; functionality, if viewed from the semantics of international capital" (Ruthrof 1997, 248).

But the apparent domestication of exported culture sometimes merely offers a few signifiers of localism while effectively being a licensed importation of values of practice and genre. In this sense, difference and a sensitivity to cultural specificity can be one more incorporative means toward the homogenization of cultural production, emblematized by that rather touching euphemism, the "multidomestic" corporation (Chartrand 1992, 153). The new marketing pharmacists prescribe cultural difference as a category of business sensitivity training. Consider a 1990s study comparing fifty nations. It put Australia close to the United States, and hence attractive in terms of modular approaches to management. On power differentials across society, the two countries ranked forty-first and thirty-eighth, respectively; on individualism, second and first; and sixteenth and fifteenth on masculinity (Hofstede 1993, 148). How nice it is to know that these places are pluralist, free, and quasi-male. Without interrogating those categories here—as if they were helpful or unhelpful, accurate or inaccurate—one can take them as directional signs based on an assumed uniformity of outlook that become tools in investment and organizational planning. They are formative knowledges, neither falsifiable nor ridiculous, but productive of the power to invest, manage, and govern. Similar logics apply to "anticosmopolitan" business or tourist travelers seeking an argot and a site for work or leisure that can be utilized with minimal but optimal adjustments to their own lives: a guidebook answering the "whether there is a Taco Bell in Mexico City" quandary (Hannerz 1990, 241). These are matters of real concern for industrial intellectuals relieved to be greeted by such signs as "Welcome to IBM-town" when they land in Bangalore, or "Nissan welcomes you to Newcastle" (quoted in Strange 1995, 294). A transnational bourgeois space is generated, not unlike the quarantined sphere of the international transit lounge. These are liminal sites that combine familiar global space with the newness of a latest home.

The mobility of the industrial intellectual turns me toward the concept of a new international division of cultural labor (NICL). It echoes the retheorization of economic dependency that emerged from West Germany in the late 1970s after the unprecedented chaos of that inflationary decade. The opportunity provided by new markets for labor and sales and the shift from the spatial sensitivities of electrics to the spatial insensitivities of electronics pushed businesses away from treating Third World countries as suppliers of raw materials. They came to be regarded instead as shadow-setters of the price of work, competing internally and with the First and Second Worlds for employment opportunities. Manufacturing practices were not only divided within the plant, but across the globe (Fröbel, Heinrichs, and Kreye 1980, 2–8, 13–15, 45–48). The mid-1980s saw offshore production by corporations exceed the amount of trade between states for the first time, as governments offered transnationals a haven from environmental controls, minimum wages, labor laws, occupational safety norms, and taxes (Strange 1995, 293; Cohen 1991, 126). Utopian formulations promise a "new economic citizenship" forged from these changes, an updated version of employee participation. Instead of concentrating on the old factory focus of a division of plant labor, workers are to match productivity and cost with specific competitors in another country. International political economy is devolved to the shop floor, allegedly empowering the labor force in the process (P. Miller and O'Leary 1993, 17).

How far can this trend go, away from the assembly of infinitely substitutable manufacturing parts? Will the deindustrialized, service-industry states once more lose jobs to the periphery, while retaining superprofits for their own ruling elite? Already, work is being done on a variety of cultural industries to examine the impact of global labor markets in advertising, architecture, and sport, trying to balance out the positives (less chauvinism and less monochromatic whiteness) and the negatives (American dominance and the deracination of peripheral suppliers) (Maguire 1994, 452, 458, 466). A quarter of Silicon Valley technicians are known to be first- or second-generation Asian migrants. And the fact that India's largest software manufacturer has more than three thousand employees who have completed graduate school, and that the country boasts eighty-five thousand chartered accountants, is advertised by the Indian Government in U.S. business pages under the slogan "3 million technical minds" (Strange 1995, 296; "Professional India"). In the fashion industry, the 1993 purchase of Yves Saint-Laurent by Elf-Aquitaine, a state-owned oil business, was not only an odd blurring of genres. The next year, much of Polo Ralph Lauren was bought by Goldman Sachs. L'Oréal now owns Lanvin, Givenchy works for LVMH, and Hermes, Versace, and Donna Karan have been floated on the stock market. In short, only Chanel of the classic global lines remains in the hands of private investors. Organic connections to the industry are off the map, as recession claims its victims. Big companies—manufacturers and banks—are the new owners, trading on the old names to use their own capital for mutual expansion into Asia and eastern Europe, which are the only opportunities for growth. The French couturiers rely on Asia for almost half their sales now ("Couture Ordinaire") (even as many fashion firms look to the same

region for docile labor and low production costs). Europe increasingly matters only for its sign value.

The audiovisual media are back where primary and secondary extractive
and value-adding industries were in the 1960s, needing to make decisions
not just about export but about the site of production. They are faced with
advances in communications technology that permit electronic off-line editing across the world, but that also enable matte effects problematizing the
very need for location shooting. In television, the trend is clearly toward a
horizontal connection to other media, a global scale of economy and administration, and a breakup of the old public-private distinctions in ownership,
control, and programming philosophy (Wedell 1994, 325; Marvasti 1994).
TV texts are fast developing as truly global trading forms. Worldwide expen-
diture in 1993 amounted to U.S.$80 billion, and the annual growth rate is
10 percent (Heilemann 1994, 4). Jay Leno's promotional spot for the pan-
European NBC Super Channel promises "to ruin your culture just like we
ruined our own." American financial institutions are long practiced at sharing risk and profit with local businesses. By the end of the 1980s, overseas
firms were crucial suppliers of funds invested in Hollywood and loans put
up against distribution rights in their countries of origin (Buck 1992, 119,
123). Joint production arrangements are well established between U.S. businesses and French, British, Swedish, and Italian concerns, with connections
to theme parks, cabling, and home video. Attempts by the French film industry in the 1980s to attract Hollywood producers may have the ultimate
effect of U.S. studio takeovers, and North American producers and networks are purchasing satellite and broadcast space across the Continent. In
eastern and central Europe, with no European Union cultural subvention,
the local industries have been decimated by Hollywood and the West since
1989. No one goes to Andrzej Wajda's films, and in Hungary technicians
survive by making Budapest resemble Maigret's Paris and medieval Britain
for French and English television (Hayward 1993, 385; Stevenson 1994, 1;
Slide 1995, 370–72). This assuredly makes for hybrid performance at the
level of the offscreen labor force!

This brings me to the implications for cultural intellectuals of such circumstances. Consider the head-to-head confrontations between France and
the United States that were waged at the conclusion to the final GATT round
in December 1993 over state support of national cinemas versus laissez-faire
conditions for Hollywood products. They exemplified an important but unstable set of oppositions that will not go away: on the one hand, sovereignty,
a oneness predicated on the subsumption of individualism by the needs of
the collectivity; on the other hand, the market, predicated on the sum of ex-

pressed desire amounting to the interests of that collectivity—the magistracy of the archive versus the economy. Both approaches—one deploying the concept of the citizen from political theory, the other borrowing the idea of the consumer from neoclassical economics—are laden with each other's political and monopoly capital baggage and interests, in a messy, logocentrically interdependent way. If the day comes when the United States complains that Japan's ideological objections to organ transplants are nontariff barriers to the export of the American heart, or takes issue with the French for prohibiting patents on DNA maps because they represent an inalienable human heritage, we shall see that debate recur on less entertaining terrain (Attali 1996, 47); for this is the lonely hour of the last instance of economic versus cultural determinations played out over the bodies of citizens, both between and within sovereign states. When I perform consumption by purchasing a ticket to a Hollywood text, what does that say about/do to my citizenship? When I perform citizenship by assenting to immigration limits in my countries of nationality, what does that say about/do to my spectatorship?

This is an era when firms are much more powerful than governments, the United States is in an increasingly asymmetrical power relationship to other countries, and there is a global fervor of deregulation. We are dealing with a triangulated form of mimetic desire. States want to emulate what they fantasize is the efficiency and effectiveness of corporate life. Firms want to rule their subjects with the disciplined policy and civic propriety of an idealized public administration. States want to look like corporations in terms of efficiency and effectiveness, at the same time as they negotiate with one another, while firms want to look like states in their own dealings. Citizens sit and watch, waiting for their governments to explain what has already been agreed between companies. The question of the modern for citizens—namely, the control of their everyday lives by forces beyond their immediate vision—is being superseded by the question of the postmodern: the control of those lives by forces beyond their knowledge. This is most obviously true in the arenas of telecommunications and illegal drugs, traditionally policy strongholds of the state, but now privatized and, frankly, American (Strange 1995, 298, 301–2, 306–7). Because of moral panics, we cannot do much about drugs: that awaits the final conquest of policy making by neoclassical economics. But we should speak about new cultural technology.

The domain of the digital references old anxieties from cultural and communications history. It is heralded as the ultimate refinement of television, a second chance, the one that puts the medium back to the origins of radio as an activity center and makes it "a good cultural object" (Boddy 1994, 116, 107). Al Gore claims that the National Information Infrastructure will "educate, promote democracy, and save lives" (quoted in Gomery 1994, 9). In short, it is the new governmentality, but inflected with the phenomeno-logical awe of a precocious child who can be returned to Eden. This re-deemed version of television will heal the wounds of the modern, reconciling private and public, labor and leisure, commerce and culture, individuality and collectivity. But although the new "digital individual" has his or her per-sona defined through computerized forms that provide some freedom of representation inside screen space, these forms also subject the person to sur-veillance and definition via governmental and corporate identification, and they operate in a privatized way that is restricted financially to the upper so-cial echelon (ibid., 17). Conventional broadcast television will continue to be what it is today for many people around the world: "a consolation prize" (Gitlin 1993, 48). By the late 1990s, the major media corporations were actively seeking to levy Web rent via gateways. The prospect of everyone becoming a performer, of all hybridities being referenced, is the utopia on offer; its dystopic other, based on a material reading of communication and cultural histories, seems more probable. What should we do about this?

We can follow the example of cultural critics who center their analysis on the conditions of making meaning as much as on its contents. When Rudolf Arnheim wrote his "Forecast of Television" in 1935, he imagined something far more splendid than later laments for television would suggest, but with the same antinomies encountered today. Arnheim predicted a global simultaneity of visual expression and experience, via the universal transmis-sion of railway disasters, professorial addresses, town meetings, boxing title fights, dance bands, carnivals, and aerial mountain views—an instantaneous montage of Broadway and Vesuvius. This common world of vision would surpass the dual limitations of linguistic interpretation and competence, with a new modesty deriving from the recognition that "we are located as one among many." But this was no naive welcome. Arnheim warned that "television is a new, hard test of our wisdom." The alternatives were enrich-ment or dormancy: a vibrant public, engaged and active; or an indolent au-dience, domesticated and private (Arnheim 1969, 160–63).

Nor was Hollywood silent on the matter. In *Murder by Television*, also from 1935 (Clifford Sanforth), the inventor of the medium, Professor Houghland, is stolidly independent from motives of personal gain. All the large media corporations are keen to obtain the new technology, but they are confounded by this free-floating intellectual's wish to keep his invention free of corporate despoliation. Houghland refuses to patent the device, so keen is he to cordon the innovation off from conventional notions of property and ensure that television can become "something more than another form of entertainment." As per Arnheim's forecast, the professor's grand demonstration joins people across the United States. Then he takes us live to Paris, London, and an unnamed Asian city. But at the moment of triumph, when television seems set to fulfill his promise that it can assure "the preservation of humanity" and "make of this earth a paradise," Houghland is killed on-screen. A doctor involved with "foreign governments" (a cable to him in code is signed "J. V. S.") uses the sound of a telephone ringing back in his office to radiate waves that merge with those from the television set, creating what Bela Lugosi later informs us is "an interstellar frequency, which is a death ray." The invention incorporates the best and the worst of human thought and guile, along with the mystery of the modern: great spirals emanate periodically from the television, suggesting a trancelike condition that never quite departs the film. That human wonder, contrasted with industrial dross and professorial anxiety, remains with us.

I return to my beginning. The summer 1993 issue of *Daedalus* was dedicated to another conference report, this time with the theme "Reconstructing Nations and States." The editor, still in office from earlier Bellagio days, welcomed the fact that it was now possible to bring "into the *Daedalus* family of authors a new generation of men and women from disparate parts of the world, including those parts only recently liberated from communist rule" (Graubard 1993, viii). Such inclusivity is a step in the right direction. But the publication these new leaders produced bore very little connection to work done in textual studies, as broadly defined. The outcome was a policy debate about distribution that is deficient in cultural content. How can people working in the domain of cultural theory and history have an impact on these discussions?

To include ourselves, we need to transcend not only traditional divisions within the humanities, but across to the social sciences, and also beyond our borders, in search of explaining and altering the distributional politics of culture as much as its textual politics. We should do so with a constant concern for the twin aspects of subjectivity and power, without denying either the Realpolitik of governmentality or the animating logic and passion of left politics (as broadly conceived). We must draw on our traditional strengths in explaining meaning, supplemented by links to those who risk most from the new international division of cultural labor in all its myriad forms, with whom we must work to influence our governments and companies away from a narrow view of international cultural corporatism. I almost forgot to mention: in 1995, *Daedalus* reissued its "psychodrama" from thirty years earlier of "men coming from different countries," so prescient did the discussion seem. The white guys keep performing over the long haul. They need watching.

Works Cited

Arnheim, Rudolf. 1969. *Film as Art.* London: Faber and Faber.

Attali, Jacques. 1996. "Hollywood vs. Europe: The Next Round." *New Perspectives Quarterly* 11: 46–47.

Axtmann, Roland. 1993. "Society, Globalization and the Comparative Method." *History of the Human Sciences* 6: 53–74.

Boddy, William. 1994. "Archaeologies of Electronic Vision and the Gendered Spectator." *Screen* 35: 105–22.

Buck, Elizabeth B. 1992. "Asia and the Global Film Industry." *East-West Film Journal* 6: 116–33.

Chartrand, Harry Hillman. 1992. "International Cultural Affairs: A Fourteen Country Survey." *Journal of Arts Management, Law and Society* 22: 134–54.

Cohen, Robin. 1991. *Contested Domains: Debates in International Labour Studies.* London: Zed Books.

"Couture Ordinaire." 1995. *Economist* 337: 79, 82.

Fröbel, Folker, Jürgen Heinrichs, and Otto Kreye. 1980. *The New International Division of Labour: Structural Unemployment in Industrialised Countries and Industrialisation in Developing Countries.* Trans. Pete Burgess. Cambridge: Cambridge University Press.

Frow, John. 1992. "Cultural Markets and the Shape of Culture." In *Continental Shift: Globalisation and Culture,* ed. Elizabeth Jacka, 7–24. Sydney: Local Consumption.

Gitlin, Todd. 1993. "Flat and Happy." *Wilson Quarterly* 17: 47–55.

Gomery, Douglas. 1994. "In Search of the Cybermarket." *Wilson Quarterly* 18: 9–17.

Graubard, Stephen R. 1993. "Preface." *Daedalus* 122: v–viii.

Hall, Stuart, and Paddy Whannell. 1965. *The Popular Arts.* New York: Pantheon.

Hannerz, Ulf. 1990. "Cosmopolitans and Locals in World Culture." *Theory, Culture and Society* 7: 237–51.

Hayward, Susan. 1993. "State, Culture and the Cinema: Jack Lang's Strategies for the French Industry 1981–93." *Screen* 34: 382–91.

Heilemann, John. 1994. "A Survey of Television: Feeling for the Future." *Economist* 330: 1–18.

Hoffmann, Stanley. 1966. "Report of the Conference on Conditions of World Order— June 12–19, 1965, Villa Serbelloni, Bellagio, Italy." *Daedalus* 95: 455–78.

Hofstede, Geert. 1993. "Cultural Dimensions in People Management: The Socialization Perspective." In *Globalizing Management: Creating and Leading the Competitive Organization,* ed. Vladimir Pucik, Noel M. Tichy, and Carole K. Barnett. New York: John Wiley.

Jacka, Elizabeth. 1992. "Introduction." In *Continental Shift: Globalisation and Culture,* ed. Elizabeth Jacka. Sydney: Local Consumption.

Maguire, Joseph. 1994. "Preliminary Observations on Globalisation and the Migration of Sport Labour." *Sociological Review* 42: 452–80.

Marvasti, A. 1994. "International Trade in Cultural Goods: A Cross-Sectional Analysis." *Journal of Cultural Economics* 18: 135–48.

Miller, Peter, and Ted O'Leary. 1993. "Accounting, 'Economic Citizenship' and the Spatial Reordering of Manufacture." *Accounting, Organizations and Society* 19: 15–43.

Miller, Toby. 1995. "Exporting Truth from Aboriginal Australia: Portions of Our Past Become Present Again, Where Only the Melancholy Light of Origin Shines." *Media Information Australia* 76 (May): 7–17.

"Professional India." 1995. *New York Times,* October 22, F13.

Pye, Lucian W. 1965. "Introduction: Political Culture and Political Development." In *Political Culture and Political Development,* ed. Lucian W. Pye and Sidney Verba. Princeton, N.J.: Princeton University Press.

Reeves, Geoffrey. 1993. *Communications and the "Third World."* London: Routledge.

Rockwell, John. 1994. "The New Colossus: American Culture as Power Export." *New York Times* January 30, H1, H30.

Ruthrof, Horst. 1997. *Semantics and the Body: Meaning from Frege to the Postmodern.* Toronto: University of Toronto Press.

Sankowski, Edward. 1992. "Ethics, Art, and Museums." *Journal of Aesthetic Education* 26: 1–15.

Slide, Anthony. 1995. "Old World, New Cinema." *Queen's Quarterly* 102: 357–74.

Stevenson, Richard W. 1994. "Lights! Camera! Europe!" *New York Times,* February 6, 1, 6.

Strange, Susan. 1995. "The Limits of Politics." *Government and Opposition* 30: 291–311.

Wedell, George. 1994. "Prospects for Television in Europe." *Government and Opposition* 29: 315–31.

A Blast from the Past

Fiona Foley

In Aboriginal Australia, there are six major seasons in the yearly cycle. It was during the Aboriginal calendar season of Midawarr (the fruiting season) that this journey unfolded.

I was air-shipped to Germany along with a number of other Australians, both indigenous and nonindigenous, in March 1995. The international guests attending the Eliza Fraser symposium in Germany were treated to a field trip. From West Berlin further into the east, on a train threading its way through a scene resembling one from Steven Spielberg's *Schindler's List,* the destination was the Leipzig Museum and the collection of the renowned German naturalist, Amalie Dietrich. It became apparent that there was another dire narrative that was seeking its own brand-new day. For the two indigenous people in the guided tour, there were flashbacks to a feature article on the front of the *Bulletin,* November 12, 1991, in which Dietrich was named the "Angel of Black Death."[1]

Amalie Dietrich, naturalist and collector, worked in the state of Queensland, Australia, from 1863 until 1873. The Leipzig collection was made up of more than 130 pieces of material culture, and eight skeletal remains from Queensland—five male and three female—as well as a male skull from the city of Rockhampton. All of the skeletal remains were destroyed during the bombing of Leipzig in World War II. Amalie Dietrich was also known to have offered financial incentives to local settlers in return for the shooting of healthy Aboriginal specimens for the assembled collection of shipping magnate Johann Caesar Godeffroy VI and his recently established museum. Aboriginal bones were used to support the new scientific

Fiona Foley, *Native Blood* series, 1994. Courtesy of the Roslyn Oxley9 Gallery.

theory of our supposed racial inferiority: the Darwinian evolutionary theory. These theories were not unlike those of the 1920s, when similar racist ideologies were embraced by Adolf Hitler and the National Socialist movement.

One of the new export industries in the Australian colonies was the shipment of Aboriginal skulls. It is estimated that between five thousand and ten thousand Aboriginal bodies were part of the international scientific trade. The insidious new science of the twentieth century is one based on the intellectual, not the physical. What has horrified me the most is the pervasive colonization of the intellect. Not content to be the body snatchers their forebears were, the nouveau colonialists colonize our indigenous intellect.

As a Badtjala woman from the largest sand island in the world, Fraser Island, Australia, I see this nouveau colonization taking place along three avenues: first, through the reconstruction of colonists' narratives nationally; second, through the use of language when using maligned buzz words such as *hybridization, reconciliation,* and *postcolonialism*; finally, through academia, where Aboriginal people are informants in the extensive research carried out by non-Aboriginal people.

The dubious status of Australian academia in not accrediting Aboriginal informants parallels the role of indigenous women on the Australian continent. The status of Aboriginal women was especially complex. They played a major role on the frontier, making significant contributions to the workforce, including stock riding, mustering, shepherding, housework, cooking, washing, and nursing, to list a few occupations.

The conquest also took place on a footing not often written about but touched on in Henry Reynolds's *With the White People,* which alludes to other ephemeral happenings: "sex-hungry males," "occupational force."[2] Aboriginal women were usually objects of desire and Anglo-Australian males could forcibly unleash their brutal lust and sire illegitimate offspring. The double injustice was that the unspoken taboo of sexual relations with Aboriginal women was never elevated to the status of marriage. This complex dichotomy always placed the black woman on the lowest economic rung of the ladder.

Alongside the virtues of women on the frontier was the need to create strong historic females in our national identity. The dilemma is that, as an indigenous woman, I cannot recall one Aboriginal heroine. The unresolved puzzle concerning the Australian heroine is the fact that she could never be black. The narrative has always puzzled me; why is it that the heroine could only be White—the White damsel in distress battling the harsh forces of nature and native savages? Her black counterpart had not left a single mark in Australian literature, yet in this landscape her skeletal remains have carbon-dated at Lake Mungo at around thirty thousand years ago.

The supposed heroine in my adulthood is the elusive narrative of Eliza Fraser. Constant public mythologizing has lionized Mrs. Fraser as a national and international heroine. In 1836, she was marooned for five weeks on Fraser Island, and her saga has been allowed to continue to this day. Mrs. Fraser's incarceration on the island would, in turn, imprison the traditional owners of Fraser Island, the Badtjala. The absence of a dialogue with the Badtjala has diligently damaged these people and put them to rest. I often wonder, when will *she* be put to rest?

In my search through Badtjala archival material, I came across a mysterious and striking image of one of my forebears. Her gaze was averted. No name. No birth. No death. The signifier in this instance is one black-and-white photograph held in the John Oxley Library, Brisbane. The real heroine of my narrative is nameless, black and defiant. She has not had a serious quarrel with the truth, unlike Mrs. Fraser. She does not appear in a Patrick White novel or in a Sidney Nolan painting.

I think of the following quote from bell hooks's *Black Looks* when I reflect on my photographic series, titled *Native Blood*: "She conquers the terror through perverse re-enactment, through resistance, using violence as a means of fleeing from a history that is a burden too great to bear."[3] I think of all the unnamed black women around the world, their unrecorded births and deaths. These marginalized women of historic deeds and their lives have never been recorded, yet they live on in our collective memories. These women are often nameless in Australia, for the space they have reclaimed, often on behalf of the communities they come from, is largely indigenous. These women I speak of include Shirley Foley, for her wisdom and foresight to reclaim land on Fraser Island and introduce Badtjala language programs, especially designed for children, into the Hervey Bay community. She is currently the coordinator (zone 2) of the Central Queensland Language Program and has completed a Badtjala dictionary.

I also speak of the artist Bunduk Marika, for her determination to bring leading Australian architect Glenn Murcutt to her community of Yirrkala to institute economical contemporary architecture suitable for northern monsoonal weather and her regeneration of native plant species in Yirrkala; and the women of Maningrida who have shared their knowledge and traveled, for weaving cultural exchanges with Aboriginal women from Queensland and South Australian communities. These women are continuing traditional and innovative weaving practices.

Women of Hindmarsh Island are also included, for standing their ground concerning Aboriginal women's religious rites, defying the development of a bridge, the South Australian Government, and a Royal Commission. These women retain their knowledge of women's secret ceremony in this tract of land and sea. They challenged the patriarchy of our Australian parliament and judicial system.

The strength of women from Central Australia who conduct business ceremonies coming from sixty thousand years of religious practices in the age of the Internet and the information superhighway must be included. In arid country and in secret places, times governed by the seasons and lunar phases, hundreds of invited Aboriginal women gather to maintain their traditional ties to land and kinship responsibilities.

Women have made a difference through sharing secret/sacred knowledge and objects. The positive outcome is a coming together that is clearly bringing about a change in verbal and nonverbal discourse between indigenous women of the continent. Linked to this is an immense appreciation of cultural leaders, most of whom, for me, are Aboriginal women from the various nations within Australia. Yet, twice in 1995 I had to contend with the English heroine Eliza Fraser, both in Australian academia and in Germany. Not one of the indigenous women mentioned earlier has had a symposium created around her life, nor is she likely to in the foreseeable future.

To recast the heroine, a perverse reenactment takes place: the black heroine of yore. The heroine in this instance is Badtjala. The only way I could come close to her was to recast her in my image. The skirt I wear in the *Native Blood* series is from Maningrida. Like the shell-and-reed necklaces, these objects were made by Aboriginal women coming from a remote Australian community. The red, black, and yellow hand-painted platform shoes symbolize the Aboriginal land-rights flag.

Unlike my forebears, my discarded symbols may possibly leave a mark on this urban landscape. The viewer has to draw her own conclusion. Yet, I live in hope that my heroine could be your heroine, as she defies all odds with an unspoken eloquence and spunk.

As history on the continent has been written by the victors, the dominant discourse has tended to be a clearly spelled-out colonialist narrative, which is linear, rather than dealing with complex histories that overlap spatial shifts in time. There has been an effective silencing.

For some, it begins with the doctrine of *terra nullius* in 1788, a Latin term meaning "land empty."

From 1788 until 1992, this false doctrine was in place concerning the indigenous populations. For the Badtjala, it begins in 1836, with the shipwreck of the *Stirling Castle* and the first Englishwoman's coming ashore at Fraser Island. A conspicuous absence is entered into by an unsuspecting nation of Badtjala. The psychological impact was great and did not afford

Fiona Foley, *Native Blood* series, 1994. Courtesy of the Roslyn Oxley9 Gallery.

the Badtjala a voice until 1964, with the publication, written by my great-uncle Wilfie Reeves, of *The Legends of Moonie Jarl.* What does this deafening SILENCE say to me? One hundred and twenty-eight years of a ruptured history, or six generations of people without a recorded existence, except on mission files. The messages are fraught with contradictory facts and public mythologizing.

At a regional level, the jarring of symbols also resound at a site on Fraser Island at Poyungan Rocks, or if one were to say it in Badtjala, Boyungan. This particular shell midden is fifteen hundred years old and contains layers of wah wong mollusc (Pipi shells). Cutting through the middle of the oldest recorded midden site on the island is a road for four-wheel drive vehicles used by local residents to access the beach and various common thoroughfares.

The static image invokes a memory of a ruptured history imbued with an immense sense of loss that has occurred through subtle and overt acts of physical and cultural genocide. In stark contrast, the artifact—in this case Badtjala cultural material collected and housed in state museums such as the South Australian Museum—bears heavily on access to knowledge for my generation of indigenous people. These objects have become so valued and precious, because of their scarcity, that they are protected through museum policy and government acts. Although the custodial guardians still inhabit the continent, they do not retain the right to house and use this material in the passing down of knowledge. At best, an appointment is made with the relevant institution, and the artifacts can be held. Photographic records may be made available to the Badtjala people on request. Ironically, these same objects will help to legitimize a race of people when they choose to seek native title on Fraser Island.

Banjo Owens was a well-known Badtjala man who was a resistance fighter. In the 1930s, he pursued a one-man struggle to reside on Fraser Island. The problem was that the Badtjala had forcibly been removed from Fraser Island in 1904. Law-enforcement officers in the 1930s saw it as their duty to abide by the previous ruling.

Banjo would row over to Fraser Island to hunt, fish, and set up camp, only to be tracked down by the local constable and taken back in his dingy to the mainland of Hervey Bay. His dingy would be chained up to a monumental gum tree, but the clever Banjo would simply return to the site with an ax to cut down the trunk and lift the padlocked chain over the stump. He would jump back in his dingy and once again return to the island. The saga would continue in this vein. Banjo's stance does not, however, negate the continuous link that other Badtajala clans have had in maintaining a custodial right through their unrecorded yet frequent visits to the island.

The season is now Barr mirri (the growth season) and the end of the journey draws closer. Successive generations of Badtjala have been afforded a voice, sometimes in mainstream spheres, at other times in local communities. As modern subversives, the oars for the dingy are still close at hand. The challenge lies in the way we shall use our Aboriginal heroes and heroines.

This brings me to Marcia Langton's paper, presented at the Global Diversity Conference in Sydney in 1995. In "Representations and Indigenous Images," Langton states, "These icons of Aboriginality are produced by Anglo-Australians, not in dialogue with Aboriginal people, but from other representations such as the noble savages or the dying race. They are inherited, imagined representations that date to the days of the colony."[4]

What has tended to take place through writings by Australian historians and academics is a gross romanticization of life in the colony based on British ignorance of the complex systems of Aboriginal languages, kinship, religion, art, and science. Overwhelmingly, one sees a glaring absence of dialogue, not only among the indigenous populations but also between the colonized and the colonizer. Yet, the populations of Australia spoke more than 250 different languages, and seven hundred separate dialect groups have been recorded. Many Aboriginal people were multilingual, able to speak and understand many different languages as well as English.

Sadly, it is very rare for Anglo-Australians to understand or speak one word of an Aboriginal language, let alone a phrase or sentence structure. Yet, our indigenous children are indoctrinated to read, write, and converse in the dominant language, thereby possibly making our systems of complex grammar defunct. Aboriginal languages are in a serious state of retrieval and maintenance nationally. The power of language is a daunting phenomenon, whose treachery reorders the subordination of the colonized.

The great chain of Australian history begins for the Eora in 1789 around the legs of the first prisoners of war, Bennelong and Colree. Governor Arthur Phillip ordered the kidnapping of two Aboriginal men. Their significant roles were as interpreter to translate English into Eora and vice versa. On November 27, 1789, Bennelong and Colbee were brought back to Government House. They were washed, shaved, clothed, and more important, shackled by the legs. The writings of Frantz Fanon echo loudly across the continent when he says, "The practice of violence binds them together as a whole, since each individual forms a violent link in the great chain, a part of the organism of violence which has surged upwards in reaction to the settler's violence in the beginning."[5] The paradigm is at play again today, bringing together the Aboriginal peoples, the Australian government, and the British monarchy.

Pemulwuy, one of Australia's first subversive activists, was an Eora man who waged a war for fourteen years. He fought the British regime from Lane Cove to Toongabbie and Parramatta. This region is better known as Sydney. He was responsible for the phrase "Tyerabarrbowaryaou," which means, "I shall never become a white man." What Pemulwuy was saying, in effect, was that he could never fence in land the way the settlers did. The boundaries are governed by natural phenomena such as tidal estuaries, watercourses, rocky outcrops, and mountain ranges.

Aboriginal informants, who were often written out of history, have never been credited for their roles in shaping Australia's economy and development as a nation. Early colonialists, escaped convicts, settler historians, and, in 1897, the government-appointed Protectors of Aborigines were the earliest recorders of a dialogue between the indigenous populations and the colonizers. Paradoxically, it is these early and scant documents that are a pivotal key in the location of a disjointed inheritance. A dialogue was initiated; however, the frontier switched strategy on numerous occasions.

In the state of Queensland, the larger scenario contains true guerrilla warfare. In 1848, the regime of "dispersal" came into force, and continued for the next three decades. Violence was the backdrop, with the imposition of the Native Police from southern states and overzealous officers. *Dispersal* was a deceptive term used in official reports to underscore what actually took place: massacres. Today, we use the term *ethnic cleansing*. It was then commonly believed that the path was smoothed for the demise of a "dying race."

As the frontier continued north and west, there was an increasing need for Aboriginal labor. Charles D. Rowley speaks of a new pact for the economic survival of the new arrivals: "professed morality in a setter democracy can be moulded by economic interest and the need to cover up awkward facts."[6] Aboriginal labor was cheap, and payment was usually made in the form of alcohol, opium, tobacco, one blanket, food, sometimes clothes. Aboriginal people provided labor for the mining fields, sugar plantations, pastoralists, and the timber and pearl industries.

Jimmy Governor (1875–1901) reminds me of Aboriginal subversive activists such as Pemulwuy and Banjo, men who stood outside the law—Aboriginal heroes who sought justice in their lifetime. Jimmy Governor dared to go against the social order of the day and married a white woman, Ethel Page, aged sixteen. The unspoken politics of sexual tensions in the colony comes into play with Governor's life. He was hanged in Paddington, Sydney, in 1901.

Although it was common for white males to have illicit intercourse with native women on a casual or semipermanent basis, the same could not be said for Aboriginal men and white women. Slighting remarks were made

Fiona Foley, *Native Blood* series, 1994. Courtesy of the Roslyn
Oxley9 Gallery.

constantly to both husband and wife. In reprisal for racist taunts in July 1990, Governor carried out a murder at the Mawbey homestead. For fourteen weeks, Governor and his brother became bushrangers.

Brian Davies, through historical accounts of events titled *The Life of Jimmy Governor,* makes an astute observation of society in Australia at the turn of the twentieth century:

> They had shed their own criminal past of convict forebears. They had built town, steeple and school where, as they perceived it, only barbarism had existed. They had every right to congratulate themselves . . . and to expect subsequent centuries to remember and acknowledge them. They were not unmindful that what they laid down then, would be their own memorial in the future—and they built well.[7]

The subject of memorials brings to mind the Australian national holiday held annually on April 25, ANZAC Day, where we remember our fallen soldiers of all wars but the very first. It is a luxury that has never been afforded to the first Australians, who died defending their land. Henry Reynolds writes that, in the state of Queensland alone,

> there is no telling the size of the Aboriginal death toll from overt violence, guesstimates of 15,000 have been made—based rather roughly upon a rule of thumb that white frontiersmen established a kill ratio of fifteen or twenty to one against the Aborigines. For comparison's sake, this is more than the number of Queenslanders killed and injured at the Sudan, the Boer Wars, and the Korean War and the Vietnam War combined.[8]

What were the casualties of the other states and territories?

In the well-known text *The Black Aesthetic,* in particular the chapter by Larry Neal, "The Black Arts Movement," when Brother Knight is calling for a new black aesthetic, he realizes, "we must create a new history, new symbols, myths and legends."[9] This philosophy has heralded a new visual language and curatorship direction within Aboriginal Australia.

What has taken place for the first time are three significant public sculptures that pay tribute to our indigenous fighters. During the bicentennial year, 1988, Djon Mundine conceived of and curated *The Aboriginal Movement,* which was installed at the Sydney Biennale and is on permanent exhibition at the National Gallery of Australia, Canberra. Ramingining artists and the surrounding communities worked toward collating two hundred hollow log coffins in a tribute to all Aboriginal people who have died defending Australia.

The year 1995 ushered in a second tribute to a specific nation of Aboriginal people, the Eora. This public sculpture, titled *Edge of Trees,* is a

ona Foley, *Native Blood* series, 1994. Courtesy of the Roslyn Oxley9 Gallery.

collaboration between Janet Laurence and myself and is placed in the fore-court of the Museum of Sydney, the previous site of the First Government House. The single most striking aspect of this work is the haunting use of the Eora language in both the written context and the spoken word on compact disc. It must be noted that the political significance of the work is that it is the oldest retrieval of an Aboriginal language since colonization in Australia.

At a site along the Brisbane River, artist Ron Hurley completed a sculpture titled *Gerrabaugh, midden.* Six timber and cast aluminum columns represent the six nations that shared an aspect of the one creation story concerning the rainbow serpent ceremony held at Coolum, as told by Willie McKenzie. A haunting visual presence is taking shape along the eastern half of the continent.

Through our memorial tributes to Aboriginal people, we have much to celebrate as a nation on the verge of maturity. The irony of the settler culture is that it has brought about many double contexts and unanswered questions, such as the Eliza Fraser saga. As a Badtjala artist reflecting on the past two centuries, for me the intensity of the gaze has increased. It is the omnipresent Aboriginal gaze that reflects the colonial gaze. What I see mirrored in the exclusive gaze of race is an inarticulate consumption of a guilty, awkward Australia.

Notes

1. David Monaghan, "Angel of Black Death," *Australian Bulletin,* November 12, 1991, 30–38.

2. Henry Reynolds, "VI Black Pioneers," in *With the White People* (Melbourne: Penguin Books, 1990), 214.

3. bell hooks, "Representations of Whiteness," in *Black Looks* (Boston: South End Press), 176.

4. Marcia Langton, "Representations and Indigenous Images," unpublished manuscript, 5.

5. Frantz Fanon, "Concerning Violence," in *The Wretched of the Earth* (Paris: Penguin Books, 1961), 73.

6. Charles D. Rowley, "The Queensland Frontiers, 1859–1897," in *The Destruction of Aboriginal Society* (Australia: Pelican Books, 1972), 175.

7. Brian Davies, "The Beginning," in *The Life of Jimmy Governor* (Sydney: Ure Smith, 1979), 18.

8. Quoted in Thomas Hardy, "The Owl and the Eagle," *Social Alternatives* 5:4 (November 1986): 18.

9. Larry Neal, "The Black Arts Movement," in *The Black Aesthetic,* ed. G. Addison Jr. (New York: Anchor Books, Doubleday, 1971).

Palimpsestic Aesthetics:
A Meditation on Hybridity and Garbage

Robert Stam

Cultural discourse in Latin America and the Caribbean has been fecund in neologistic aesthetics, both literary and cinematic: "lo real maravilloso americano" (Alejo Carpentier), the "aesthetics of hunger" (Glauber Rocha), "Cine imperfecto" (Julio Garcia Espinosa), the "creative incapacity for copying" (Paulo Emilio Salles Gomes), the "aesthetics of garbage" (Rogério Sganzerla), the "salamander" (as opposed to the Hollywood dinosaur) aesthetic (Paul Leduc), "termite terrorism" (Gilhermo del Toro), "anthropophagy" (the Brazilian modernists), "Tropicália" (Gilberto Gil and Caetano Veloso), "rasquachismo" (Tomás Ibarra-Frausto), and Santeria aesthetics (Arturo Lindsay). Most of these alternative aesthetics revalorize by inversion what had formerly been seen as negative, especially within colonialist discourse. Thus ritual cannibalism, for centuries the very name of the savage, abject other, becomes with the Brazilian *modernistas* an anticolonialist trope and a term of value. Even "magic realism" inverts the colonial view of magic as irrational superstition. At the same time, these aesthetics share the jujitsu trait of turning strategic weakness into tactical strength. By appropriating an existing discourse for their own ends, they deploy the force of the dominant against domination.

I would like to focus on three related aspects of these aesthetics: (1) their constitutive hybridity; (2) their chronotopic multiplicity; and (3) their common motif of the redemption of detritus. After arguing the special qualifications of the cinema for realizing such a hybrid, multitemporal aesthetic, I will conclude with the case of the Brazilian "aesthetics of garbage" as the point of convergence of all these themes, and specifically examine three films literally and figuratively "about" garbage.

First, hybridity. Although hybridity has been a perennial feature of art and cultural discourse in Latin America—highlighted in such terms as *mestizaje, indianismo, diversalite, creolite, raza cósmica*—it has recently been recoded as a symptom of the postmodern, postcolonial, and postnationalist moment.[1] The valorization of hybridity, it should be noted, is itself a form of jujitsu, because within colonial discourse the question of hybridity was linked to the prejudice against race mixing, the "degeneration of blood," and the putative infertility of mulattoes. But if the nationalist discourse of the 1960s drew sharp lines between First World and Third World, oppressor and oppressed, postnationalist discourse replaces such binary dualisms with a more nuanced spectrum of subtle differentiations, in a new global regime where First World and Third World are mutually imbricated.[2] Notions of ontologically referential identity metamorphose into a conjunctural play of identifications. Purity gives way to "contamination." Rigid paradigms collapse into sliding metonymies. Erect, militant postures give way to an orgy of "positionalities." Once secure boundaries become more porous; an iconography of barbed-wire frontiers mutates into images of fluidity and crossing. A rhetoric of unsullied integrity gives way to miscegenated grammars and scrambled metaphors. A discourse of "media imperialism" gives way to reciprocity and "indigenization." Colonial tropes of irreconcilable dualism give way to postcolonial tropes drawing on the diverse modalities of mixedness: religious (syncretism), botanical (hybridity), linguistic (creolization), and human-genetic *(mestizaje)*.

Although hybridity has existed wherever civilizations conflict, combine, and synthesize, it reached a kind of violent paroxysm with the European colonization of the Americas. The *conquista* shaped a new world of practices and ideologies of mixing, making the Americas the scene of unprecedented combinations of indigenous peoples, Africans, and Europeans, and later of immigratory diasporas from all over the world. But hybridity has never been a peaceful encounter, a tension-free theme park; it has always been deeply entangled with colonial violence. Although for some hybridity is lived as just another metaphor within a Derridean free play, for others it is lived as pain and visceral memory. Indeed, as a descriptive catchall term, *hybridity* fails to discriminate between the diverse modalities of hybridity, such as colonial imposition (for example, the Catholic church constructed on top of a destroyed Inca temple), or other interactions such as obligatory assimilation, political co-optation, cultural mimicry, commercial exploitation, top-down appropriation, bottom-up subversion. Hybridity, in other words, is power-laden and assymetrical. Hybridity is also co-optable. In Latin America, national identity has often been officially articulated as hybrid, through hypocritically integrationist ideologies that have glossed over subtle racial hegemonies.

Brazilian composer-singer Gilberto Gil calls attention to the power-laden nature of syncretism in his 1989 song "From Bob Dylan to Bob Marley: A Provocation Samba." The lyrics inform us that Bob Dylan, after converting to Christianity, made a reggae album, thus returning to the house of Israel by way of the Caribbean. The lyrics set into play a number of broad cultural parallels, between Jewish symbiology and Jamaican Rasta-farianism, between the Inquisition's persecution of Jews (and Muslims) and the European suppression of African religions ("When the Africans arrived on these shores / there was no freedom of religion"), ultimately contrasting the progressive syncretism of a Bob Marley (who died "because besides being Black he was also Jewish") with the alienation of a Michael Jackson, who "besides turning white . . . is becoming sad." Gil celebrates hybridity and syncretism, then, but articulates them in relation to the asymmetrical power relations engendered by colonialism. For oppressed people, artistic syn-cretism is not a game but a painful negotiation, an exercise, as the song's lyrics put it, both of "resistance" and "surrender."[3]

Second, chronotopic multiplicity. Current theoretical literature betrays a fascination with the notion of simultaneous, superimposed spatiotempo-ralities. The widely disseminated trope of the palimpsest, the parchment on which are inscribed the layered traces of diverse moments of past writing, contains within it this idea of multiple temporalities. The postmodern moment, similarly, is seen as chaotically plural and contradictory, while its aesthetic is seen as an aggregate of historically dated styles randomly re-assembled in the present. But this oxymoronic space-time is not found only in recent theoretical literature. It was anticipated in Walter Benjamin's "revo-lutionary nostalgia," in Ernst Bloch's conjugation of the now and the "not yet," in Fernand Braudel's multiple-speed view of history, in Louis Althusser's "overdetermination" and "uneven development," in Raymond Williams's "residual and emergent" discourses, in Fredric Jameson's "nostalgia for the present," and in David Harvey's "time-space compression." Bakhtinian dia-logism, in the same vein, alludes to the temporally layered matrix of com-municative utterances that "reach" the text not only through recognizable citations but also through a subtle process of dissemination. In a very suggestive formulation, Mikhail Bakhtin evokes the multiple epochs inter-textually "buried" in the work of Shakespeare. The "semantic treasures Shakespeare embedded in his works," Bakhtin writes, were created and collected through the centuries and even millennia: they lay hidden in the language, and not only in the literary language, but also in those strata of the popular language that before Shakespeare's time had not entered literature, in the diverse genres and forms of speech communication, in the forms of a mighty national culture (primarily carnival forms) that were shaped through millennia, in theatre-spectacle genres (mystery plays, farces, and so forth), in plots whose roots go back to prehistoric antiquity.[4]

Bakhtin thus points up the temporally palimpsestic nature of all artistic texts, seen within a millennial *longue durée*.[5] Nor is this aesthetic the special preserve of canonical writers, because dialogism operates within all cultural production, whether literate or nonliterate, highbrow or lowbrow. Rap music's aesthetic of sampling and cut'n'mix, for example, can be seen as a streetsmart, low-budget embodiment of Bakhtin's theories of temporally embedded intertextuality, because rap's multiple strands derive from sources as diverse as African call-and-response patterns, disco, funk, the Last Poets, Gil Scott Heron, Muhammed Ali, doo-wop groups, skip-rope rhymes, prison and army songs, signifying, and "the dozens," all the way back to the griots of Nigeria and Gambia.[6] Rap bears the stamp and rhythm of multiple times and meters; as in artistic collage or literary quotation, the sampled texts carry with them the time-connoted memory of their previous existences.

The third shared feature of these hybrid bricolage aesthetics is their common leitmotif of the strategic redemption of the low, the despised, the imperfect, and the "trashy" as part of a social overturning. This strategic redemption of the marginal also has echoes in the realms of high theory and cultural studies. One thinks, for example, of Jacques Derrida's recuperation of the marginalia of the classical philosophical text, of Bakhtin's exaltation of "redeeming filth" and of low "carnivalized" genres, of Benjamin's "trash of history" and his view of the work of art as constituting itself out of apparently insignificant fragments, of Gilles Deleuze and Félix Guattari's recuperation of stigmatized psychic states such as schizophrenia, of camp's ironic reappropriation of kitsch, of cultural studies' recuperation of subliterary forms and "subcultural styles," and of James Scott's "weapons of the weak."

In the plastic arts, the "garbage girls" (Mierle Laderman Ukeles, Christy Rupp, Betty Beaumont) deploy waste disposal as a trampoline for art. Ukeles, for example, choreographed a "street ballet" of garbage trucks. (One is reminded of the "dance of the garbage can lids" in the Donen-Kelly musical *It's Always Fair Weather*.) Betty Beaumont makes installation art on toxic wastes using government surplus materials.[7] Joseph Cornell, similarly, turned the flotsam of daily life—broken dolls, paper cutouts, wineglasses, medicine bottles—into luminous, childlike collages. In the cinema, an "aesthetics of garbage" performs a kind of jujitsu by recuperating cinematic waste materials. For filmmakers without great resources, raw-footage minimalism reflects practical necessity as well as artistic strategy. In a film such as *Hour of the Furnaces,* unpromising raw footage is transmogrified into art, as the alchemy of sound-image montage transforms the base metals of titles, blank frames, and wild sound into the gold and silver of rhythmic virtuosity. Compilation filmmakers such as Bruce Conner, Mark Rappaport, and Sherry Milner/Ernest Larsen rearrange and reedit preexisting filmic materials, while trying to fly below the radar of bourgeois legalities. Craig Baldwin, a San Francisco film programmer, reshapes outtakes and public domain materials into witty compilation films. In *Sonic Outlaws,* he and his collaborators argue for a media *détournement* that deploys the charismatic power of dominant media against itself, all the time displaying a royal disregard for the niceties of copyright. Baldwin's anti-Columbus Quincentennial film *O No Coronado!* (1992), for example, demystifies the conquistador whose desperate search for the mythical Seven Cities of Cibola led him into a fruitless, murderous journey across what is now the American Southwest. To relate this calamitous epic, Baldwin deploys not only his own staged dramatizations but also the detritus of the filmic archive: stock footage, pedagogical films, industrial documentaries, swashbucklers, tacky historical epics.

In an Afro-diasporic context, the "redemption of detritus" evokes another, historically fraught strategy—specifically, the ways that dispossessed New World blacks have managed to transmogrify waste products into art. The Afro-diaspora, coming from artistically developed African cultures but now of freedom, education, and material possibilities, managed to tease beauty out of the very guts of deprivation, whether through the musical use of discarded oil barrels (the steel drums of Trinidad), the culinary use of throwaway parts of animals (soul food, *feijoada*), or the use in weaving of throwaway fabrics (quilting).[8] This "negation of the negation" also has to do with a special relationship to official history. As those whose history has been destroyed and misrepresented, as those whose very history has been dispersed and diasporized rather than lovingly memorialized, and as those whose history has often been told, danced, and sung rather than written, furthermore, oppressed people have been obliged to re-create history out of scraps and remnants and debris. In aesthetic terms, these hand-me-down aesthetics and history making embody an art of discontinuity—the heterogeneous scraps making up a quilt, for example, incorporate diverse styles, time periods, and materials—whence their alignment with artistic modernism as an art of jazzistic "breaking" and discontinuity, and with postmodernism as an art of recycling and pastiche.[9]

Alternative aesthetics are multitemporal in still another sense, in that they are often rooted in nonrealist, non-Western cultural traditions featuring other historical rhythms, other narrative structures, and other attitudes toward the body and spirituality. By incorporating paramodern traditions into clearly modernizing or postmodernizing aesthetics, they problematize facile dichotomies such as traditional and modern, realist and modernist, modernist and postmodernist. Indeed, the projection of Third World cultural practices as untouched by avant-gardist modernism or mass-mediated postmodernism often subliminally encodes a view of the Third World as "underdeveloped," or "developing," as if it lived in another time zone apart from the global system of the late-capitalist world.[10] A less stagist conception would see all the "worlds" as living the same historical moment, in mixed modes of subordination or domination. Time in all the worlds is scrambled and palimpsestic, with the premodern, the modern, and the postmodern coexisting globally, although the "dominant" might vary from region to region.

The world's avant-gardes are also characterized by a paradoxical and oxymoronic temporality. Just as the European avant-garde became "advanced" by drawing on the "primitive," so non-European artists, in an aesthetic version of "revolutionary nostalgia," have drawn on the most traditional elements of their cultures, elements less "premodern" (a term that embeds modernity as telos) than "paramodern." In the arts, the distinction archaic/modernist is often nonpertinent, in that both share a refusal of the conventions of mimetic realism. It is thus less a question of juxtaposing the archaic and the modern than deploying the archaic in order, paradoxically, to modernize, in a dissonant temporality that combines a past imaginary communitas with an equally imaginary future utopia. In their attempts to forge a liberatory language, alternative film traditions draw on paramodern phenomena such as popular religion and ritual magic. In African and Afro-diasporic films such as *Yeelen* (Senegal), *Jitt* (Zimbabwe), *Quartier Mozart* (Cameroun), *The Amulet of Ogum* (Brazil), *Patakin* (Cuba), *The Black Goddess* (Nigeria), and *The Gifted* (the United States), magical spirits become an aesthetic resource, a means for breaking away from the linear, cause-and-effect conventions of Aristotelian narrative poetics, a way of flying beyond the gravitational pull of verism, of defying the "gravity" of chronological time and literal space.

The cinema, I would argue, is ideally equipped to express cultural and temporal hybridity. The cinema is temporally hybrid, for example, in an intertextual sense, in that it "inherits" all the art forms and millennial traditions associated with its diverse matters of expression. (The music or pictorial art of any historical period can be cited, or mimicked, within the cinema.) But the cinema is also temporally hybrid in another, more technical sense. As a technology of representation, the cinema mingles diverse times and spaces; it is produced in one constellation of times and spaces, it represents still another (diegetic) constellation of times and places, and is received in still another time and space (theater, home, classroom). Film's conjunction of sound and image means that each track not only presents two kinds of time, but also that they mutually inflect one another in a form of synchresis. Atemporal static shots can be inscribed with temporality through sound.[11] The panoply of available cinematic techniques further multiplies these already multiple times and spaces. Superimposition redoubles the time and space, as do montage and multiple frames within the image. The capacity for palimpsestic overlays of images and sounds facilitated by the new computer and video technologies further amplifies possibilities for fracture, rupture, polyphony. An electronic "quilting" can weave together sounds and images in ways that break with linear single-line narrative, opening up utopias (and dystopias) of infinite manipulability. The "normal" sequential flow can be disrupted and sidetracked to take account of simultaneity and parallelism. Rather than an Aristotelian sequence of exposition, identification, suspense, pathos, and catharsis, the audiovisual text becomes a tapestry. These media are capable of chameleonic blendings à la *Zelig,* digital insertions à la *Forrest Gump,* and multiple images/sounds à la *Numéro Deux.* These new media can combine synthesized images with captured ones. They can promote a "threshold encounter" between Elton John and Louis Armstrong, as in the 1991 Diet Coke commercial, or allow Natalie Cole to sing with her long-departed father. Potentially, the audiovisual media are less bound by canonical institutional and aesthetic traditions; they make possible what Arlindo Machado calls the "hybridization of alternatives."

The cinema in particular, and audiovisual media in general, is in Bakhtinian terms "multichronotopic." Although Bakhtin develops his concept of the "chronotope" (from *chronos,* time, and *topos,* place) to suggest the inextricable relation between time and space in the novel, it also seems ideally suited to the cinema as a medium where "spatial and temporal indicators are fused into one carefully thought-out concrete whole." (It also spares us the absurdity of "choosing" between time and space as theoretical focus.) Bakhtin's description of the novel as the place where time "thickens, takes on flesh, becomes artistically visible" and where "space becomes charged and responsive to the movements of time, plot and history" seems in some ways even more appropriate to film than to literature, for whereas literature plays itself out within a virtual, lexical space, the cinematic

chronotope is quite literal, splayed out concretely across a screen with specific dimensions and unfolding in literal time (usually twenty-four frames
per second), quite apart from the fictive time-space specific films might construct. Thus, cinema embodies the inherent relationality of time *(chronos)*
and space *(topos)*; it is space temporalized and time spatialized, the site where
time takes place and place takes time.

The multitrack nature of audiovisual media enables them to orchestrate
multiple, even contradictory, histories, temporalities, and perspectives. They
offer not a "history channel," but rather multiple channels for multifocal,
multiperspectival historical representation. What interests me especially here
is a kind of matching between representations of the palimpsestic, multi-
nation state and the cinema as a palimpsestic and polyvalent medium that
can stage and perform a transgressive hybridity. Constitutively multiple, the
cinema is ideally suited for staging what Néstor García Canclini, in a very
different context, calls "multitemporal heterogeneity."[12] The fact that dominant cinema has largely opted for a linear and homogenizing aesthetic where
track reinforces track within a Wagnerian totality in no way effaces the
equally salient truth that the cinema and the new media are infinitely rich in
polyphonic potentialities.[13] The cinema makes it possible to stage temporalized cultural contradictions not only within the shot, through mise-en-
scène, decor, costume, and so forth, but also through the interplay and contradictions between the diverse tracks, which can mutually shadow, jostle,
undercut, haunt, and relativize one another. Each track can develop its own
velocity; the image can be accelerated while the music is slowed, or the
sound track can be temporally layered by references to diverse historical periods. A culturally polyrythmic, heterochronic, multiple-velocity, and con-
trapuntal cinema becomes a real possibility.

We catch a glimpse of these possibilities in Glauber Rocha's *Terra em
Transe* (Land in anguish, 1967), a baroque allegory about Brazilian politics,
specifically the 1964 right-wing coup d'état that overthrew João Goulart. Set
in the imaginary land of Eldorado, the film offers an irreverent, "unofficial"
representation of Pedro Álvares Cabral, the Portuguese "discoverer" of Brazil.
More important for our purposes, the film exploits temporal anachronism as
a fundamental aesthetic resource. The right-wing figure of the film (named
Porfirio Díaz, after the Mexican dictator) arrives from the sea with a flag and
a crucifix, suggesting a foundational myth of national origins. Dressed in
an anachronistic modern-day suit, Díaz is accompanied by a priest in a
Catholic habit, a sixteenth-century conquistador, and a symbolic feathered
Indian. Díaz raises a silver chalice, in a ritual evoking Cabral's "first Mass,"
but in an anachronistic manner that stresses the continuities between the

conquest and contemporary oppression; the contemporary right-winger is portrayed as the latter-day heir of the conquistadores. But Rocha further destabilizes time and space by making Africa a textual presence. The very aesthetic of the sequence, first of all, draws heavily from the Africanized forms of Rio's yearly samba pageant, with its polyrythyms, its extravagant costumes, and its contradictory forms of historical representation; indeed, the actor who plays the conquistador is Clóvis Bornay, a historian specializing in carnival "allegories," and a well-known figure from Rio's carnival. Second, the Mass is accompanied not by Christian religious music but by Yoruba religious chants, evoking the "transe" of the Portuguese title. Rocha's suggestive referencing of African music, as if it had existed in Brazil prior to the arrival of Europeans, reminds us not only of the "continental drift" theory that sees South America and Africa as once having formed part of a single landmass, but also of the theories of Ivan van Sertima and others that Africans arrived in the New World "before Columbus."[14] The music suggests that Africans, as those who shaped and were shaped by the Americas over centuries, are in some uncanny sense also indigenous to the region.[15]

At the same time, the music enacts an ironic reversal, because the chants of exaltation are addressed to a reprehensible figure. Although Eurocentric discourse posits African religion as irrational, the film suggest that in fact it is the European elite embodied by Porfirio Díaz that is irrational, hysterical, entranced, almost demonic. The presence of a *mestiço* actor representing the Indian, furthermore, points to a frequent practice in Brazilian cinema during the silent period, when Indians, whose legal status as "wards of the state" prevented them from representing themselves, were often represented by blacks. Whereas in the United States white actors performed in blackface, in Brazil blacks performed, as it were, in "redface." That the entire scene is a product of the narrator-protagonist's delirium as he lies dying, finally, as the past (the "discovery") and the future (the coup d'état) flash up before his eyes, adds still another temporalized layer of meaning. Here temporal contradiction becomes a spur to creativity. The scene's fractured and discontinuous aesthetic stages the drama of life in the colonial "contact zone," defined by Mary Louise Pratt as the space in which "subjects previously separated" encounter each other and "establish ongoing relations, usually involving conditions of coercion, radical inequality, and intractable conflict."[16] Rocha's neobaroque Afro-avant-gardist aesthetic here figures the discontinuous, dissonant, fractured history of the nation through equally dissonant images and sounds.

Brazilian cinema proliferates in the signs and tokens of hybridity, drawing on the relational processes of Brazil's diverse communities. Rather than merely reflect a preexisting hybridity, Brazilian cinema actively hybridizes, it stages and performs hybridity, counterpointing cultural forces through surprising, even disconcerting, juxtapositions and counterpoints. At its best, it orchestrates not a bland pluralism but rather a strong counterpoint between in some ways incommensurable yet nevertheless thoroughly coimplicated cultures. The opening sequence of *Macunaima,* for example, shows a family whose names are indigenous, whose epidermic traits are African and European and mestizo, whose clothes are Portuguese and African, whose hut is indigenous and backwoods, and whose manner of giving birth is indigenous. The plot of *Pagador de Promessas* (The given word, 1962) revolves around the conflicting values of Catholicism and *candomblé,* evoked through the manipulation of cultural symbols, setting in motion a cultural battle, for example, between *berimbau* (an African instrument consisting of a long bow, gourd, and string) and church bell, thus synecdochically encapsulating a larger religious and political struggle. *Tent of Miracles* (1977) counterposes opera and samba to metaphorize the larger conflict between Bahia's white elite and its subjugated mestizos, between ruling-class science and Afro-inflected popular culture.

Latin America, for García Canclini, lives in a postmodern "time of bricolage where diverse epochs and previously separated cultures intersect."[17] In the best Brazilian films, hybridity is not just a property of the cultural objects portrayed but rather inheres in the film's very processes of enunciation, its mode of constituting itself as a text. The final shot of *Terra em Transe* exemplifies this process brilliantly. As we see the film's protagonist Paulo wielding a rifle in a Che Guevara-like gesture of quixotic rebellion, we hear a sound track composed of Heitor Villa-Lobos, *candomblé* chants, samba, and machine-gun fire. The mix, in this feverish bricolage, is fundamentally unstable; the Villa-Lobos music never really synchronizes with the *candomblé* or the gunfire. We are reminded of Alejo Carpentier's gentle mockery of the innocuous juxtapositions of the European avant-gardists— for example, Lautréamont's "umbrella and a sewing machine"—which he contrasts with the explosive counterpoints of indigenous, African, and European cultures thrown up daily by Latin American life and art, counterpoints where the tensions are never completely resolved or harmonized, where the cultural dialogue is tense, transgressive, not easily assimilated.

Another way that Brazilian culture is figured as a mixed site is through the motif of garbage. Garbage, in this sense, stands at the point of convergence of our three themes of hybridity, chronotopic multiplicity, and the redemption of detritus. Garbage is hybrid, first of all, as the diasporized, heterotopic site of the promiscuous mingling of rich and poor, center and periphery, the industrial and the artisanal, the domestic and the public, the durable and the transient, the organic and the inorganic, the national and the international, the local and the global. The ideal postmodern and post-colonial metaphor, garbage is mixed, syncretic, a radically decentered social text. It can also be seen as what Charles Jencks calls a "heteropolis" and Edward Soja, following Michel Foucault, a "heterotopia," that is, the juxta-position in a real place of "several sites that are themselves incompatible."[18] As a place of buried memories and traces, meanwhile, garbage is an example of what David Harvey calls the "time-space compression" typical of the acceleration produced by contemporary technologies of transportation, communication, and information. In Foucault's terms, garbage is "hetero-chronic"; it concentrates time in a circumscribed space. (Archaeology, it has been suggested, it simply a sophisticated form of garbology.)[19] The garbage pile can be seen as an archaeological treasure trove precisely because of its concentrated, syndechocic, compressed character. As congealed history, garbage reveals a checkered past. As time materialized in space, it is coagu-lated sociality, a gooey distillation of society's contradictions.

As the quintessence of the negative—expressed in such phrases as "talk-ing trash," "rubbish!" and "cesspool of contamination"—garbage can also be an object of artistic jujitsu and ironic reappropriation. An ecologically aware recycling system in Australia calls itself "reverse garbage." (The subversive potential of garbage as metaphor is suggested in Thomas Pynchon's novel *The Crying of Lot 49,* where the heroine collects hints and traces that reveal the alternative network of W.A.S.T.E. as a kind of counterculture outside of the dominant channels of communication.) In aesthetic terms, garbage can be seen as an aleatory collage or surrealist enumeration, a case of the defini-tive by chance, a random pile of objets trouvés and papiers collés, a place of violent, surprising juxtapositions.[20]

Garbage, like death and excrement, is a great social leveler; the trysting point of the funky and the shi-shi. It is the terminus for what Mary Douglas calls "matter out of place." In social terms, it is a truth teller. As the lower stratum of the socius, the symbolic "bottom" or cloaca maxima of the body politic, garbage signals the return of the repressed; it is the place where used condoms, bloody tampons, infected needles, and unwanted babies are left, the ultimate resting place of all that society both produces and represses, se-cretes and makes secret. The final shot of Luis Buñuel's *Los Olvidados,* we may recall, shows the corpse of the film's lumpen protagonist being uncere-moniously dumped on a Mexico City garbage pile; the scene is echoed in Hector Babenco's *Kiss of the Spider Woman,* where Molina's dead body is tossed on a garbage heap while the voice-over presents the official lies about his death. Grossly material, garbage is society's id; it steams and smells below the threshold of ideological rationalization and sublimation. At the same time, garbage is reflective of social prestige; wealth and status are correlated with the capacity of a person (or a society) to discard commodities, that is, to generate garbage. (The average American discards five pounds of garbage per day.) [21] Like hybridity, garbage too is power-laden. The power elite can gentrify a slum, make landfill a ground for luxury apartments, or dump toxic wastes in a poor neighborhood.[22] They can even recycle their own fat from rump to cheek in the form of plastic surgery.

It is one of the utopian, recombinant functions of art to work over dystopian, disagreeable, and malodorous materials. Brazil's *udigrudi* (underground) filmmakers of the 1960s were the first, to my knowledge, to speak of the "aesthetics of garbage" *(estética do lixo)*. The movement's film manifesto, Sganzerla's *Red Light Bandit* (1968), began with a shot of young *favelados* dancing on burning garbage piles, pointedly underlined by the same *candomblé* music that begins Rocha's *Terra em Transe*. The films were made in the São Paulo neighborhood called "boca de lixo" (mouth of garbage), a red-light district named in diacritical contrast with the high-class red-light district called "boca de luxo" (mouth of luxury). Brazilian plastic artist Regina Vater played on these references in her mid-1970s work *Luxo/Lixo* (Luxury/garbage) where she photographically documented the quite different trash discarded in neighborhoods representing different social classes.

For the underground filmmakers, the garbage metaphor captured the sense of marginality, of being condemned to survive within scarcity, of being the dumping ground for transnational capitalism, of being obliged to recycle the materials of the dominant culture.[23] If the early 1960s trope of hunger—as in Rocha's "aesthetics of hunger"—evokes the desperate will to dignity of the famished subject, token of the self writ large of the Third World nation itself, the trope of garbage is more decentered, postmodern, postcolonial. Three recent Brazilian documentaries directly address the theme of garbage. Eduardo Coutinho's *O Fio da Memoria* (The thread of memory, 1991), a film made as part of the centenary of abolition commemoration, reflects on the sequels of slavery in the present. Instead of history as a coherent, linear narrative, the film offers a history based on disjunctive scraps and fragments. Here the interwoven strands or fragments taken together become emblematic of the fragmentary interwovenness of black life in Brazil.

One strand consists of the diary of Gabriel Joaquim dos Santos, an elderly black man who had constructed his own dream house as a work of art made completely out of garbage and detritus: cracked tiles, broken plates, empty cans. For Gabriel, the city of Rio represents the "power of

Still from Eduardo Coutinho's *O Fio da Memoria* (The thread of memory), 1991.

wealth," while his house, constructed from the "city's leftovers," represents the "power of poverty." Garbage thus becomes an ideal medium for those who themselves have been cast off, broken down, who have been "down in the dumps," who feel, as the blues line had it, "like a tin can on that old dumping ground." A transformative impulse takes an object considered worthless and turns it into something of value. Here the restoration of the buried worth of a cast-off object analogizes the process of revealing the hidden worth of the despised, devalued artist himself.[24] At the same time, we witness an example of a strategy of resourcefulness in a situation of scarcity. The trash of the haves becomes the treasure of the have-nots; the dank and unsanitary is transmogrified into the sublime and the beautiful. What had been an eyesore is transformed into a sight for sore eyes. The burned-out lightbulb, wasted icon of modern inventiveness, becomes an emblem of beauty.

With great improvisational flair, the poor, tentatively literate Gabriel appropriates the discarded products of industrial society for his own recreational purposes, in procedures that inadvertently evoke those of modernism and the avant-garde: the Formalists' "defamiliarization," the Cubists' "found objects," Bertolt Brecht's "refunctioning," the situationists' *détournement*. This recuperation of fragments also has a spiritual dimension in terms of African culture. Throughout West and Central Africa, "the rubbish heap is a metaphor for the grave, a point of contact with the world of the dead."[25]

Enoch in *Boca de Lixo* (The scavengers), 1992.

The broken vessels displayed on Kongo graves, Robert Farris Thompson informs us, serve as reminders that broken objects become whole again in the otherworld.[26]

The title of another "garbage" video, Coutinho's documentary *Boca de Lixo* (literally "mouth of garbage," but translated as "The scavengers," 1992) directly links it to the "aesthetics of garbage," because its Portuguese title refers to the São Paulo red-light district where the "garbage" films were produced. The film centers on impoverished Brazilians who survive thanks to a garbage dump outside of Rio, where they toil against the backdrop of the outstretched ever-merciful arms of the Christ of Corcovado. Here the camera is witness to social misery. Ferreting through the garbage, the participants perform a triage of whatever is thrown up by the daily lottery of ordure, sorting out plastic from metal from food for animals. Because many of the faces are female and dark-skinned, the film reveals the feminization, and the racialization, of social misery. Here we see the end point of an all-permeating logic of commodification, logical telos of the consumer society and its ethos of planned obsolescence. Garbage becomes the morning after of the romance of the new. (Italo Calvino's story "Invisible Cities" speaks of a city so enamored of the new that it discards all of its objects daily.) In the dump's squalid phantasmagoria, the same commodities that had been fetishized by advertising, dynamized by montage, and haloed through backlighting are stripped of their aura of charismatic power. We are confronted with the seamy underside of globalization and its facile discourse of one world under a consumerist groove. The world of transnational capitalism and the "posts," we see, is more than ever a world of constant, daily immiseration. Here we see the hidden face of the global system, all the sublimated agonies masked by the euphoric nostrums of "neoliberalism."

If *O Fio da Memoria* sees garbage as an artistic resource, *Boca de Lixo* reveals its human-existential dimension. Here the garbage dwellers have names (Jurema, Enoch), nicknames ("Whiskers"), families, memories, and hopes. Rather than take a miserabilist approach, Coutinho shows us people who are inventive, ironic, and critical, who tell the director what to look at and how to interpret what he sees. While for Coutinho, the stealing of others' images for sensationalist purposes is the "original sin" of TV reportage,[27] the garbage dwellers repeatedly insist that "Here nobody steals," as if responding to the accusations of imaginary middle-class interlocutors. Instead of the suspect pleasures of a condescending "sympathy," the middle-class spectator is obliged to confront vibrant people who dare to dream and talk back and even criticize the filmmakers. The "natives," in this ethnography of garbage, are not the object but rather the agents of knowledge. At the end of the film, the participants watch themselves on a VCR, in a reflexive gesture that goes back to the African films of Jean Rouch and that is now familiar from "indigenous media."

Rather than pathetic outcasts, the film's subjects exist on a continuum with Brazilian workers in general; they encapsulate the country as a whole; they have held other jobs, they have worked in other cities, they have labored in the homes of the elite. They have absorbed and processed the same media representations as everyone else. They have "lines out" to the center; they disprove what Janice Perlman calls the "myth of marginality." A vernacular philosopher in the film tells the filmmakers that garbage is a beginning and an end in a cyclical principle of birth and rebirth—what goes around comes around. Garbage is shown as stored energy, containing in itself the seeds of its own transformation. Garbage becomes a form of social karma, the deferred rendezvous between those who can afford to waste and those who cannot afford not to save what has been wasted. Those who live off garbage also decorate their homes with it. While the elite waste food almost as a matter of principle, the poor are obliged to lick clean their own plates, and those of others.[28]

Jorge Furtado's *Isle of Flowers* (1989) brings the "garbage aesthetic" into the postmodern era, while also demonstrating the cinema's capacity as a vehicle for political/aesthetic reflection. Rather than an aestheticization of garbage, here garbage is both theme and formal strategy. Described by its

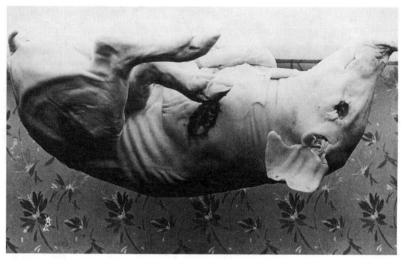

Still from Jorge Furtado's *Isle of Flowers,* 1989.

author as a "letter to a Martian who knows nothing of the earth and its social systems," Furtado's short uses Monty Python-style animation, archival footage, and parodic/reflexive documentary techniques to indict the distribution of wealth and food around the world. The "isle of flowers" of the title is a Brazilian garbage dump where famished women and children, in groups of ten, are given five minutes to scrounge for food. But before we get to the garbage dump, we are given the itinerary of a tomato from farm to supermarket to bourgeois kitchen to garbage can to the "Isle of Flowers." Furtado's edited collage is structured as a social lexicon or glossary, or better, surrealist enumeration of key words such as *pigs, money,* and *human beings.* The definitions are interconnected and multichronotopic; they lead out into multiple historical frames and historical situations. In order to follow the trajectory of the tomato, we need to know the origin of money: "Money was created in the seventh century before Christ. Christ was a Jew, and Jews are human beings." As the audience is still laughing from this abrupt transition, the film cuts directly to the photographic residue of the Holocaust, where Jews, garbage-like, are thrown into death-camp piles. (The Nazis, one is reminded, had their own morbid forms of recycling.) Throughout, the film moves back and forth between minimalist definitions of the human to the lofty ideal of freedom evoked by the film's final citation: "Freedom is a word the human dream feeds on, that no one can explain or fail to understand."

This summary, however, gives little sense of the experience of the film, of its play with documentary form and expectations. First, the film's visuals—

old TV commercials, newspaper advertisements, health-care manuals—themselves constitute a kind of throwaway, visual garbage. (In the silent period of cinema, we are reminded, films were seen as transient entertainments rather than artistic durables and therefore as not worth saving; during World War I, they were even recycled for their lead content.) Many of the more banal shots—of pigs, tomatoes, and so forth—are repeated, in defiance of the cinematic decorum that suggests that shots should be (1) beautiful and (2) not repeated. Second, the film, whose preamble states that "this is not a fiction film," mocks the positivist mania for factual detail by offering useless, gratuitous precision: "We are in Belem Novo, city of Porto Alegre, state of Rio Grande do Sul. More precisely, at thirty degrees, twelve minutes and thirty seconds latitude south, and fifty-one degrees eleven minutes and twenty-three seconds longitude west." Third, the film mocks the apparatus and protocols of rationalist science, through absurd classificatory schemata ("Dona Anete is a Roman Catholic female biped mammal) and tautological syllogisms ("Mr. Suzuki is Japanese, and therefore a human being"). Fourth, the film parodies the conventions of the educational film, with its authoritative voice-over and quizlike questions ("What is a history quiz?"). The overture music is a synthesized version of the theme song of *Voice of Brazil,* the widely detested official radio program that has been annoying Brazilians since the days of Brazilian president Getúlio Vargas. Humor becomes a kind of trap; the spectator who begins by laughing ends up, if not crying, at least reflecting very seriously. Opposable thumbs and highly developed telencephalon, we are told, have given "human beings the possibility of making many improvements in their planet"; a shot of a nuclear explosion serves as illustration. Thanks to the universality of money, we are told, we are now "Free!"; a snippet of the "Hallelujah Chorus" punctuates the thought.

Furtado invokes the old carnival motif of pigs and sausage, but with a political twist; here the pigs, given inequitable distribution down the food chain, eat better than people.[29] In this culinary recycling, we are given a social examination of garbage; the truth of a society is in its detritus. The socially peripheral points to the symbolically central. Rather than having the margins invade the center, as in carnival, here the center creates the margins, or better, there are no margins; the tomato links the urban bourgeois family to the rural poor via the sausage and the tomato within a web of global relationality.[30]

In these films, the garbage dump becomes a critical vantage point from which to view society as a whole. It reveals the social formation as seen "from below." As the overdetermined depot of social meanings, as a concentration of piled-up signifiers, garbage is the place where hybrid, multichronotopic relations are reinvoiced and reinscibed. Garbage defines and illuminates the world; the trash can, to recycle Leon Trotsky's aphorism, is history. Garbage offers a database of material culture off of which one can read social customs or values. Polysemic and multivocal, garbage can be seen literally (garbage as a source of food for poor people, garbage as the site of ecological disaster), but it can also be read symptomatically, as a metaphoric figure for social indictment (poor people treated like garbage, garbage as the "dumping" of pharmaceutical products or of "canned" TV programs, slums—and jails—as human garbage dumps). These films reveal the "hidden transcripts" of garbage, reading it as an allegorical text to be deciphered, a form of social colonics where the truth of a society can be "read" in its waste products.

Notes

This essay originated as a talk presented at the second installment of the "Hybrid Cultures and Transnational Identities" conference held at UCLA March 7–8, 1997. The session was organized by Randal Johnson.

1. For those of us working in the area of Latin American culture, where "hybridity" and *mestizaje* have been critical commonplaces for decades, it is always a surprise to learn that Homi Bhabha, through no fault of his own, has been repeatedly "credited" with the concept of "hybridity."

2. For more on "post-Third Worldism," see Ella Shohat and Robert Stam, *Unthinking Eurocentrism: Multiculturalism and the Media* (London: Routledge, 1994), and Ella Shohat, "Post-Third Worldist Culture: Gender, Nation and the Cinema," in *Feminist Genealogies, Colonial Legacies, Democratic Futures,* ed. M. Jacqui Alexander and Chandra Talpade Mohanty (New York: Routledge, 1997).

3. The mutually enriching collaborations between the diverse currents of Afro-diasporic music, yielding such hybrids as "samba reggae," "samba rap," "jazz tango," "rap reggae," and "roforenge" (a blend of rock, forro, and merengue) in the Americas offer examples of "lateral syncretism," that is, syncretism on a "sideways" basis of rough equality. Diasporic musical cultures mingle with one another, while simultaneously also playing off the dominant media-disseminated tradition of First World, especially American, popular music, itself energized by Afro-diasporic traditions. An endlessly creative multidirectional flow of musical ideas thus moves back and forth around the "Black Atlantic" (Paul Gilroy), for example, between cool jazz and samba in bossa nova, between soul music and ska in reggae. Afro-diasporic music displays an anthropophagic capacity to absorb influences, including Western influences, while still being driven by a culturally African bass note.

4. Mikhail Bakhtin, "Response to a Question from the *Novy Mir* Editorial Staff," in *Speech Genres and Other Late Essays* (Austin: University of Texas Press, 1986), 5.

5. Ibid., 3.

6. See David Toop, *The Rap Attack: African Jive to New York Hip Hop* (New York: Pluto Press, 1984).

7. See Lucy Lippard, "The Garbage Girls," in *The Pink Glass Swan: Selected Feminist Essays on Art* (New York: New Press, 1995).

8. In his fascinating intervention at the "Hybrid Cultures and Transnational Identities" conference, Teshome Gabriel showed slides of the salvage art of African-American artist Lefon Andrews, who uses paper bags as his canvas and dry leaves for paint. Gabriel demonstrated the method by showing the audience a paper bag and some leaves, revealing them to be the basic materials that went into the beautiful artifacts pictured in the slides.

9. The African-American environmental artist known as "Mr. Imagination" "has created bottle-cap thrones, paintbrush people, cast-off totems, and other pieces salvaged from his life as a performing street artist" (Charlene Cerny and Suzanne Seriff, eds., *Recycled, Reseen: Folk Art from the Global Scrap Heap* [New York: Harry N. Abrams, 1996], 8).

10. Commenting on the Afro-Brazilian musical group Olodum, which contributed to Paul Simon's compact disk *The Spirit of the Saints,* Caetano Veloso remarked in an interview that "It is not Paul Simon who brings modernity to Olodum; no, Olodum is itself modern, innovative" (interview with Christopher Dunn in *Transition* [fall 1996]).

11. See Michel Chion, *Audio-Vision: Sound on Screen* (New York: Columbia University Press, 1994), especially the first chapter, "Projections of Sound on Image."

12. See Néstor García Canclini, *Hybrid Cultures: Strategies for Entering and Leaving Modernity* (Minneapolis: University of Minnesota Press, 1995).

13. Ella Shohat and I call attention to the vast corpus of films that explore these potentialities in our *Unthinking Eurocentrism.*

14. See Ivan van Sertima, *They Came Before Columbus* (New York: Random House, 1975).

15. A 1992 samba pageant presentation, Kizombo, also called attention to the putative pre-Columbian arrival of Africans in the New World, both in the lyrics and through gigantic representations of the Mexican Olmec statues with their clearly Negroid features.

16. Mary Louise Pratt, *Imperial Eyes: Travel Writing and Transculturation* (London: Routledge, 1992), 7.

17. See Néstor García Canclini, "Los estudios culturales de los 80 a los 90: perspectivas antropológicas y sociológicas en América Latina," *Iztapalapa: Revista de Ciencias Sociales y Humanidades* 11:24: 24.

18. See Christopher Jencks, *Heteropolis: Los Angeles, the Riots and the Strange Beauty of Hetero-Architecture* (London: Academy Editions, 1993), and Edward W. Soja, *Thirdspace: Journeys to Los Angeles and Other Real-and-Imagined Places* (Oxford: Blackwell, 1996).

19. Another form of garbology is the study of celebrity garbage (for example, that of Bob Dylan or O. J. Simpson), for purposes of psychological investigation.

20. For a survey of recycled art from around the world, see Cerny and Seriff, *Recycled, Reseen.*

21. Artist Milenko Matanovic has developed a project called "Trash Hold" in which

high-profile participants drag especially designed bags of their garbage around with them for a week, at the end of which the participants gather to recycle. See Lippard, *The Pink Glass Swan*, 265.

22. For more on the discourse of garbage, see Michael Thompson, *Rubbish Theory: The Creation and Destruction of Value* (Oxford: Oxford University Press, 1979); Judd H. Alexander, *In Defense of Garbage* (Westport, Conn.: Praeger, 1993); William Rathje and Cullen Murphy, *Rubbish! The Archeology of Garbage* (New York: HarperCollins, 1992); and Katie Kelly, *Garbage: The History and Future of Garbage in America* (New York: Saturday Review Press, 1973).

23. For an analysis of Brazil's *udigrudi* films, see Ismail Xavier, *Allegories of Underdevelopment: "Aesthetics and Politics in Modern Brazilian Cinema* (Minneapolis: University of Minnesota Press, 1997).

24. My formulation obviously both echoes and Africanizes the language of Fredric Jameson's well-known essay "Third World Literature in the Era of Multinational Capitalism" (*Social Text* 15 [fall 1986]).

25. Wyatt MacGaffey, "The Black Loincloth and the Son of Nzambi Mpungu," in *Forms of Folklore in Africa: Narrative, Poetic, Gnomic, Dramatic* (Austin: University of Texas Press, 1977), 78.

26. See Robert Farris Thompson and Joseph Cornet, *The Four Moments of the Sun: Kongo Art in Two Worlds* (Washington, D.C.: National Gallery, 1981), 179.

27. Quoted in *Revista USP* 19 (September–November 1993): 148.

28. Juan Duran-Luzio has kindly given me a copy of a Costa Rican "garbage novel," Fernando Contreras Castro's *Unica mirando al mar* (Unica looking toward the sea) (San José: Farben, 1994). In the novel, the protagonist's husband writes to the president of the republic concerning the fate of those who live off the garbage dumps.

29. The pig, as Peter Stallybrass and Allon White point out, was despised for its habits: "its ability to digest its own and human faeces as well as other 'garbage'; its resistance to full domestication; its need to protect its tender skin from sunburn by wallowing in the mud" (*The Politics and Poetics of Transgression* [Ithaca, N.Y.: Cornell University Press, 1986]), 45.

30. Jorge Furtado's *Esta não e a sua vida* (This is not your life, 1992) prolongs the director's reflections on the nature of documentary, posing such questions as: How does the documentarist find a topic? What does it mean to "know" about someone's life? How much has the spectator learned about someone's life by seeing a documentary? How does one film one's subject?

The Daughters of Gandhi: Africanness, Indianness, and Brazilianness in the Bahian Carnival

Barbara Browning

Friday is the day of Oxalá, Big Daddy in the Sky, and on this Friday that opens the carnival of Bahia, Brazil, my sister *sócias* of the carnival group the Daughters of Gandhi and I convene in the old part of the city to offer him libations and ask for peaceful festivities. The oldest Daughters sing, and we clap and respond, and then our chests are splashed with a cool, gritty mixture of cornmeal and water that will leave us smelling sweet like corn all that afternoon and evening, despite the oppressive heat. Our offerings constitute a secular ritual. The scene is a moment of marked solemnity in the most profane of contexts: carnival, five days of extreme political and sexual expressivity. But sacred and secular expressions infect each other in Brazil and force us to rethink the distinction.

Brazilian culture is highly syncretic—mixing not only African traditions with indigenous and European ones, but also mixing certain distinct African traditions with one another. The African religion observed in Bahia is called, broadly, *Candomblé,* but there is a wide range of variation in its practice. *Candomblé,* like Santeria in the Caribbean, is largely derived from Yoruba beliefs and is centered on the worship of divinities called the *orixás.* Although this is true of all houses of *Candomblé,* some houses appear to have syncretized greater and lesser influences from other traditions. The houses held to be the "purest," that is, conforming most closely to Yoruba convention, are said to be of the *nagô* or *kêtu* "nation." Those with greater Dahomean influence are *gege* nation, and those of Bantu inflection are *angola.* This talk of nations is somewhat misleading, however; these terms were applied by Europeans during the slave trade, and they referred not to the cultural origins

79

of the Africans they held hostage but to the ports out of which they were shipped. They were, in effect, trade names, which were adopted over the years by Africans in Brazil in order to distinguish cultural differences. Of course, Yoruba beliefs also encountered European beliefs in Brazil, as well as indigenous ones. It has been suggested that Catholicism in Latin America, as opposed to Protestantism in the North, allowed for a greater degree of syncretism (Raboteau 1978, 87–89). In particular, the saints may be perceived as another form of dispersed or fragmentary divinity, like the *orixás*.

Candomblé is the product of a violent cultural encounter. It demands not only a comparison of Catholic and Yoruba beliefs, but their mutual approximation. When Africans in Brazil first assimilated the *orixás* to Catholic saints—and Olorun to the Christian God—it was out of necessity and fear of retribution. *Candomblé* worshipers use the names of Saint Barbara and Iansã as interchangeable terms for the same principle. European-pressed chromolithographs of the Catholic saints are said to be representations of the *orixás*. But whereas the saints are, for the most part, depicted as white, the *orixás* are recognized as being African in origin.

There is some debate surrounding the classification of Yoruba belief as mono- or polytheistic, because it contains the notion of a supreme god— Olorun, the god of gods. Olorun is the one divinity that can never be represented. It is not even possible to refer to him obliquely through matter, as he is the truth beyond human knowledge. The other *orixás* represent the fragmentary bits of divine truth accessible to us. They are abstract principles— of justice, seduction, aggression, epidemia, and so on—and they manifest themselves in the objects of nature: stones, trees, water, meteorological phenomena, animals, and the human body. They accomplish this last manifestation through what is often referred to as "possessional dance," a phrase that has accrued an unfortunate association with horrific, inaccurate images produced by the Western media. Participation in *Candomblé* dance is not passive submission to a violent force but involves study and commitment to an ethos. It is what allows humans moments of intimacy with the divine. Still, incorporating *orixá* energy does require an acknowledgment that humans do not fully determine their own significance in the world.

Through divination, a priestess or priest in *Candomblé* can determine the particular *orixás* (generally three, in descending order of dominance) that "guide one's head," or influence one's life trajectory. The initiation process in *Candomblé* prepares one to incorporate all of one's *orixás*. It involves a tremendous amount of training, and yet this is not considered dance training as it is usually understood in Western culture. When one dances the *orixás'* choreographies, one recognizes oneself as an object, not a subject, of art. The dancer in *Candomblé* is not considered to be an artist. Individual creativity is not admired as a characteristic of the worshiper. The community may take pleasure in the excellence of a body as a vessel for an *orixá*; physical strength and beauty may be appreciated by other worshipers, as they will be appreciated by the *orixá*. But what animates the religious dance is not personal genius. Often an old or feeble body contains so much *axé* (spiritual energy) that its motion in the dance far exceeds what should be physically possible. When observers of a ceremony see this kind of transformation, they recognize the body as divinely gorgeous.[1] The study of the *orixá* dances marks one not as an artist but as a committed member of a community seeking a collective experience of divinity.

If the individual body in *Candomblé* expresses the belief of the community, the carnival is a context in which community affiliation becomes much more apparent, at least to Western eyes. Carnival in Rio de Janeiro is famous, of course, not only for its extravagance, but also for its spectacular inversions of racial and economic hierarchies: poor black women and men, mostly domestic workers and manual laborers, parade in regal European attire. In Bahia, carnival may still be the site of utopian fantasies, but those fantasies are African and explicitly political.

Carnival in Bahia is not a pageant, but a participatory street party. Since the early 1980s, the dominant element of Bahian carnival has been the *blocos afro,* or African blocs. Some of the blocs consist of thousands of members, with massive, complex, and perfectly rehearsed drum corps. One of the best-known blocs is called Olodum, a variant of the name of the god of gods. The first bloc, Ilê Aiyê, was founded in 1974, the year Portugal's former African colonies gained independence. Few Bahians cite African decolonization as the occasion for Ilê Aiyê's founding. The more common explanation is that it was a response to the racial discrimination of a predominantly white group called the Internacionais. Ilê Aiyê's charter (alone among the *blocos*) defiantly stipulates that only blacks can join. This policy continues, despite revisions in the Internacionais' racial policy.

There are other types of carnival groups. The daughters of Gandhi, the organization of which I am a member, is an *afoxé*. The daughters of Gandhi are unusual in that we are an all-women group, but we are affiliated with the largest, most famous group of this kind, the Sons of Gandhi. The *afoxés* are generally more modest in size than the *blocos* and are linked to houses of *Candomblé*. less apparently political, they are united by spiritual belief and practice. As is the case in the houses of *Candomblé,* the *afoxés* have members of all races. Yet, Bahians readily and regularly acknowledge the African roots of the *afoxés*.

Perhaps the most difficult carnival groups to decipher are the *blocos de índio,* or Indian blocs. They are hard-partying, "Indian"-identified samba crews (I will come back to the significance of this identification). The Indian blocs, in contrast to the other groups, have been viewed as unorganized, even misdirected, violent expressions of racial and class frustration (Dunn 1992). In a way, however, they raise some of the most important issues in the carnival, including the significance of racial displacement and sexual violence.

Finally, there are the *trios elétricos,* hyperamplified, super high-speed, hokey pop-rock ensembles aboard huge floats, followed by masses of pom-pom-shaking kids. The Internacionais are among them. These electrified rockers, almost all white, used to dominate the scene, at least in terms of volume. But with the development of the *blocos afro* in the 1980s, with their brilliant musical merger of samba with the deep funk of the *afoxés* and other New World rhythms, the carnival took on a definitively African inflection. Today, the *trios* do covers of *bloco afro* hits, and, in what to some ears is a sorry cross-fertilization, some of the *blocos afro* are electrifying and popifying their sound.

"Cross-fertilization" is, of course, a metaphor for cultural mixing and syncretism. It is not a particularly sexy phrase, but it hints at one of the ways that cultural mixing is typically discussed in Brazil—through figures of sexual mixing. Racial and cultural identity are worked out in terms of sex, and sexuality is often figured in racial terms. An example that could be read in either (or both) of these two directions is the name used to refer to any woman who dances samba professionally, either in tourist shows or atop the Rio carnival floats. Regardless of her color, she is a *mulata.* I myself am white and blue-eyed, and I have danced samba professionally beside jet-black women, but in the context of our dancing, we were all called *mulatas.* Samba itself is used by Brazilians as a figure for racial mixing in Brazil—and, by extension, for Brazilianness itself. The woman who dances it at once represents literal racial mixing and cultural syncretism. She is also, of course, a highly sexualized figure. This sexual figure is part of a long history of such metaphors, which began with the Portuguese colonists' letters describing Brazil as a sexy earthly paradise populated by shamelessly (innocently) naked Indian maids. But it also corresponds to contemporary Western stereotypes of Brazilian sensuality. Internal and external stereotypes of Brazilian sexuality are sometimes difficult to distinguish, and always difficult to disentangle. As Richard Parker has observed, "Brazilians view themselves as sensual beings not simply in terms of their individuality . . . but on a social or cultural level—as sensual individuals, at least in part, by virtue of their shared *brasilidade,* or 'Brazilianness'" (Parker 1991, 7).

Sexuality is a significant element of the carnival, and not merely in simple, ecstatic moments of personal abandon. The tourists who flock to Brazil

at carnival time anticipate an orgiastic celebration in which individual in-
hibitions are transported from the everyday to the erotic and exotic. But all
sexual exchanges during the carnival—from the theatrical presentation of
the bikinied *mulatas* bumping and grinding on the floats in Rio to the actual
screwing of a Bahian transvestite and a German tourist behind a stalled *trio
elétrico*—are exchanges within a system of racial, economic, and sexual politics. The stereotyped perception of Brazilian dance as uniformly erotic—
be it samba or the hyped and supersexualized, international version of the
lambada[2]—does not account for the complex historical and cultural meanings of those dances in Brazil. However, the juxtaposition of perceived pantomimes of sexual motion with literal acts of sex during the carnival demands that one acknowledge the erotic aspect of the dances. It also demands
that one read sex as a gesture choreographed into a dance signifying larger
social issues.

Perhaps the most pressing of these is economic: the carnival inversion of
rich and poor expresses itself not only in costume, but also in sexual exchange. Middle-class whites and poor blacks spend the rest of the year in
rigid awareness of their economic roles, and virtually every white household
has a domestic servant of color. But during the carnival, men and women
who would never socialize together are pressed body to body in the street. It
is true that many middle-class whites refrain from participating in the Bahian
street carnival, preferring the private "balls" at hotels and country clubs.
But many, especially the young, put themselves in the thick of things. In a
sweaty, spontaneous, deep, and prolonged kiss, in the massaging of breasts
or buttocks that is part of the dance, economic disparity seems momentarily
healed in a sexual gesture. It is not, of course. Nonetheless, what this demonstrates is that the dances of the carnival are not mere pantomimes of sexuality. Sexual acts themselves are incorporated into the choreography—acts
that can be read for larger significances.

Economic and racial inversions are not the only inversions allowed to
occur in the carnival. There is also a free play of gender roles, particularly for
men. On the first night of the Bahian carnival, for those not scheduled to go
out with an official group, the traditional game is transvestism, for both men
and women. Men generally take a more enthusiastic part in the switch. On
the first night of carnival, men with lurid eye makeup, inflated breasts, and
wobbly high heels fill the square. A man's participation in this event is no
indication of his year-round sexual behavior, although it is a moment that
suggests that the *machista* stereotype of Brazilian straight men covers a more
complex sexual identity (Parker 1991).

Some of these men, however, are occasional or full-time cross-dressers.

The carnival is understood to be their moment of glory—the brief period in which their sexuality and validity are acknowledged. They are not just tolerated but celebrated. Bahia has a large and famous transvestite population, consisting mostly of poor men, black or of mixed race. Many are on hormonal medication, easy to procure in a town where pharmacists regard prescriptions as unnecessary scraps of paper. During the year, Bahian transvestites attract a kind of licentious attention from straight men that is difficult to characterize. They are whistled and hooted at in a manner that seems ironic, aggressive, affectionate, and genuinely sexual all at once. But in the carnival, men and women alike applaud their beautiful adolescent-looking breasts, which they expose, for once, with a kind of maternal dignity and pride. In the carnival, they seem to offer a suck of the milk of human tolerance. However, their permanently carnivalized position in Brazilian society is hardly one of acceptance.

The celebration of the transvestite (*travesti* in Portuguese) takes place not only in the street carnival, but in the expensive carnival balls as well. I have a clipping from a newspaper account of a 1984 "gay ball" in the exclusive French Meridien Hotel:

> The gay ball, at the Meridien on Thursday, was an apotheosis. Inside the hotel, the salon was full with some costumes actually bought in New York, as was the case of the Royal Peacock, which won in the category of luxury. Outside of the hotel, the evening gang, a fantastic multitude of three hundred people, did not shift a foot until dawn, staying to applaud the transvestites passing by.
>
> There were even tears of emotion, such as those of a public functionary who took her son, a shy *bichinha* [diminutive of *queen*], to the ball. When they passed through the aisle formed by the evening gang, they were applauded. "Ai, my son, my eye is full of water. I'm going to cry in there, I never thought it could all be so beautiful. The people applauded me and my son." They were dressed in Sumerian sarongs, both of them.

The term *gay ball* recalls the events of the same name depicted in Jennie Livingston's film *Paris Is Burning*. The gay balls of Harlem are a black and Latino cultural phenomenon. Although enormous interest was provoked by the film's illustration of the complex sexual identity politics of the competing "houses," surprisingly little has been noted about the specific cultural traditions that frame the balls. The most obvious connection would be with the carnival traditions of black and mixed-race communities throughout the New World. Perhaps a more telling connection could be made to spiritual communities such as *Candomblé*.

I said that initiation into *Candomblé* prepares one to incorporate one's *orixás* in dance. But not everyone is equipped to receive divine energy. Although it is not the case in Yorubaland, or even in many parts of Brazil, in Bahia (the center of *Candomblé* activity), it is widely accepted that women are significantly more receptive to the *orixás* than are men. The exception to this rule is the homosexual man. Actually, the very term *homosexual* is one that needs to be opened up to reconfiguration in the context of *Candomblé* (for that matter, so are the terms *woman* and *man*).

The important issue of sex and sexuality in *Candomblé* is certainly underplayed in the ethnographic literature, but it is by no means news. Ruth Landes published her scientific study "A Cult Matriarchate and Male Homosexuality" for the *Journal of Abnormal and Social Psychology* in 1940, and followed it in 1947 with a more popular account in *City of Women*. Landes quotes Edison Carneiro, who first introduced her to a ceremony: "No upright man will allow himself to be ridden by a god, unless he does not care about losing his manhood. . . . Some men do let themselves be ridden, and they become priests with the women; but they are known to be homosexuals" (Landes 1947, 37). Carneiro himself was somewhat more circumspect about homosexuality in his own writings on *Candomblé,* but both the ethnographic community and popular knowledge have long held this to be a truism. In fact, the sexuality of men who incorporate divinity is further specified. In her scientific paper, Landes noted in greater detail that most male cult leaders and followers in Bahia were "passive homosexuals of note" (1940, 386). Roger Bastide, similarly, noted the common occurrence of "passive pederasty" among initiates (1961, 309).

The understanding of homosexuality as a category of persons in Brazilian popular culture is highly complicated. In some circles, it is not a category as such. The anthropologists Peter Fry and, more recently, Richard Parker have attempted to translate and historicize Brazilian connotations of sexuality. As Fry has shown, the traditional folk model of sexuality is based on types and positions of sexual activity. There are no "heterosexuals" and "homosexuals" per se; rather, there are those who, in popular parlance, "eat" and those who "give"—the former signifying taking the penetrative position in sex, the latter the penetrated. Obviously, the figure marks the distinction that Landes and Bastide called "active" and "passive." This opposition was the primary one used in Brazil to configure sexuality until the beginning of the twentieth century, when medical models began to focus on sexual object choice. Enter the categories of hetero-, bi-, and homosexuality. In the late 1960s, with the increased coalescence and politicization of a gay community in Brazil, a third categorization emerged stressing acknowledgment of one's sexual orientation, and the validity of gay sexual expressions, be they "active" or "passive." This third phase corresponds largely to popular North American and European notions of sexuality.

Educated Brazilians (that is, those educated in Western social beliefs) distinguish between straights and gays according to choice of opposite-sex or same-sex partners. But those whose social education takes place outside of Western institutions still hold firmly to the active/passive, eat/give model: in fact, that model is still operative in the upper classes, even as it is negotiated with another system.

Women's sexuality in *Candomblé* is more infrequently discussed. Regardless of its manifestation, female sexuality is apparently not problematic in the way male sexuality can be—although it is sometimes suggested that older, less sexually active women are more suited to devotion to the saints than their younger counterparts. Lesbianism or bisexuality among women appears not to be disruptive in the way that male penetrative sexuality is. This corresponds to the lack of interest in female transvestism in the carnival, mentioned earlier. Perhaps this comes from a phallocentric society's inability to conceive of women's sexuality *as* penetrative, or "active." Men who "eat" are termed *homens* (men), whereas those who "give" are *bichas* (properly, a small creature or parasite): the word itself has a feminine ending, and takes the feminine article.

What at first glance appears to be a constellation of figures seems highly readable: women and *bichas* are not only passive and penetrable in the sexual context, they are so in the spiritual context as well. Although proscriptions of sexuality are specific to *Candomblé* practice in Bahia, J. Lorand Matory (1988) has demonstrated that the metaphor of male sexual and spiritual penetrability exists in Yorubaland as well. Those who receive spiritual energy are "mounted" *(montados)* as horses are mounted by riders (see Maya Deren's *Divine Horsemen*) and as *bichas* are mounted by *homens*.

Yet, *Candomblé* may provide a more complex way of thinking about sexuality. In fact, the metaphors themselves are at odds with one another. The penetrator is he who eats—figurally consuming, absorbing the one who gives. Doesn't this reverse the notion of penetration? Even if the metaphor is anthropophagic, the person who "gives" is accorded the power of materializing and separating from a part of the self, which is, presumably, the body. To allow oneself to be eaten can be seen as, in itself, a penetrative act. The term *bicha* also inverts the penetration metaphor, as a parasite is one who both penetrates and consumes another's body.

Judith Butler has turned to anthropological discourse to open up the configuration of gender and sexuality. Citing Mary Douglas, who observed that the boundaries of the body often stand for social boundaries across cultures, Butler writes: "The construction of stable bodily contours relies upon fixed sites of corporeal permeability and impermeability. Those sexual practices in both homosexual and heterosexual contexts that open surfaces and orifices to erotic signification or close down others effectively reinscribe the boundaries of the body along new cultural lines" (1990, 132). In fact, in Brazil, the delineation of the sexual body is by no means fixed. The permeability of that body to *orixá* energy may be read as a metaphor for shifting social boundaries. The priestess, on the other hand, might prefer to read the reinscription of boundaries—social change—as the outward manifestation of the mobility of the *orixás*.

Gay men have a privileged place in *Candomblé*. Along with women, they are capable of embodying principles, in the same way that participants in the Harlem gay balls attempt to "be real"—whether that means a "real" butch queen or a "real" military man. The priest in *Candomblé* occupies the role generally reserved for the priestess or *mãe de santo*—mother of saints. Likewise, Harlem house leaders are called, explicitly, mothers of the houses' children.

Judith Butler has mapped what is really at stake in the gay balls and in transvestism generally: "Drag fully subverts the distinction between inner and outer psychic space and effectively mocks both the expressive model of gender and the notion of a true gender identity. . . . *In imitating gender, drag implicitly reveals the imitative structure of gender itself—as well as its contingency*" (1993, 137; emphasis in the original). Although the embodiment of the *orixás* in *Candomblé* is not imitative, it does demonstrate the irrelevance of the specific body in establishing "real" gender. Butler goes on to ask of drag: "Does this mean that one puts on a mask or a persona, that there is a 'one' who precedes that 'putting on,' who is something other than its gender from the start? Or does this miming, this impersonating, precede and form the 'one' operating as its formative precondition rather than its dispensable artifice?" (ibid., 230). To this, the priestess would surely respond that here is no "one," but several, probably conflicting principles in operation; and the body itself is *both* their formative precondition *and* their dispensable artifice.

Transvestism surrounds the Bahian street carnival and is perhaps the centerpiece of the balls. But transvestites are not integrated into the organized processional groups—the *blocos afro*, Indian samba clubs, *afoxés*, or *trios elétricos*. The *blocos* present their kings and queens, skilled African dancers aboard their floats, and these kings seem to be grand representatives of black masculine ideals. Yet, there is an unspoken understanding that although the study of the athletic *Candomblé* choreographies does not indicate femininity in a man, the genuine incorporation of *orixá* energy in real

Candomblé dance is usually achieved only by women or gay men. But in the carnival, the choreographies are secularized and highly stylized. The explicit message of these dances is not one of shifting gender roles. Still, the *blocos afro* and especially the *afoxés,* more insistently rooted in *Candomblé,* hold open a place for the *bicha.* I used to go to the rehearsals of a small *afoxé* group in the old part of town. The group's artistic director was a tough-acting street fighter who barked out orders like a sergeant. He was the epitome of the *machão:* ur-macho, violent, inflexible. He stampeded us through our choreographies to the sound of his stamping foot and thunderous claps. But he always acknowledged the expertise of a young, plump *bicha* with plucked eyebrows who swam through the moves of the female *orixás* of seduction with supreme grace. Our leader accorded him a special place in our midst. We would watch as he practiced the goddess's solo without music, gliding through her liquid gestures.

Candomblé is a discreet domain that accommodates gays throughout the year. During the carnival, they literally come out in a secular moment that is temporally bracketed and therefore unthreatening. The carnival appears to be a temporarily closed circle in the way that *Candomblé*'s circle of faith is both spatially and culturally closed. The *terreiro,* the physical grounds of a house of *Candomblé,* is a sanctuary. My own *mãe de santo,* the woman who baptized me into *Candomblé,* would express mild, ironic disdain for homosexual priests; yet, as a black woman in Brazil, she, like them, and like the mothers of the Harlem gay balls, found a sanctuary in her house. She was such a powerful personality that it was hard for me to imagine her shying away from any conflict or difficulty. But I remember her frank face as she told me: "The world outside is crazy. They think I'm crazy for living in here—but I'm not crazy. I lived out there, I know what goes on." It made perfect sense to me.

Transvestism is not the only "coming out" that occurs in the carnival. In effect, the *afoxés* constitute the coming out of the houses of *Candomblé.* The *afoxés* take *Candomblé* rhythms and choreographies into the street. The dancers, in this context, are not animated by divine energy, but rather by cultural pride. Although the *afoxés* are less explicitly politicized than the *blocos afro,* they certainly demonstrate the unity of the African religious community. Here, virtuosity is not just the domain of the *orixás.* Although the gods do not come down, at least not usually, the dance achieves a heightened intensity. Still, the *afoxés* are not about the skills of individual dancers. The energy that infuses the bodies is that of community solidarity, and of precisely the cultural values that in another context are called by the *orixás'* names: justice, female strength, seduction, and political power.

As the rhythms and dances of the *afoxés* are further syncretized by the *blocos afro,* they become more culturally complex, and yet they appear more politically readable. As already noted, the houses of *Candomblé* are distinguished by "nation" even as Yoruba beliefs dominate the religion. The *blocos afro* are dedicated to celebrating African nations in a different sense. Every year, each *bloco* celebrates a particular culture in the carnival. A group may sing songs in praise of Senegal, for example, mentioning great figures in Senegalese history, but in the same breath it may invoke the *orixás* of *Candomblé.* This is by no means a question of misinformation. The carnival composers research carefully the distinctive cultures of which they write. But for black Bahians, the Yoruba *orixás* signify a commitment to their Africanness generally. At the same time, they incorporate African diasporic rhythms—reggae, mambo, merengue—into their own music, acknowledging its complex origins, and articulating it all through the samba. The brilliance is in balancing African nationalism with attention to cultural specificity: one's own and others'.

Not all critics have perceived this process as fruitful. In the only book-length, English-language study of the Bahian carnival, *African Myth and Black Reality in Bahian Carnival,* Daniel Crowley laments the "naive Pan-Africanism" of both the *afoxés* and the *blocos afro* (1984, 2). By leaping arbitrarily between African and diasporic cultures, Crowley asserts, the *blocos* lose sight of certain historical and political realities. Christopher Dunn, however, has challenged Crowley's critique:

> At one level one might ask, what is the "real" African past? . . . To some extent, all histories must rely on mythic prefigurations in order to render the past meaningful and coherent. In this sense, the *afoxés* and *blocos afro* are not so much spreading misinformation about Africa, as constructing a powerful, grass-roots discourse which challenges traditional notions and myths of Africans and their descendants in Brazil. (1992, 12)

Although the *bloco afro* composers avail themselves of the published histories and ethnographies of African states and cultures, they are aware of the woeful inadequacy of many of these accounts.

Western historiographers are increasingly sensitive to this kind of critique (Feierman 1993). If Western linear accounts of an African past have proven themselves insufficient, then why is it surprising to find Afro-Brazilians offering a nonlinear account? The Bahian carnival rewrites African history in terms that are meaningful to its participants. This inscription includes the *orixás,* even in accounts of non-Yoruba cultures. From the perspective of the composers, the *orixás* are the *only* universal, trans-historical terms. Much of the West's confusion regarding the Afro-Brazilian worldview generally seems to stem from an inability—or a refusal—to take the *orixás* seriously as legitimate principles that precede and exceed culture, even as Western conventions, including linear narrative, are regarded as universal.

Beyond retelling history, the *blocos* are educating the Bahian public about contemporary political issues at home and abroad. Their interest in the political struggles of African states is, again, not a "naive Pan-Africanism," but is a reasoned recognition that, as largely underclass Brazilians, the members share many difficulties (individual and communal) with their African brothers and sisters. This affiliation is not simply racial. Perhaps the instance that illustrated this most clearly was Olodum's choice, in 1990, to celebrate not an African nation but as the northeastern region of Brazil itself. The *nordeste* is understood as delimiting not merely a geographic terrain, but a terrain of character as well. The very name of the area evokes images of agricultural and human devastation. The northeast is regularly racked by drought. It has by far the lowest per capita income and the highest mortality rate in the country. Although technically the entire state of Bahia is included in the region, the word *nordeste* is usually used to signify the interior of the region—seemingly a world apart from the lush, coastal state capital of Salvador where the carnival takes place. There is another difference. Although the *nordeste* is also known for racial mixing, the predominant component is indigenous, not African.

This was certainly not the first moment of black cultural affiliation with indigenous Brazilians. In fact, in some houses of *Candomblé,* they are even a part of the pantheon. The *Candomblé* houses of the *angola* nation worship entities known as *caboclos,* which is a word for indigenous people. The *caboclos* are not *orixás,* but they are powerful spiritual figures. They do not follow the same law of penetrability as the *orixás*—which is to say, they can be embodied by men or women, regardless of their sexual preferences or practices. Jim Wafer has noted that *angola* houses generally entertain only male *caboclo* spirits, and yet this means that the *caboclos,* "at least in their materialized form, live in an exclusively masculine world. But a world in which there is only one sex is a world that is sexually undifferentiated." In this way, Wafer suggests, the *caboclo* "resists dichotomization. . . . This is perhaps why it is difficult to locate the realm of the *caboclos* on the spirit-matter continuum" (Wafer 1991, 106). Unlike the *orixás,* who manifest themselves in human bodies but are, as it were, closed themselves (they do not, for example, eat food, and their motion is choreographically prescribed), the *caboclos* freely socialize, drink like fish, samba with people, and generally comport themselves like rude party animals.

Wafer's book focuses on sexual dichotomization and its subversion in *Candomblé*. But the *caboclo* is an interesting figure because he also resists racial classification. Indigenous culture is also part of the violent history that produced the syncretism of *Candomblé*. The *caboclo* both marks a "real" indigenous influence on African culture, and the figural appropriation of the European figure of the "wild Indian." The *caboclo* is revered in black Brazilian culture because, as Rául Lody (1977) has argued, he ironically has come to represent black resistance—wildness as the refusal to be controlled or contained. At the same time, he figures black solidarity with another national population under siege: actual women and men whose historical and contemporary problems resemble those of blacks.

The *caboclo* is not the only black figure for indigenous affiliation. Of the "Indian"-identified carnival groups mentioned earlier, the most famous are the Apaches and the Comanches. These groups are made up mostly of black members. The Apaches and Comanches are, of course, North American "Indian" references, and they play on the images of Wild West films, known as "bang-bang" pictures in Brazil. The costumes of these groups resemble those cinematic getups as well.

One can hardly help but compare the *blocos de índio* to the Indian organizations of the New Orleans Mardi Gras. Also a black institution, the Mardi Gras Indians combine a literal, cultural, and political affiliation with a metaphoric one. Members of the Mardi Gras Indian groups have asserted that there exists a genuine racial link as well. Although some cultural contact and intermarriage between blacks and Native Americans in Louisiana certainly did and does take place, most students of the Mardi Gras find the association a politically significant but semifictional narrative (Lipsitz 1988; Kinser 1990; Berry, Foose, and Jones 1986). In fact, much like the *blocos de índio,* the Mardi Gras Indians appear to have been modeled on the Wild West carnival shows of the late nineteenth century. The Mardi Gras Indians have developed a complex language of their own, which renders their songs nearly indecipherable to those outside of the community. They are also difficult to read in another sense: as George Lipsitz has put it, the Mardi Gras Indian phenomenon "projects a cultural indeterminacy" (1988, 102). Neither "really" Indian nor "purely" African, its complexity is the point.

The choice of an American Indian stereotype in Brazil is more complicated still. It sets askew the process of carnivalization by putting it in an international context. If the indigenous Brazilians were colonized by the Portuguese in the sixteenth century, Brazil in the twentieth century found itself under American pressures both economic and cultural. The influence of the "bang-bang" is a case in point. The choice of a black Brazilian to portray himself as an Apache marks him as the conquered but dangerous "other" in a game involving not only the whites of his own culture, but Americans as well.

Not only the costumes recall Western films: the behavior of these groups seems patterned after the lawless, hooting trouble making of their cinematic counterparts. The Apaches are especially known for violent rampages. In the late 1970s, some members of the mostly male group surprised a women's carnival group (no longer in existence) and sexually molested dozens of them. It was a scandal that cast the *blocos de índio* in a terrible light, and the Apaches nearly went under. It is difficult to recuperate any meaning from such an episode. Dunn's own assessment of the Indian blocs contrasts with his extremely sympathetic account of the *blocos afro*: "The notoriously rowdy and sometimes violent *blocos índio* [*sic*] rebelled against white Bahian society, yet failed to articulate themselves politically" (1992, 14). And Daniel Touro Linger has written generally of acts of violence during the carnival:

> Whether one discovers in Carnival political inspiration or political reverie, carnival counterposes a utopian world vision to a socially constructed, culturally imagined, and experientially insistent "real world" infused by competition, hierarchy, frustration, and violence.
>
> But ironically, within Carnival itself this real world resurges in its most concentrated form. (1992, 13)

It is tempting to read the violent episode of the sexual attack as a concentrated form of the misogyny of everyday life in Brazil. The fact that the notorious Apache attack took sexual form, however, makes it not only especially horrific, but especially linked to stereotypical representations of dangerous Indians. Fear of indigenous North Americans' cultural and racial difference has always been linked to a sexual threat: the defilement of white womanhood. Although the women attacked were not in the majority white, they became figurally "whitened" in the event, coming to represent the object of an Indian threat. There are obvious and justified objections to this suggestion. Scandalously little attention is given in both the Brazilian and U.S. media to the reality of sexual violence against women of color. It is perhaps even more disturbing that a woman raped can certainly not be accounted for as "mere" representation; the individual responsibility for such acts can not be elided by metaphors. But acts of violence, and perhaps especially acts of sexual violence, do take place in a context of racial significa-

tions. Although the figure of the Indian—the Apache of American cinema—
is a highly fictionalized representation, the sexual attack seems in retrospect
to have demonstrated the literal fallout of racist representations.

Depictions of the violence and savagery of indigenous Brazilians and
North Americans of course did not begin with Wild West shows and shoot-
'em-up pictures. The earliest colonial documents countered all those sexy
earthly paradise stories with grave warnings about cannibalism. In fact cannibalism and sexuality seem inextricably linked in these accounts. Richard
Parker has brilliantly suggested that the carnival itself cannibalizes Brazilian
society's myth of miscegenation as a sexual and racial fusion, spitting it back
out as a "juxtaposition of differences" (1991, 163). And he reminds us of the
cannibal reference in that grounding sexual metaphor of "those who eat":

> Given all of the sexual and sensual connotations of the act of eating in
> Brazilian culture, the symbolism of anthropophagy is especially well
> suited to the semantic structure of the *carnaval.* The transgression of a
> food taboo can easily be linked to the transgression of sexual taboos in
> a symbolic construct focused on devouring the flesh of another human
> body in order to incorporate it within one's own. As a symbol of incor-
> poration, then, anthropophagy can be invested with layers of meaning
> ranging from cannibalism itself, to the act of sexual intercourse, to the
> mixture of the races and cultures that is taken as definitive of Brazilian
> reality. (Ibid., 149)

Brazilians understand themselves in the eyes of the world not only as mythic
sexual beings, but also as cannibals. The carnival provides its own version of
cannibalistic inversions, and they involve sexual as well as racial stereotypes.

Syncretism, like cannibalism, is the absorption of one body—this time
a body of belief—into another. *Candomblé* is a syncretic system, where
names and images of Catholic saints have been absorbed into a body of
African beliefs. The carnival groups offer an even more complex syncretism.
My own carnival group, the Daughters of Gandhi, and our brother organization, the Sons of Gandhi, perform a kind of secular syncretism by associat-
ing the Yoruba principle of peace, the *orixá* Oxalá, with Mahatma Gandhi.
Gandhi is also, of course, a symbol of dignity and resistance in the face of
colonial oppression. The Sons and Daughters of Gandhi give another meaning to an African affiliation with Indians—this time, with the great Indian
liberator. Of course, Gandhi is never embodied in *Candomblé*. But he does
manifest himself during the carnival: a frail, bespectacled fellow, dead ringer
for the original, says he receives Gandhi's spirit for five days every year. He
rides the float surveying his followers and sometimes walks among us. I got

to know Gandhi quite well myself, as he makes it a habit to get very friendly with his Daughters. Gandhi patted me on the ass! Gently, very gently.

The Sons and Daughters of Gandhi are an alternative version of the Indian nation. We seem to be in stark contrast to the Apaches and the Comanches, but in a way we are all just offering another way of telling a story about Brazil. According to Homi Bhabha: "Counter-narratives of the nation that continually evoke and erase its totalizing boundaries—both actual and conceptual—disturb those geological maneuvers through which 'imagined communities' are given essentialist identities" (1990, 300). The Bahian carnival, I think it is fair to say, blows the lid off any fixed notion of Brazilianness—as well as Indianness and Africanness.

This evocation and erasure of national boundaries is parallel to the evocation and erasure of sexual boundaries, even the very boundaries of the individual body. The subversion of national and sexual borders occurs in *Candomblé* as well, but in the carnival it is made public, and often violent. Race, sex, sexuality, violent struggle—none of these are isolated systems of signification. If the carnival appears to bring these issues to a head, it is simply making manifest the social violence motivated by racism, sexism, and heterosexism that is sometimes difficult to identify as such.

"Os Filhos de Gandhy pedem paz": the Sons of Gandhi ask for peace. This is the banner of my brother organization, and it is a calming phrase that recurs to me at troublesome moments. Carnival in Bahia can be a terrifying event. There may be many levels of significance, but the violence is absolutely real. The world outside the carnival, too, is sometimes brutal beyond belief. So we invoke Mahatma Gandhi, Oxalá, Jesus Christ—whatever it takes to make sense of all this.

Notes

1. Maya Deren, writing about the related and similar religious dances of Haiti, noted that the gods of *vodun,* the *loa,* are always perceived as the authors of glorious motion: "For if the mark of a man's dedication to the *loa* is selfless anonymity, the mark of a *loa*'s devotion to man is his most elaborated, realized manifestation. Therefore, virtuosity is the province of divinity. Only the loa are virtuosi" (Deren 1970, 230).

2. The lambada was danced for several years in northeastern Brazil before its international explosion as a "dirty dance." Its earlier incarnation was as a simple couple's dance, something like merengue with a doubled beat. Two French promoters exported the dance, and added some slam-dunk dips and exaggerated hip action. It became a kind of caricature of Latin sexiness, and was reimported to Brazil, where it burned out on the hype almost as fast as it did abroad. For a while, though, every Rio health club had packed lambada classes, with Brazilian couples earnestly learning the choreographies of their own stereotyped sexuality.

Works Cited

Bastide, Roger. 1961. *O Candomblé da Bahia*. São Paulo: Editora Nacional.

Berry, Jason, Jonathon Foose, and Tad Jones. 1986. *Up from the Cradle of Jazz*. Athens: University of Georgia Press.

Bhabha, Homi K., ed. 1990. *Nation and Narration*. New York: Routledge.

Browning, Barbara. 1996. *Samba: Resistance in Motion*. Bloomington: Indiana University Press.

Butler, Judith. 1990. *Gender Trouble: Feminism and the Subversion of Identity*. New York: Routledge.

____. 1993. *Bodies That Matter: On the Discursive Limits of "Sex."* New York: Routledge.

Crowley, Daniel. 1984. *African Myth and Black Reality in Bahian Carnival*. Los Angeles: Museum of Cultural History, UCLA Monograph Series, no. 25.

Deren, Maya. 1970. *Divine Horsemen: The Living Gods of Haiti*. New York: Dell; reprint, New Paltz, N.Y.: Documentext, McPherson, 1983.

Dunn, Christopher. 1992. "Afro-Bahian Carnival: A Stage for Protest." *Afro Hispanic Review* 5:11: 1–3; 1–19.

Feierman, Steven. 1993. "African Histories and the Dissolution of World History." In Robert H. Bates, V. Y. Mudimbe, and Jean O'Barr, eds., *Africa and the Disciplines: The Contributions of Research in Africa to the Social Sciences and Humanities*, 167–212. Chicago: University of Chicago Press.

Fry, Peter. 1982. "Da hierarquia á igualdade: A construção da homosexualidade no Brasil." In *Para inglês ver: Identidade e política na cultura brasileira*, 87–115. Rio de Janeiro: Zahar Editores.

Kinser, Sam. *Carnival, American Style: Mardi Gras at New Orleans and Mobile*. 1990. Chicago: University of Chicago Press.

Landes, Ruth. 1940. "A Cult Matriarchate and Male Homosexuality." *Journal of Abnormal and Social Psychology* 35: 3: 386–97.

____. 1947. *City of Women*. New York: MacMillan.

Linger, Daniel Touro. 1992. *Dangerous Encounters: Meanings of Violence in a Brazilian City*. Stanford, Calif.: Stanford University Press.

Lipsitz, George. 1988. "Mardi Gras Indians: Carnival and Counter-Narrative in Black New Orleans." *Cultural Critique* 10: 99–121.

Lody, Raúl. 1977. *Samba de Caboclo*. Rio de Janeiro: Funarte.

Matory, J. Lorand. 1988. "Homens montados: Homosexualidade e simbolismo da possessão nas religiões afro-brasileiras." In *Escrividão e invenção da liberdade: Estudos sobre o negro no Brasil*, ed. J. J. Reis, 215–31. São Paulo: Brasiliense.

Parker, Richard. 1991. *Bodies, Pleasures, and Passions: Sexual Culture in Contemporary Brazil*. Boston: Beacon Press.

Raboteau, Albert. 1978. *Slave Religion*. New York: Oxford University Press.

Wafer, Jim. 1991. *The Taste of Blood: Spirit Possession in Brazilian Candomblé*. Philadelphia: University of Pennsylvania Press.

Floating Signification:
Carnivals and the Transgressive Performance of Hybridity

Awam Amkpa

Days before carnival in inner-city communities in Britain, huge sound systems make their distinctive musical pronouncements in street corners and various housing projects or estates. Calypso, reggae, ragamuffin, jungle, hip-hop, ska, and other forms of music inscribed with a determined desire for conditions of *being, becoming,* and *belonging* to various imaginations and constructions of *home* dominate the energies of the revelers. For these people, the celebratory cultural activities and constant hegemonic reminder of *not belonging, not being at home,* and destitution evoke a counterspirit of relentless assertiveness of their presence through music and dance. Apart from diverse auditory tropes, aromas of cooking and deep frying varieties of tropical food mix with distinct smells of smokable herbs to provide complementary olfactory dimensions to the proceedings. Longer daylight hours also make such occasions big revelries where adults and children of various shades of black dance, talk, watch, and perform to the music and moment. In such cities as London, Leeds, Bristol, and Birmingham, nights before the parades of extraordinary floats and costumes are typified by a manic release of energy through dance parties and other smaller events preceding the grand occasion of declaring their "presence" to one another and to other citizens outside the communities. As dawn breaks, "Jouvay!" Carnival begins! Masquerades built surreptitiously over months and those built openly by different community groups are released into orderly narratives and routes set by organizers.

With bands and masquerades on floats, the music, singing, dancing, and whistling build up to performances that are simultaneously individual and collective processions. On floats, one sees elaborate masquerades that are symbolic representations of fantasies of grandeur and beauty, or simply satires of reality. Beside the floats are dancers with uniform costumes shuffling and swaying to steel drum music. According to Errol Hill and Rex Nettleford's description of its Caribbean antecedent, the processions entail:

> Mobilizing masses of people in marches, with their feet keeping a basic rhythm while the upper parts of the body in polyrhythmic counterpoint curve myriad designs in space, produces a different kind of kinesthetic quality and visual impact than that of the American modern dance or the European classical ballet, both of which are rooted in the cultural realities of their respective habitats.[1]

Despite similarities in performance styles between carnivals in the Caribbean and England, or between such practices in English cities, it is difficult to offer a totalizing descriptive archaeology for such displays. What is of interest in this essay is not so much the commonality of styles as the discursiveness and corporeality of the occasions in processes of identity formation and politics in England. As a practice developed in the Caribbean, these carnivals have come to incorporate other minorities and postcolonial subjects forced to live in inner-city communities.

For such communities defining the habitat of Britain's postcolonial subjects with ancestral roots in Africa, the Caribbean, and South Asia, summertime signifies moments of invitation to "perform identity." This is unlike most times, when such identities, as festering reminders of England's imperial escapades, are well policed, criminalized, and demonized by racist institutions and organizations. Such invitation to "identify" is a hegemonic concession and indeed is rationalized as incorporating Britain's marginals into a formulaic "multiculturalism." It is important to stress the Manichaean world implied by such invitations; for those occasions are not so much a legitimization of diversity as eloquent pointers to a metaphor of singularity that these people are excluded from. In Robert Young's equally cynical words: "Today's self-proclaimed mobile and multiple identities may be a marker not of contemporary social fluidity and dispossession but of a new stability, self assurance and quietism. . . . multiplicity must be set against at least a notional singularity to have any meaning."[2] Through institutions and organizations, such invitations suture carnivals onto the dominant ideology and its idea of what identities are diverse and multiple as opposed to those that are singular.

The term *Carnival* has come to mean different things to different communities and historical epochs. In academic circles, Mikhail Bakhtin and V. N. Volosinov's theses are usually invoked to explain its structure, contiguity, and subversive relationship to dominant culture.[3] Although this essay assumes most of their postulations, it is suspicious of the totalizing descriptions their theses offer and seeks to analyze the specificity of such practices among England's black population. To England's postcolonial communities, there is no better time to enunciate tropes of *home,* reconstruct *memory,* and perform *remembering* in contexts overdetermined by hundreds of years of denigration and lack of access to resources for effective citizenship. Such occasions allow a reentry into historical and cultural trauma through performances that are themselves not simply processes of recovering original experiences but a recapitulating practice of questioning the singularity of identity that the English state implies and denies them. To these *unhomed* people, any cultural event allowed by the dominant culture becomes an occasion for simultaneously denouncing their subordination, performing insubordination, and enunciating varieties of subjectivity that not only challenge but are likely not to be acceptable to the dominant culture.

As preparations and rehearsals get under way for the various carnivals in which alterity and hybrid identities are flaunted through masquerades, flamboyant costumes, and music, a major question in the imaginations of the participants is, Will the state perform its hegemonic presence by parading cohorts of racist police? In such situations, according to Frantz Fanon, "the symbols of social order—the police, the bugle calls, the waving flags—are at once inhibitory and stimulating; for they do not convey the message "Don't budge': rather they cry out 'Get ready to attack.'"[4] Will individuals from the community, for various reasons of performing dissident subjectivity, construct narratives challenging and undermining those organized by community leaders, taunt the police to repressive actions? Whatever the case, the presence of the state's repressive apparatus is structured into their performance strategies and attitudes and delineates the boundaries of possibilities.

Who are the dominant occupants of English inner cities and what constitutes their given and taken identities before, during, and after such carnivals? Unlike in the United States, the population of black communities is smaller and has specific migratory patterns simultaneously attached to the evolution of England's national and dominant culture, as well as its former colonized spaces in the Caribbean, Asia, and Africa. "Blackness" in England is a wider discursive front that by the 1970s meant postcolonial peoples from the Caribbean, Africa, and South Asia. The intense cultural chauvinism informing Thatcherite England in the 1970s produced an atmosphere of affiliatory and coalitional politics that made the term *black* include people of Asian descent. Apart from an enforced habitation and consequent hybridity in the "spatial margins" of imperial England (also named and formulated by the colonizing process as Jamaica, Barbados, Trinidad, India, Pakistan, Bangladesh, Nigeria, Ghana, South Africa, etc.), the migrations of peoples from these areas into working-class and ghettoized communities in England underscore the levels of enforced hybridity and consequent epistemological violence and conflicts in processes of self-description.

Studies stressing hybridity as a critical check on particularist and essentialist discourses draw significant attention to identity formation as a process of socialization rather than mere events of "becoming," and such cautionary narratives are woven into this essay. Although works by Frantz Fanon, Homi Bhabha, Mikhail Bakhtin, and Stuart Hall, looked closely into the subject and historicity of hybridity, it is still pertinent to continue to critically examine the particulars of hybridity and the states of epistemological violence generated by diverse colonial discourses and histories foundational to black communities in England. For those who perform in carnivals, the colonial and postcolonial relationships generated by contacts with imperial England produce two major discursive obstacles to generating cultural power, knowledge, and strategies of defining selfhood.

The first obstacle is a consequence of the historic process of enforced mixture of diverse people wherein language and conventions of representations and communication have to be formulated anew to make socialization within and outside such communities possible. Within such reconfigurations of conventions of representation and communication, people inscribe struggles for *being* and *becoming* by deliberately "pidginizing" and "creolizing" the dominant European languages and their cultural practices such as music and dance. "Pidginization" introduces formal rules of other languages onto a dominant one, thereby contesting its structures of enunciating meaning, whereas "creolization" as a syncretic process produces an amalgam of linguistic structures, thereby transforming them into a new one. Within performative cultural practices such as dance, masks, and music, acts of compacting, subverting, and limiting the dominant language and its cultural practices evoke different traumas of colonial and postcolonial encounters, as well as competing and overlapping myths of origination. Producing these trauma and myths in carnivals provides ready sites for negotiating and contesting ethnicity and other differences, sometimes to the detriment of formulating an effective anticolonial bloc through representational acts. The metaphors as multiple signifiers produce what Stuart Hall refers to as a "sliding chain of signification."[5] Thus, the practices of culture for such communities reflect a permanent revolution of conventions of representation. Whatever the particulars, the simultaneous actions of *pidginization* and *creolization* are transgressive of colonial cultures, as communities deliberately reinvent their hybrid cultures and systems of representation. This transgressive enunciation of self- and community identities gives postcolonial people in England the "cultural capital" for dissent and authority in what Pierre Bourdieu terms the "structuring structure" of culture.[6]

The second obstacle is spatial and geographic. The spaces for enunciating subjectivity are historically limited by colonialist and postcolonial discourses despite their potential oppositional tropes. For most postcolonial peoples, the process of citizenship even in their so-called countries of origin is as problematic as the same process in England, which on the whole constitutes the metropolitan center of their existence. The question of the *nation they come from* and the *nation they have come to* as sites of enunciating subjectivity and citizenship remains a key signifier to the typologies of hybridity experienced by such people. What and who is a Jamaican in Jamaica and England? Or a Barbadian in Barbados and England? Or indeed a Nigerian, or an Indian in the colonized and postcolonial countries and England? As *places* within the *Place,* or nations whose identities are articulated into England's political economy and dominant culture, immigrants to England realize how limited spaces of enunciation are. The geographic and spatial limitation features in the content and forms of the performances witnessed. Having historically contested inner cities with white working classes all over the country, the performance of carnivals continues to be restricted to such spaces. Carnivalesque dissidence by black people cannot be performed in, say, Hyde Park in London, despite its reputation as a place for "free and dissident speech."

These issues further complicate processes of hybridity within such communities. The movement of identity formation within black communities is forced to happen sideways, downwards, and backwards. Limited in its movement outward, black identity has a limited capacity to effectively hybridize the white dominant culture with its tropes of hybridity, fluidity, and quests for equity and social justice. Despite these limitations, processes of negotiating these and other obstacles make carnivals by black people in England recognizable forms of political calculations and strategic actions toward identity politics. Indeed, recognition of the enforced hybridity of identity politics and the proactive willingness within such communities to create affiliatory politics is central to the hybridity in carnivals and other cultural practices such as popular music, dance, and fashion.

Although a signifier known and promoted as "black" is used in determining levels of *belonging* in England, heterogeneous discourses of gender, class, sexuality, ethnicity, and generational issues are precariously sutured onto such an almost overperformed dominant racial signifier. Historically, it has been in the interest of the hegemony to hierarchize these discourses and subordinate them to the racial discourse as its signification not only produces slippery discursive fields contradicting a wider and more effective anti-hegemonic affiliation, but also makes dissent from these heterogeneous and insubordinate discourses containable.

Varieties of contradictory discourses weave themselves into cultural practices such as carnivals. There is no homogeneous and stable notion of blackness projected in the events. Rather, a spectrum of multiple discourses and critical relationships between individuals and groups within the communities highlights the complexity of their hybrid identities. There are individuals who, as self-designated spokespersons of their communities, use the occasion of carnivals to commoditize black culture, sanitizing their constructs of any political meanings. Paul Gilroy identifies them as "traffickers of black culture" who strive to "deny that their chosen commodity has any political dimensions at all."[7] Consequently,

> the anti-political approach is even stronger where
> the signs of blackness have been specially packaged
> in order to cross over to white consumers, many of
> whom take pleasure in the transgression and dangerousness
> which these once forbidden commodities express, without
> discovering a similar enthusiasm for either the company
> of real live black people or the history of their struggles
> against slavery, for citizenship and towards personal and
> social autonomy.[8]

There are also those who see themselves as authors of a "pure" narrative of masculinist and phallocentric blackness and whose contributions to the carnivals evoke a "repulsion and attraction" syndrome for participants. Added to these are the squeamish antiessentialists who masquerade their political apathy in narratives of denial of the hegemonic exclusion of people because of skin pigmentation and postcolonial heritage. Despite these contradictory examples, there are individuals and groups who genuinely recognize and participate in the cultural politics of their communities, stressing affiliations of their subjectivities and differences, as well as desires for an equitable distribution of power locally and globally. The list is endless, and what it suggests is that numerous signifiers are performed in carnivals that are neither fixed nor fixable, but rather mark identities in flux. Kobena Mercer puts it succinctly when he asserts: "No one has a monopoly or exclusive authorship over signs they share in common: rather, elements from the same system of signs are constantly subject to antagonistic modes of appropriation and articulation."[9]

As enunciating texts, carnivals are what Kobena Mercer refers to as "floating signifiers."[10] They are fluid significations of identities in complex relationships with one another, complementary and contradictory with one another and the dominant culture, as their meanings cross and bleed into one another. This is so because carnivals, as cultural practices, are structures within which *heteronomous* and *autonomous* identities cohabit and inscribe their desires for being. By *heteronomous,* I am extending Pierre Bourdieu's notion of the term as it suggests cultural practices soliciting diverse attention to the black arts produced in carnivals. While they seek diverse attraction, *autonomous* art and cultural practices display individualistic chauvinism as nonconformity and offense stress dissident subjectivities. Thus, the floating signifiers we see and become simultaneously perform heteronomous and autonomous desires for spectacle and spectating, and such relationships are usually tense and on the verge of developing into antagonism and scuffles.

We must remember that in the histories of contemporary English cultures, the concept of "blackness" and its celebration are themselves subversions of the imperial logic and fantasies of the dominant culture. Ever since black people in the diaspora began displaying their subordination and insubordination to the dominant culture, thereby inverting the "given" images of racial differentiation, the organization of countertexts on a large scale such as carnivals has always carried with it both risks of repression and contradictory representations fitting into the wishes of the hegemony. By the 1970s, carnivals were simply defined by the mainstream culture as opportunities for releasing "black excess." Tourists in London and other cities are forever warned about the dangers of crossing into black communities, let alone when they openly celebrate their displacement! Over the years, the media has created a notoriety for the carnivals as sites for "barbaric violence," "drugs," and "licentiousness."

For those who watch, spectatorship can be a tourist experience whereby their panoptic gaze confirms their identities and superiority in economic, ethnic, and, most of all, gendered terms. For others, the carnivals offer an occasion for the voyeuristic envy of those whose subordination is more visual, and whose defiance to domination is more assertive. For some others, it can be an opportunity to confirm their voluntary assimilation or liberal recognition of "otherness" performed by people politically defined as "near self," and whose communities are inhabited by the unemployed, unskilled, homeless, criminalized, and culturally marginalized. Carnivals and their sites of performance may also present those outside such communities with arenas for performing texts they cannot otherwise perform in their own communities.

Because numerous bodies present their hieroglyphs to people they share their communities with, and those who have "migrated" to these communities to view them, ambivalence characterizes each text. Marginality is displayed and beautified like a festering sore of the tropes of domination. In performance, the participants do not disguise the texts defining them. Every derogatory sign exhibited about themselves is at the same time a signifier of the dominant culture. Secondariness is performed as primariness and conventions of representations and enunciating subjecthood are performed as heteroglossia, spectatcularly presented through masks, dance, and music. "Otherness" is fetishized by performance and spectatorship, while gazes that are countertextual and signify limits of the dominant culture dominate the performances.

Various discursive issues at play range from shouting aloud with body narratives the pride of ethnic origin, to the anarchic display of spaces other than those prescribed by definitions of ethnic marginality. In the processes of sharing narratives with spectators, authority is willingly dismantled and disrupted, and social meaning loudly signifies melancholy, displacement, and alienation.

Regarding those who share politically, ideologically, and culturally in the multiple discourses of the carnivals, spectatorship is recognized as an interactive performance. History denies significant strata of these communities the luxury of formulating any "distance" between art and their lives, or between the practice of culture and the politics of culture in contemporary England. On such occasions, the performance of spectacles and the spectacle of spectating offer a context for desiring. Fanon's assertion underscores the significance of such desires:

> As soon as I desire I am asking to be considered.
> I am not merely here and now, sealed into thingness.
> I am for somewhere else and for something else.
> I demand that notice be taken of my negating activity
> insofar as I pursue something other than life; insofar
> as I do battle for the creation of a human world—that
> is a world of reciprocal recognitions. In the world in
> which I travel, I am endlessly creating myself. And it
> is going beyond the historical, instrumental hypothesis
> that I will initiate my cycle of freedom.[11]

Such is the temperament echoed in the carnivals that black and postcolonial subjects in English inner cities enact as they struggle to reproduce themselves as social agents in contemporary England. As contexts for the performances of texts of social and political reality, these carnivals provide spaces for challenging the homogeneous identities imposed by the dominant culture on subordinated social formations and their localities. Through performing constellations of semiotic texts, they provide occasions for celebrating heterogeneous identities and their intertextual relationships in the development of subject positions in spaces circumscribed by the state. This is not to suggest that these carnivals are terminal events or annual rituals that are solely paradigmatic of the lives and struggles of the black communities. Such performative acts only act as artifacts within the processes of practicing what Michel de Certeau refers to as "everyday life" in a society for whom black populations are offensive reminders of the triumphalist narratives of imperial England.[12]

Race, ethnicity, class, gender, and sexuality denote the definitions and differentiations of people from our illustrative communities. Theirs is a history that has its roots in the development of the European bourgeoisie, modernity, and capitalism from its mercantile to its contemporary finance and corporate form. That history whose narratives enabled the denigration, physical removal, epistemological violence, and denial of the humanity of people from Africa, South Asia, and the Caribbean through slavery, indentured labor, colonialism, and immigrations planted the seedlings that are germinated in the performances displayed on British streets in the summer. It is such history that makes them attractive for those wishing to reconstruct the imperial history of the dominant English Self, and in pinning down how others define their Otherness.

Strategies for more intensive incorporation and neutralization of the political effectiveness of such carnivals by black communities have become more established in recent years. Transnational corporations are beginning to sponsor some of the festivals and are contributing to creating a "Disneyfied" mass commercialized audience under the guise of bogus multiculturalisms and tourist leisures. The Notting Hill carnival in London is a case in point. In Thatcherite Britain, multiculturalism was reinvented as a stabilizing process of reducing the dynamism of rapidly mutating cultures from postcolonial subjects. Will these carnivals still provide sites for transgressive texts or will transgressions of dominance and marginality seek alternative sites? As their practices destabilize hitherto stable categorizations of who is negated in radial, ethnic, sexual, gendered, or class terms, these carnivals draw significant attention to the complex routes of black identities in diaspora and the effectiveness of their theatrical performances.

Because this form of exercising cultural politics is becoming increasingly systematized, it is important to note that as long as triumphalist and ethnocentric narratives by the English dominant culture continue to operate by excluding communities denigrated for nearly four hundred years, practices such as carnivals will remain inspiring locations for textualizing and confronting social reality, not only for the racially deprived, but also for those denied full participation in society on grounds of their gender, class, and sexuality.

As we smell, eat, drink, dance, watch, and perform our spectatorships, how much empowerment or subordination we experience will depend on our getting out there to see and participate in textualizing our realities and the participation of others in them. This is not only within the arenas of carnivals, but in spaces that generally define our political lives and culture.

Notes

1. Errol Hill and Rex Nettleford, "Implications for Caribbean Development," in *Caribbean Festival Arts,* ed. John W. Nunely and Judith Bettelheim (Seattle: University of Washington Press, 1988), 186.

2. Robert Young, *Colonial Desire: Hybridity in Theory, Culture and Race* (London and New York: Routledge, 1995), 4.

3. Mikhail Bakhtin, *The Dialogic Imagination* (Austin: University of Texas Press, 1981); Mikhail Bakhtin, *Rabelais and His World* (Bloomington: University of Indiana Press, 1984); V. N. Volosinov, *Marxism and the Philosophy of Language* (New York: Seminar Press, 1973).

4. Frantz Fanon, *Black Skin, White Masks* (London: Pluto Press, 1986), 41.

5. An interview with Stuart Hall, "On Postmodernism and Articulation," in D. Morley and K. Chen, eds., *Stuart Hall* (London and New York: Routledge, 1996), 137.

6. Pierre Bourdieu, *The Field of Cultural Production* (New York: Columbia University Press, 1993).

7. Paul Gilroy, *Small Acts* (London: Serpent's Tail Press, 1993), 4.

8. Ibid., 4–5.

9. Kobena Mercer, "'1968': Periodising Politics and Identity," in *Cultural Studies,* ed. Lawrence Grossberg, Cary Nelson, and Paula Treichler (London: Routledge, 1992), 427.

10. Ibid.

11. Fanon, *Black Skin, White Masks,* 218, 231.

12. On the notion of the practice of everyday life, see Michel de Certeau, *The Practice of Everyday Life* (Berkeley: University of California Press, 1984).

Hybridity and Other Poems

Shani Mootoo

Hybridity

Point of convergence
Union of way back then, back home and home
Where I depend neither on memory or desire
Where I am neither mendhi, baigan, or steelpan
Nor
Mindless of these

Seamless juncture
As in mulligatawny that cooks long and slow
Neither Jeera, cardamom, hurdi, nor clove
stand alone

Hybridity
As in: "offspring of tame sow and wild boar
Child of freeman and slave"*
Some concoction, some new stew or callallaoo
Spotted variegated deformed crude new

Calcottawarima
Persimangorangegrapear
Pomeracappleplummecythere
Gorakpurcarapachaimavancouverlaromainottawa
Coconutcashewpeachskookumuckalapaninaananaani

Where neither Nepalese great-grandmother
Mother, lover, nor government can define I
Nor
am I
Mindless of these

*Oxford English Dictionary, 7th ed., "hybrid"

"It is a crime." Photo-based work, 1994.

Bu' A A!

Hardi aloo "Sita Gita Meethai!"
Paymee pone doorma.
Aloo dhal tabanka?
Baigan peewah, junjhut mamguy.

Jeera jhundi, "Gulab jamon chokha,"
Anchar roti, pelau baigan bayta!
Chundy aloo dal paratha?
Pomerac chataigne peewah.

"Doodoose sapodilla peera cokeeyea."
Pooja, busup-shirt joovay.
Googlie junjhut calalloo,
Pholourie—Pandit Panday!

Mauby: sagaboy pelau pone,
Shadow-benny sorrell pastel.
Cookoo, la jablesse, jagabat?
Careete corailee parang!

Moko jumbie bara,
Agoutie.
Chip-chip ackra!

For Naan
who made the incredible journey from Nepal to
Trinidad to be a bride, and never,
in all her years there, spoke a word of English.

The requested moment precisely,
the alarm clock radio blurts out, CBC Vancouver,
fluorescent red glow pries me awake to hear read
a letter from two flight attendants from New West
                    ON HOLIDAY
Pawing the foothills of the Nepalese Himalayas
enamoured of the simple primitive lives of the Nepalese
of beautiful smiles white teeth
of brass bells tinkling tinkling
on beasts of burden as they trek over
this pass that summit—
how they wished to remain as long as they could
before returning to civilization—
if you're planning a trip keep in mind it costs only ten rupees,
or thirty cents, for a bed per night. What a deal!

They brought back trophies of authentic Kula Valley topi.

Images I have hoarded jealously
from *National Geographic*'s favorite topic
span panoramic across my mind.
But how it irks me to know the color of the hills
before the snow blues everything
to know of pebbly faces creviced as the hills around
to know of Naan's girlhood clothing swirling
dusty red dandelion saffron
sequins iridescent and beads of glass
to know of yaks, yak butter, remote mountain culture
to know of these, how it irks me
from travelogues, adventure journals and PBS tv.

How it beserks me
that I have exoticized
my great-grandmother's land
by my yearnings.
That someone else continues to relentlessly
tame conquer colonize gaze objectify leave paw marks
where I can only dream of an embrace

but this is how I know the look and lay of Naan's land.

If I were to do the white thing and pilgrimage there
would my cousins, I wonder, gladly see Naan in me?
and I, Naan in them?
Do I dare wear a Topi?
It's been so long that I who have minable traces
of authentic Nepalese swirling in the heritage river,
Surely *I* appropriate if I dare to wear
a topi from the Kulu Valley.

Let me suggest something.
When my presence in this land irks you
when your eyes froth spit curse because of me
brown as I am
other as I am
ancestor of the pebbly face
Remember how you love to haughtily climb all over
my great-grandmother's mountains, this pass that summit
simple primitive lives beautiful smiles white teeth
brass bells tinkling tinkling beasts of burden trek
remember how you are charmed by my Naan's quaint ways
(as long as she stays in her place)
And remember how you love to photograph all of this
in another land.

All the Hindi I Know

Acha
Chalo
Aap ke naam kya hai?
Bayti bayta,
Meera naam Shani hai.
Dhadi Dhada,
Nahi
Hai

The Autoethnographic Performance:
Reading Richard Fung's Queer Hybridity

José Esteban Muñoz

In the Caribbean we are all performers.
—Antonio Benítez-Rojo

The Queen's English, Too: Queer Hybridity and the Autoethnographic Performance

Are queens born or made? The royal visit sequence of Richard Fung's *My Mother's Place* (1991) undoes the "either/or" bind that such a question produces. A sequence from the film's beginning narrates the moment when the pasty specter of a monarch born to the throne helps to formulate an entirely different type of queen. A flickering sound and image connotes an 8mm camera, the technology used before the advent of amateur video cameras. A long black car leads a procession as schoolchildren, mostly black girls and boys wearing white or light blue uniforms, look on. At the center of the procession, we can easily identify the British queen. The voice-over narration sets the scene:

> Under the watchful eyes of the priests we stand for ages on the side-walk, burning up in our school uniforms. Then quickly they pass, and all you see is a long white glove making a slow choppy motion. We wave the little flags we were given and fall back into class. White socks on our arms, my sister and I practice the royal wave at home. After Trinidad and Tobago got our independence in 1962, Senghor, Salessi, and Indira Gandhi also made visits. We were given school holidays just like we got for the queen and Princess Margaret, but my mother never took pictures of them.

The young Chinese Trinidadian's identification with the queen is extremely complicated. Practicing the royal wave, in this instance, is an important example of a brand of dissidence that Homi Bhabha has defined as "colonial mimicry": "Mimicry emerges as the representation of a difference that is itself a process of disavowal. Mimicry is thus the sign of the double articulation; a complex strategy of reform, regulation, and discipline, which 'appropriates' the other as it visualizes power."[1] The modalities of difference that inform this royal gesture are structured not only around the colonized/colonizer divide, but also a gay/straight one. This moment of protodrag "flaunting" not only displays an ambivalence to empire and the protocols of colonial pedagogy, but also reacts against the forced gender prescriptions that such systems reproduce. This mode of mimicry is theatrical inasmuch as it mimes and renders hyperbolic the symbolic ritual that it is signifying upon. This brief "visualization" of power is representative of Fung's cultural performance. Fung's video "visualizes" the workings of power in ethnographic and pornographic films, two discourses that assign subjects such as Fung, colonized, colored, and queer, the status of terminally "other" object. Many of the performances that Fung produces are powerful disidentifications with these othering discourses.

Eve Kosofsky Sedgwick has defined the term *queer* as a *practice* that develops for queer children as

> the ability to attach intently to a few cultural objects, objects of high or popular culture or both, objects whose meaning seemed mysterious, excessive or oblique in relation to the codes most readily available to us, [which] became a prime resource for survival. We needed for there to be sites where meanings didn't line up tidily with each other, and we learn to invest these sites with fascination and love.[2]

Thus, to perform queerness is to constantly disidentify, to constantly find oneself thriving on sites where meaning does not properly "line up." This is equally true of hybridity, another modality where meaning or identifications do not properly line up. The postcolonial hybrid is a subject whose identity practices are structured around an ambivalent relationship to the signs of empire and the signs of the "native," a subject who occupies a space between the West and the rest.

This is not to say that the terms *hybridity* and *queerness* are free of problems. Ella Shohat attempts to temper the celebratory aura that currently envelops the word *hybridity*: "As a descriptive catchall term, 'hybridity' *per se* fails to discriminate between diverse modalities of hybridity, for example, forced assimilation, internalized self-rejection, political co-optation, social conformism, cultural mimicry, and creative transcendence."[3] It would be dangerous to collapse the different modalities of hybridity we encounter in the First World and its neocolonial territories, and in the various diasporas to which the diversity of ethnically marked people belong. Queerness, too, has the capacity to flatten difference in the name of coalition. Scholars working with these antiessentialist models of identity need to resist the urge to give in to crypto-essentialist understandings of these terms that eventually position them as universal identificatory sites of struggle. Despite some of the more problematic uses of the terms *hybridity* and *queerness,* I take the risk of melding them when discussing the work of cultural producers such as Fung because hybridity helps one understand how queer lives are fragmented into various identity bits: some of them adjacent, some of them complementary, some of them antagonistic. The hybrid—and terms that can be roughly theorized as equivalents, such as the Creole or the mestizo—are paradigms that help account for the complexities and impossibilities of identity, but, except for a certain degree of dependence on institutional frames, what a subject can do from her or his position of hybridity is, basically, open-ended. The important point is that identity practices such as queerness and hybridity are not a priori sites of contestation but, instead, spaces of productivity where identity's fragmentary nature is accepted and negotiated. It is my understanding that these practices of identification inform the reflexivity of Fung's work.

The concept of hybridity has also been engaged by theorists outside of the field of postcolonial or critical race studies. Bruno Latour, the French philosopher of science, has argued that the hybrid is a concept that must be understood as central to the story of modernity. Latour contends that the moderns, the denizens and builders of modernity, are known not for individual breakthroughs such as the invention of humanism, the emergence of the sciences, the secularization and modernization of the world, but instead with the conjoined structure of these historical movements. Latour writes:

> The essential point of the modern constitution is that it renders the work of mediation that assembles hybrids invisible, unthinkable, unrepresentable. Does this lack of representation limit the work of mediation in any way? No, for the modern world would immediately cease to function. Like all other collectives it lives on that blending. On the contrary (and here the beauty of the mechanism comes to light), *the modern constitution allows the expanded proliferation of the hybrids whose existence, whose very possibility, it denies.*[4]

Latour's formulation explains the way in which modern culture produces hybrids while at the same time attempting to elide or erase the representation or signs of hybridity. I want to suggest that Latour's formulation might also give us further insight into empire's panicked response to the hybrids it continuously produces. Empire's institutions, such as colonial pedagogy, are in no small part responsible for the proliferation of hybrid identities, but it is in colonialism's very nature to delineate clearly between the West and the rest. Its terms do not allow for the in-between status of hybridity. The work of hybrid cultural producers such as Fung might thus be understood as a making visible of the mediations that attempt to render hybridity invisible and unthinkable: in both *My Mother's Place* and *Chinese Characters* (1986), Fung works to make hybridity and its process comprehensible and visible.

Fredric Jameson has contended that "The visual is essentially pornographic, which is to say it has its end in rapt, mindless fascination."[5] But some visuals are more pornographic than others. The epistemological affinity of ethnography and pornography has been explained in Bill Nichols, Christian Hansen, and Catherine Needham's "Ethnography, Pornography and the Discourses of Power," which maps various ways in which the two regimes of ethnography and pornography share a similar discourse of dominance.[6] Both discourses are teleologically cognate insofar as they both strive for the achievement of epistemological utopias where the "Other" and knowledge of the "Other" can be mastered and contained. Ethnotopia can be characterized as a world of limitless observation, where "we know them," whereas pornotopia is a world where "we have them," "a world of lust unlimited."[7] At the end of that essay, the writers are unable to imagine a new symbolic regime or practice where these genres can be reformulated differently, in ways that actively attempt to avoid the imperialist or exploitative vicissitudes of these cinematic genres. My project here is to explicate the ways in which Richard Fung's work invites the viewer to push this imagining further. Fung challenges the formal protocols of such genres through the repetition and radical reinterpretation of such stock characters as the "native informant"[8] and the racialized body in porn. I will consider two of Fung's videos, *My Mother's Place* and *Chinese Characters*. The former traces the Fung family's migratory history in the Asian diaspora through a series of interviews with Rita Fung, the artist's mother; the latter considers the role of the eroticized Asian Other in the discourse of gay male pornography.

A consideration of the performativity of Fung's production sheds valuable light on his project. Reiteration and citation are the most easily identifiable characteristics of this mode of performativity. I will suggest that by its use of such strategies as voice-over monologues, found familial objects such as home-movie footage, and the technique of video keying, Fung's work deploys a practice of performativity that repeats and cites, *with a difference,* the generic fictions of the native Other in ethnography and the Asian "bottom"[9] in fetishizing, North American, specialty porn. The definition of "performative" that I am producing is not meant as an overarching one, but as a working definition designed to deal with the specificity of Fung's productions. This operative understanding of performativity is informed, to some degree, by the work of Judith Butler. In *Bodies That Matter: On the Discursive Limits of Sex,* Butler explains that, if a performative succeeds, "that action echoes prior actions, and accumulates the force of authority through the repetition or citation of a prior, authoritative set of practices. What this means, then, is that a performative 'works' to the extent that it draws on and covers over the constitutive conventions by which it is mobilized."[10] In this quotation, Butler is answering a rhetorical question put forward by Jacques Derrida when he considers whether or not a performative would work if it did not "repeat a 'coded' or iterable utterance . . . if it were not identifiable in some way as a 'citation.'"[11] Butler, in her analysis, is in agreement with Derrida as she understands a performative as working only if it taps into the force of its site of citation, the original that is being repeated, while it draws on and, in time, covers the conventions that it will ultimately undermine. Although Butler's essay is concerned specifically with the performative charge of queerness, its ability to redo and challenge the conventions of heterosexual normativity, it can also explicate the workings of *various* "minority" identifications. Homi Bhabha defines the power of performance in the postcolonial world as the "'sign of the present,' the performativity of discursive practice, the *récits* of the everyday, the repetition of the empirical, the ethics of self-enactment."[12] The repetition of the quotidian in Bhabha, like citation and repetition in Butler, elucidates Fung's own ethics of self-enactment.

Fung's performances work as "autoethnography," inserting a subjective, performative, often combative, "native I" into ethnographic film's detached discourse and gay male pornography's colonizing use of the Asian male body. I will be suggesting that through acts like postcolonial mimicry and the emergence of a hybridized and queerly reflexive performance practice, the social and symbolic economy that regulates otherness can be offset.

The movement of personal histories into a public sphere is typical of autoethnography. Françoise Lionnet describes the way in which autoethnography functions in written cultural production as a "skepticism about writing the self, the auto-biography, turning it into the allegory of the ethnographic project that self-consciously moves from the general to the particular to the general."[13] These movements from general to specific, and various shades in between, punctuate Fung's work. Lionnet, in her study of folk anthropologist and novelist Zora Neale Hurston, conceives of autoethnography as a mode of cultural performance. She explains that autoethnography is a "text/performance" and "transcends pedestrian notions of referentiality, for the staging of the event is part of the process of 'passing on,' elaborating cultural forms, which are not static and inviolable but dynamically involved in the creation of culture itself."[14] The creation of culture in this style of performance is always already braided to the production of self in autoethnography insofar as culture itself is the field in which this "figural anthropology" of the self comes to pass.[15] Mary Louise Pratt also employed the term *autoethnography* in her study of travel writing on the imperial frontier. In this study, Pratt lucidly outlines the differences between ethnography and autoethnography:

> I use these terms [*autoethnography* and *autoethnographic expression*] to refer to instances in which colonized subjects undertake to represent themselves in ways which engage with the colonizer's own terms. If ethnographic texts are a means in which Europeans represent to themselves their (usually subjugated) others, autoethnographic texts are those the others construct in response to or in dialogue with those metropolitan representations.[16]

Conventional video and documentary style can, in the case of Fung and in the light of Pratt's definition, be understood as the "colonizer's terms" that are being used to address the metropolitan form. But in Fung's case these terms work to address more than just the metropolitan form and the colonizer. The terms are also meant to speak to the colonized in a voice that is doubly authorized, by both the metropolitan form and subaltern speech. I am not proposing an explanation where form and content are disentangled; more accurately, I mean to imply that the metropolitan form is inflected by the power of subaltern speech, and the same is equally true in reverse. Fung's cultural work elucidates a certain imbrication—that the metropolitan form needs the colonial "other" to function. Autoethnography is a strategy that seeks to disrupt the hierarchical economy of colonial images and representations by making visible the presence of subaltern energies and urgencies *in* metropolitan culture. Autoethnography worries easy binarisms such as colonized and the colonizer or subaltern and metropolitan by presenting subaltern speech through the channels and pathways of metropolitan representational systems.

Lionnet's and Pratt's theorizations are useful tools in understanding the tradition of autobiographical film that has flourished in North America since 1968.[17] The practice of combining evidentiary sound/image cinema with narratives of personal history has been especially prevalent in video documentary production since the advent of widespread independent video production in the late 1960s. Video technology provided disenfranchised sectors of the public sphere with inexpensive and mobile means to produce alternative media. Video documentary practices were adopted by many different minority communities that might be understood as counterpublics. Native Americans, African-Americans, Asians, Latina/os, feminists, gay men, and lesbians all made considerable contributions to the field of documentary video. In the 1980s, AIDS/HIV activist groups such as ACT-UP made use of this technology and the practices of documentary in politically adroit ways.[18]

We might consider this modality as an intensification of what Jim Lane has called the "personal as political trend" in post-1960s autobiographical film.[19] Lane registers a diminishing production of overtly political cinema in the face of what he understands as the more privatized identity politics of the 1970s and 1980s. Such a dichotomy would be of little use when considering trends in video production, a medium that has always found political relevance precisely in the politics of identity and different minority communities.

This strain of autobiographical documentary is best illustrated in recent work by numerous queer video artists. Fung's practice shares an autoethnographic impulse with the work of Sadie Benning and the late Marlon Riggs, to identify only two examples from a larger field. Riggs excavated an African-American gay male image that has been elided in the history of both black communities and queer communities.[20] Benning's confessional experimental videos produce an interesting ethnography of white queer youth culture.[21] In both these examples, the artists inhabit their videos as subjects who articulate their cultural location through their own subcultural performances as others: poetic teen angst monologues in the case of Benning, and, from Riggs, vibrant snap diva virtuosity that includes, but is not limited to, dance, music, and monologues.

The queer trend that I am identifying is in many ways an effort to reclaim the past and put it in direct relationship with the present. Autoethnography is not interested in searching for some lost and essential experience, because it understands the relationship that subjects have with their own pasts as complicated yet necessary fictions. Stuart Hall provides a formulation that addresses this complicated relationship between one's identity and one's past:

> Far from being eternally fixed in some essentialized past, they [identities] are subject to the continuous play of history, culture and power. Far from being grounded in a mere "recovery" of the past, which is

waiting to be found and which, when found, will secure our sense of ourselves into eternity, identities are the names we give to the different ways in which we are positioned by, and position ourselves within, narratives of the past.[22]

A subject is not locating her or his essential history by researching a racial or cultural past; what is to be located is in fact just one more identity bit that constitutes the matrix that is hybridity. This relationship between a past and a present identity is articulated through a voice-over near the end of *My Mother's Place,* when Fung explains that his mother "connects me to a past I would have no other way of knowing. And in this sea of whiteness, of friends, enemies and strangers, I look at her and know who I am." The past that Rita makes available to Richard is not an essentialized racial past, but instead a necessary fiction of the past that grounds the video artist in the present.

Fung's relationship with and love for his mother are at the center of *My Mother's Place.* The video paints an endearing portrait of Rita Fung as a woman who came of age during colonialism and took her identifications with the colonial paradigm with her to the moment of decolonization. It is shot in Canada and Trinidad and is composed of a series of "interviews" and recollections that form a decidedly personal register. This video portrait of his mother is a queer son's attempt to reconstruct and better understand his identity formation through equally powerful identifications, counteridentifications, and disidentifications with his mother and her own unique relationship to the signs of colonization. The tape relies on its documentary subject's ability to tell her own story in a witty and captivating fashion.

The opening of *My Mother's Place* includes a section subtitled "Reading Instructions." This depicts a sequence of women, mostly academics and activists, mostly women of color, sitting in a chair in front of a black background on which photographs of different women's faces are projected. After the women pronounce on various critical issues including imperialism, gender, political action, and exile, the screen is filled with captions that loosely define the cluster of talking heads on the screen. The descriptions include: teacher, writer, sociologist, arts administrator, feminist, poet, Jamaican, English, Indian, friends. The visual text is accompanied by Fung's voice-over saying "these women have never met my mother." This "not lining up" of sound and image is not meant to undermine any of the women's interviews. More nearly it speaks to the ways in which identification with neither his mother nor his academic friends and colleagues suffices. This moment where things do not line up is a moment of reflexivity that is informed by and through the process of queerness *and* hybridity. It is a moment where hybridity is not a fixed positionality but a survival strategy that is essential for both queers and postcolonial subjects who are subject to the violence that institutional structures reproduce.

This skepticism and ambivalence that Lionnet identifies as being characteristic of autoethnography can be located throughout Fung's project. Fung employs various tactics to complicate and undermine his own discourse. During a sequence toward the middle of the video, the artist once again employs home-movie footage. The 8mm home video instantly achieves a texture reminiscent of childhood. In viewing the section from the tape, the spectator becomes aware of the ways in which the videographer supplies contradictory information on three different levels: the visual image, the voice-over, and the written text that appears on the screen. The visual image shows a young Rita Fung strolling the garden in her 1950s-style *Good Housekeeping* dress and red pillbox hat. She does not look directly at the camera. Her stride is calm and relaxed. There is a cut and Rita Fung re-appears, her back to the camera as she walks off, holding the hand of a little boy. The little boy is wearing a white button-down oxford and black slacks. He holds on tightly to his mother's hand. The next cut shows both mother and son smiling and walking toward the camera. This is the first view the spectator has of the narrator. The voice-over scene matches the image by narrating a family history:

> It's Sunday after Mass. Dressed in satin, she looks like the woman in the *Good Housekeeping* magazine that arrives from the States. During the week she is off to work while I go to school. She wears a pencil behind her right ear and her desk is near the Coke machine. When she is not at the shop she is washing clothes, cooking, sitting on a box in the garden, cutters in hand, weeding. In the evening she is making poppy sauce or making cookies to sell. We dropped six cookies at a time in a plastic bag while we watched *Gunsmoke* on TV. When I bring home forms from school she puts "housewife" down as occupation. The women in *Good Housekeeping* are housewives. In the afternoon they wait at home to serve cookies and milk to their children. Mom was never home when I got home from school.

When this segment of narration concludes, the flickering sound of home projector fades and is replaced by the film's nondiegetic score. Text appears over the image of young Richard and Rita Fung. It reads: "These pictures show more about my family's desire than how we actually lived." The voice-over narration then continues: "But in all the family pictures this is the only shot that shows what I remember." The image that follows this statement is of a young Richard wearing shorts and a T-shirt, still holding on to his mother's hand as they both dance. A new title is superimposed over the image and this text responds to the last bit of narration by explaining: "We're doing the twist." The next image shows an uncoordinated little Richard dancing and jumping barefoot in his backyard. He looks directly at the camera and sticks his tongue out. His manner is wild and effeminate. The narrator then introduces the last installment of text in this segment by saying: "And me, well, you can see from these pictures that I was just an ordinary boy doing ordinary boy things." The screen is then once again covered with text. The story superimposed over the image is one that is familiar to many children who showed cross-dressing tendencies in early childhood: "One day Mom caught me in one of her dresses and threatened to put me out in the street. . . . I was scared but it didn't stop me." When Fung betrays the visual image as a totally imaginary ideal that was more about his parents' fantasy life than about what really happened, he is disavowing the colonial fantasy of assimilation that his family's home movies articulated. In this scene, and throughout *My Mother's Place,* the "Queen's English" is spoken by a mimic man, a subject who has interpolated the mark of colonial power into his discourse but through repetition is able to disarticulate these traditional discourses of authority. The term coined by Bhabha to describe the condition of the colonized subject, "not quite/not white," aptly depicts the overall effect of the "all-American" home-movie footage. The statements disseminated through the visual text are directly connected with Fung's then protoqueer identity as an effeminate boy, the type of queer child whom Sedgwick describes as a subject for whom meaning does not neatly line up. He was not, as his voice-over suggested, "an ordinary boy doing ordinary boy things"; he was, in fact, a wonderfully swishy little boy who, among other things, liked to dress in his mother's *Good Housekeeping*-style dresses, liked the fictional moms on television who baked cookies for their children. I would also suggest that we might understand the actual storytelling practice of the film, the not lining up of image, sound, and text, as something that is decidedly queer about Fung's production. This not lining up of image and sound is a deviation from traditional documentary, which is chiefly concerned with sound and image marching together as a tool of authorization. The not-lining-up strategy was employed in different ways in Fung's earlier videotape *Chinese Characters,* achieving similar disidentificatory effects. Although the two tapes deal with vastly different subjects, they nonetheless, on the level of process and practice, share significant strategical maneuvers that once again are indebted to a predominantly queer wave in documentary production.

Transfiguring the Pornographic

The reassertions of agency that Fung displays in *My Mother's Place,* the way in which he asserts the natives' authority in the ethnographic project, are not entirely different from those that are achieved in *Chinese Characters.* This videotape performs an intervention in the field of mainstream pornography by adding an Asian male presence where it has routinely been excluded. This experimental documentary interviews gay Asian men about their relationships to pornography. The documentary subjects reflect on the way in which pornography helped mold them as desiring subjects. The tape also includes a narrative sequence in which a young Asian man penetrates the white gay male field of pornography by being video-keyed into an early porn loop.

The mainstream gay pornography that has dominated the market, produced by California-based companies such as Catalina, Falcon, and Vivid Video, has contributed to a somewhat standardized image of the porn performer. It is paradoxical that the promise of pornotopia, the promise of lust unlimited, desire without restriction, is performed by a model who generally conforms to a certain rigid set of physical and racial characteristics. This standardized porn model is a paler shade of white, hairless, and usually young and muscled. He is the blueprint that is later visualized infinitely at gay male identity hubs such as gyms and dance clubs. The mainstream porn image, throughout the late 1980s and early 1990s, continued to evolve into an all-too-familiar clean-shaven Anglo twenty-something clone. Although the pornography with which Fung interacts in his interventionist video performances is not quite as homogenized as today's pornography, the porn loops he riffs on still display the trace of this white normative sex clone. The point here is not to moralize about how such an image might be harmful, for it is my belief that it is a futile project to deliberate on the negativity or positivity of images within representational fields.[23] Instead, it is far more useful to note the ways in which Fung transfigures porn through his practices. His video production illuminates the normative logics of porn productions by deploying, through an act of postcolonial mimicry, a disidentification with a popularized ideal: the Asian gay male body. Fung's disidentification with the generic and racially inflected protocols of porn opens up a space that breaks down the coherence of white domination in the gay male erotic imaginary. This disidentification accesses possibilities, through the unlikely vehicle of the Orientalized body, that are ultimately sex- and pornography-positive, but nonetheless rooted in a struggle to free up the ethnocentric conceit that dominates the category of the erotic in the pornographic imaginary. By "ethnocentric conceit" I mean the troubling propensity of representing standardized white male beauty as a norm, and the tendency in erotic representation to figure nonwhite men as exotic kink.

It is important to note here the powerful connection between gay male porn and gay male culture. Richard Dyer, in an often-cited essay on gay male pornographic production, has pointed out that gay male pornography is analogous to gay male sexuality in more general terms.[24] Understanding pornography as an analog to broader aspects of gay male culture makes even more sense today, as pornography, during the AIDS pandemic, is one of the few completely safe and sex-positive, identity-affirming spaces/practices left to gay men. Fung's critique of porn, or the one that is being offered here, should not be understood as antipornographic; rather, by unveiling the ethnocentric bias at work in the pornographic imaginary that is collectively produced by the porn industry, one can better understand the larger problem of white normativity and racism within North American gay male culture.

In her essay "The She-Man: Postmodern Bi-Sexed Performance in Film and Video," Chris Straayer described the process of this reenacting of historically denied agency in Fung's work. "Fung uses technology to intervene in conventional positioning," she explains. "First he video-keys himself into a pornographic film where he then poses as the lure for a desiring 'stud.'"[25] Straayer's description is evocative of the way in which the terrain of pornography becomes a contact zone,[26] one in which the ideological (visualized in Fung's technological reinsertion into the representational field) and the epistemological (pornography's need to carnally know the Other) collide.

The ideological effect is visible in a scene from *Chinese Characters* where an actual Chinese character is video-keyed into an exclusively white gay male porn film. The Asian male body, after being keyed into the grainy seventies porn loop, proceeds to take what seems like a leisurely stroll in an outdoor sex scene. The act of taking a leisurely walk is designed to connote casual tourism. The touristic pose taken here is quite different from the usual options available to gay men of color in the pornography industry. This performatively reappropriates the position of the white male subject who can touristically gaze at minority bodies in such tapes as *Orient Express* (1990), *Latin from Manhattan* (1992), or *Blackshaft* (1993).[27] The newly subjectivized Other who has been walking through this scene then comes face to face with a character from this porn loop. The white male reaches out to the Asian male who, by the particular generic protocols of this vanilla porn subgenre, would be excluded from that symbolic field. Donning a "traditional" dome-shaped Asian field-worker's hat, the Asian male subject plays with his own nipples as he then materializes in a California poolside orgy. Such a performance of autoeroticism, within a symbolic field such as the 1970s white male porn loop, realigns and disrupts the dominant stereotype insofar as it portrays the Asian male body not as the perpetually passive bottom who depends on the white male top, but instead as a subject who can enjoy scopic pleasure in white objects while at the same time producing his own pleasure.

Fung later, in a print essay, deals with the marginal genre of interracial porn, especially tapes featuring Asian men.[28] In this essay, Fung explains that the Asian male body in interracial videotapes is almost always cast as the passive bottom who depends on the white male top to get off. I find it significant that this inquiry into interracial porn follows an initial engagement with porn's exclusionary and racially biased image hierarchy (the critique that *Chinese Characters* produces). Within the logic of porn, a subfield such as racially integrated or exclusively nonwhite tapes is roughly equivalent to other modalities of kink such as bondage, sadomasochism, shaving, and so on. The point here is that, because of white normativity of the pornotopic field, race *counts* as a different sexual practice (that is, doing sadomasochism, doing Asians). Thus, race, like sadomasochism, is essentially a performance. An observation of Fung's practices reveals that the Asian men in his tapes essentially repeat Orientalized performances with a difference through the video insertions and interviews they perform in the tape.

Chinese Characters narrates another cultural collision through different representational strategies. What seems like a traditional Chinese folktale is first heard as the camera lyrically surveys what appears to be a Chinese garden. When the visual image abruptly cuts to a full body shot of an Asian man trying on different outfits, the nondiegetic "traditional" Chinese music is replaced by a disco sound track that signifies that one has entered a gay male subculture. For a brief period we continue to hear the folktale with the disco sound track. When the folktale expires, we hear the sound track of a porn trailer that announces the names of recognizable white porn performers/ icons, such as Al Parker. The announcer's voice produces a typical raunchy rap that eventually fades as a techno disco beat rises in volume. The Asian man finally chooses his outfit and commences his cruise. The filaments of the artist's hybridized identity, in this brief sequence, are embodied in sound and performance. The gay man's body literally bridges these different sound messages: traditional Chinese music, the heavy accent of a Chinese-American retelling what seems to be an ancient fable, the voice of the white porn announcer as he describes the hot action, and the techno beat that eventually emerges as the score for the gay man's cruise. On the level of the visual, the fact that the subject is dressing during the scene identifies it as a moment of queer hybrid self-*fashioning*. Both the performances of drag and striptease are signified upon during this sequence. Rather than taking off his clothing, as in the traditional striptease, the process of revealing an "authentic" self, the Asian male about to commence his cruise continuously dresses and redresses, enacting a kind of counter-striptease that does not fetishize a material body but instead mediates on the ways in which, through costume and performance, one continuously *makes* self. Each outfit that is tried on displays a different modality of being queer; all the ensembles depict different positions on a gay male subcultural spectrum. All of it is disguise and the sequence itself works as a catalog of various queer modalities of self-presentation.

Of these different disguises, the Orientalized body is one of the most important. Fung's critique is not simply aimed at the exclusion of Asians from pornographic video and, in turn, other aspects of a modern gay lifeworld. It is also, through a mode of mimicry that I understand as disidentificatory, a challenge to the limited and racist understandings of the gay male body in pornography. *Orientalism* is a powerful critical term first coined by Edward Said in his influential study of that name. Said described Orientalism as "a style of thought that is based on an ontological and epistemological division made between 'the Orient' and (most of the time) 'the Occident.'"[29] The totalizing implications of Said's theory have been critiqued by many scholars. Bhabha, in perhaps the most famous of these challenges to Said's analysis of Orientalism, points to the ambivalence of power in colonial discourse, arguing that Said's narrative of Orientalism posited all agency and power on the side of the "Occident," ignoring the ways in which the colonized might gain access to power and enact self against and within the colonial paradigm.[30] Lisa Lowe has made a significant contribution to the development of the theoretical discourse on Orientalism by further describing the phenomenon with a special attention to its nuanced workings:

> I do not construct a master narrative or a singular history of orientalism, whether of influence or of comparison. Rather, I argue for a conception of orientalism as heterogeneous and contradictory; to this end I observe, on the one hand, that orientalisms consist of uneven orientalist situations across different cultural and historical sites, and on the other, that each of these orientalisms is internally complex and unstable. My textual readings give particular attention to those junctures at which narratives of gendered, racial, national and class differences complicate and interrupt the narrative of orientalism, as well as to the points at which orientalism is refunctioned and rearticulated against itself.[31]

Fung's engagement with Orientalism can be understood to operate in a way similar to Lowe's. Orientalism in *Chinese Characters,* like the signs of colonial power in *My Mother's Place,* are refunctioned by Fung's disidentification with these cultural referents. Disidentification is the performative re-citation of the stereotypical Asian bottom in porn, and the trappings of colonial culture. In this instance, we have a useful example of the way in which disidentification engages and recycles popular forms with a difference. Fung's strategy of disidentification reappropriates an ambivalent yet highly charged set of images—those representing the queer Asian body in porn—and remakes them in a fashion that explores and outlines the critical ambivalences that make this image a vexing site of identification and desire for Asian gay men and other spectators/consumers with antiracist political positions. The erotic is not demonized but instead used as a site for critical engagement. Documentary, in the case of Fung's production, is a reflexive practice inasmuch as it aims to rearticulate dominant culture and document a history of the other, an Orientalized other that remakes otherness as a strategy of enacting the self that is undermined and limited by Orientalist and colonialist discourses.

Finding Fung

Specific scenes, postcolonial or decolonized spaces such as Fung's Trinidad or the Asian community in Toronto, enable these sorts of rearticulations by functioning as contact zones, locations of hybridity that, because their location is liminal, allow for new social formations that are not as easily available at the empire's center.

The Caribbean basin is an appropriate setting for *My Mother's Place* in that it is a "contact zone," a space where the echoes of colonial encounters still reverberate in the contemporary sound produced by the historically and culturally disjunctive situation of temporal and spatial copresence that is understood as the postcolonial moment.

Pratt elaborates one of the most well developed theories of contact zones. For Pratt, the "contact" component of contact zone is defined as a perspective: "A 'contact' perspective emphasizes how subjects are constituted in and by their relations to each other. It treats the relations among colonizers and colonized, or travelers and 'travelees,' not in terms of separateness or apartheid, but in terms of copresence, interaction, interlocking understanding and practices, often within radically asymmetrical relations of power."[32]

For Pratt, a contact zone is both a location and a different path to thinking about asymmetries of power and the workings of the colonizer/colonized mechanism. Both videotapes I have analyzed in this essay stage copresences that are essentially instances of contact: the contact between a colonized queer boy (and his mother) with the signs of empire and imperialism like the queen, *Good Housekeeping* magazine, and *Gunsmoke* in *My Mother's Place,* and, in the case of *Chinese Characters,* the contact between the Asian male body in pornotopia and the whiteness of the industry that either relegates him to the status of perpetual bottom or excludes him altogether.

It would also be important to situate the artist's own geography in this study of contact zones. Fung's Trinidad is considered a contact zone par excellence in part because its colonial struggle has been well documented by postcolonial thinkers such as C. L. R. James who have written famous accounts of the island's history of colonization.[33] Fung's status as Asian in a primarily black and white colonial situation further contributes to Fung's postcolonial identity. An Asian in such a setting, like an Asian in the already subcultural field of (white-dominated) gay male culture, is at least doubly a minority and doubly fragmented from the vantage point of dominant culture. Canada, on the other hand, has not received extensive consideration as a postcolonial space.[34] A settler colony, Canada's status as not quite First World and not quite Second World positions it as a somewhat ambiguous postcolonial site. Canada, for example, is an importer of U.S. pornography. It is, therefore, on the level of the erotic imaginary, colonized by a U.S. erotic image hierarchy.[35] The geographic location of Fung's production is significant when considering the hybridity of his representational strategies. Fung's *place,* in both Canada, Trinidad, gay male culture, documentary practice, ethnography, pornography, the Caribbean and Asian diasporas, is not quite fixed; thus, this work is uniquely concentrated on issues of place and displacement.

Furthermore, these zones are all productive spaces of hybridization where complex and ambivalent *American* identities are produced. The process by which these hybrid identity practices are manufactured is one that can be understood as syncretism. Many Latin American and U.S. Latino critics have used the term not only to explicate a complex system of cultural expressions, but also to describe the general character of the Caribbean. The Cuban theorist of postmodernism, Antonio Benítez-Rojo, uses the term *supersyncretism,* which for him arises from the collision of European, African, and Asian components within the plantation. For Benítez-Rojo, the phenomenon of supersyncretism is at its most visible when one considers performance:

> If I were to have to put it in a word I would say performance. But performance not only in terms of scenic interpretation but also in terms of the execution of a ritual. That is the "certain way" in which two Negro women who conjured away the apocalypse were walking. In this "certain kind of way" there is expressed the mystic or magical (if you like) loam of civilizations that contributed to the formation of Caribbean culture.[36]

Benítez-Rojo's description is disturbing insofar as it reproduces its own form of Orientalism by fetishizing the conjuring culture of Cuban Santeria and its mostly black and often female practitioners in a passing lyrical mention. There is, nonetheless, a useful refunctioning of this formulation. Instead of Benítez-Rojo's example, consider the acts that Fung narrates: the way in which a protoqueer Chinese Trinidadian boy with a sock on his hand mimics the queen's wave, a gesture that is quite literally the hailing call of empire. Fung's videos are especially significant in that through such acts and performances they index, reflect on, and are reflexive of some of the most energized topics and debates confronting various discourses, such as cultural studies, anthropology, queer theory, and performance studies. In the end, white sock sheathed over his hybrid's hand like a magical prophylactic, protecting him from the disciplinary effect of colonial power, the queer gesture of Fung's wave deconstructs and ruptures the white mythologies of ethnotopia and pornotopia.[37]

Notes

I would like to thank Jane Gaines, Katie Kent, Mandy Merck, Eve Kosofsky Sedgwick, Gustavus Stadler, and Sasha Torres for their suggestions on earlier versions of this essay.

1. Homi K. Bhabha, *The Location of Culture* (New York and London: Routledge, 1994), 86.

2. Eve Kosofsky Sedgwick, *Tendencies* (Durham, N.C.: Duke University Press, 1993), 3.

3. Ella Shohat, "Notes on the Post-Colonial," *Social Text* 31–32 (1992): 110.

4. Bruno Latour, *We Have Never Been Modern,* trans. Catherine Porter (Cambridge: Harvard University Press, 1993), 34; emphasis added.

5. Fredric Jameson, *Signatures of the Visible* (New York and London: Routledge, 1992), 1.

6. This coauthored essay appears in Bill Nichols's collection *Representing Reality: Issues and Concepts in Documentary* (Bloomington and Indianapolis: Indiana University Press, 1991), 201–28.

7. For further discussion of "pornotopia," see Linda Williams, *Hardcore: Power, Pleasure, and the 'Frenzy of the Visible'"* (Berkeley and Los Angeles: University of California Press, 1989).

8. The idea of the "native informant" has been discredited in contemporary anthropology and is now only written within scare quotes. The idea of indigenous people serving as informants to First World ethnographers has been critiqued throughout anthropology, critical theory, and postcolonial studies.

9. In contemporary gay culture, *top* and *bottom* are words used to describe people's sexual proclivities. Women or men who prefer to be penetrated in the economy of sexual acts are bottoms; those whose identification is connected with acts of penetration are

usually referred to as tops. The words *top* and *bottom* do not capture the totality of one's sexual disposition, but instead work as a sort of cultural shorthand. Asian gay men, as will be explained later in this essay, are stereotypically labeled as strictly bottoms in the erotic image hierarchy of North American gay porn.

10. Judith Butler, *Bodies That Matter: On the Discursive Limits of Sex* (New York and London: Routledge, 1993), 226–27.

11. Jacques Derrida, *Limited Inc.,* trans. Samual Weber and Jeffery Mehiman (Evanston, Ill.: Northwestern University Press, 1988), 18.

12. Bhabha, *The Location of Culture,* 245.

13. Françoise Lionnet, *Autobiographical Voices: Race, Gender, and Self-Portraiture* (Ithaca, N.Y., and London: Cornell University Press, 1989), 99–100.

14. Ibid., 102.

15. The phrase "figural anthropology" is developed in the work of Michel Serres, *The Parasite,* trans. Lawrence R. Schehr (Baltimore: Johns Hopkins University Press, 1982), 6.

16. Mary Louise Pratt, *Under Imperial Eyes: Travel Writing and Transculturation* (New York and London: Routledge, 1992), 6–7.

17. Jim Lane has argued for the utility of literary theories of autobiography when considering the historical and theoretical underpinnings of autobiographical film. Lane's article also provides a good gloss of the autobiographical film after 1968. See "Notes on Theory and the Autobiographical Documentary Film in America," *Wide Angle* 15:3 (1993): 21–36.

18. For a historical overview of documentary video, see Deirdre Boyle, "A Brief History of American Documentary Video," in Dough Hall and Sally Jo Fifer, eds., *Illuminating Video: An Essential Guide to Video Art* (New York: Aperture Bay Area Video Coalition, 1990), 51–70. Boyle's most significant elision in the summary is the omission of gay, lesbian, queer, and HIV/AIDS activist video documentary.

19. Lane, "Notes on Theory."

20. See Marcos Becquer, "Snapthology and Other Discursive Practices in *Tongues Untied,*" *Wide Angle* 13:2 (1991), for a fine reading of Riggs's black and queer performance and production.

21. Chris Holmlund has discussed Benning's videos as autoethnographies in "When Autobiography Meets Ethnography and Girl Meets Girl: The 'Dyke Docs' of Sadie Benning and Su Friedrich," unpublished manuscript, presented at Visible Evidence, Duke University, September 1993.

22. Stuart Hall, "Cultural Identity and Cinematic Representations," in Mbye Cham, ed., *Ex-Iles: Essays on Caribbean Cinema* (Trenton, N.J.: African World Press, 1992), 1333.

23. Michelle Wallace has argued forcefully against the trend to produce negative/positive critiques in critical race theory in her book *Invisibility Blues: From Pop to Theory* (New York and London: Verso, 1990), 1–13.

24. Richard Dyer, "Male Gay Porn: Coming to Terms," *Jump Cut* 30 (1985): 27–29.

25. Chris Straayer, "The She-Man: Postmodern Bi-Sexed Performance in Film and Video," *Screen* 31:3 (1990): 272.

26. The term *contact zone* is borrowed from Pratt, *Under Imperial Eyes,* 6–7.

27. The tradition of white male spectators, firmly positioned in a superior hierarchical position, dates back to the very first photographic male pornography. An article on six gay male pornographic photographs, retrieved from the Kinsey Institute for Research in Sex, Gender, and Reproduction, identifies an Orientalist motif in the images of two men with turbans and "Oriental" robes having oral and anal sex in front of the artificial backdrop of exoticized palm trees. The article's author argues that Orientalism has long occupied an important position in gay male pornography (Todd D. Smith, "Gay Male Pornography and the East: Re-orienting the Orient," *History of Photography* 18:1 [1994]).

28. See Richard Fung, "Looking for My Penis: The Eroticized Asian in Gay Video Porn," in *How Do I Look?: Queer Film and Video* (Seattle: Bay Press, 1991), 145–60. In this essay, Fung explains an Orientalism that Edward Said's seminal study could not imagine. Fung surveys the different racist constructions of Asian men that dominate gay male pornography, and tentatively imagines a pornography that affirms rather than appropriates Asian male sexuality.

29. Edward Said, *Orientalism* (New York: Random House, 1979), 2–3.

30. Homi K. Bhabha, "The Other Question: The Stereotype of Colonial Discourse," *Screen* 24:6 (1983); reprinted in Bhabha, *The Location of Culture.* Tom Hastings offers the most interesting and sustained critique of the heterosexist blind spots in Said's study in his "Said's Orientalism and the Discourse of (Hetero)Sexuality," *Canadian Review of American Studies* 23:1 (1992): 130.

31. Lisa Lowe, *Critical Terrains: French and British Orientalism* (Ithaca, N.Y., and London: Cornell University Press, 1991), 5.

32. Pratt, *Under Imperial Eyes,* 7.

33. See, for example, C. L. R. James, *Beyond a Boundary* (London: Stanley Paul, 1963).

34. Vijay Mishra and Bob Hodge touch on Canada's ambiguous postcolonial status in their essay "What Is Post-Colonialism?" *Textual Practices* 15:3 (1991): 339–414. Canada is also covered in the important primer by Bill Ashcroft, Gareth Griffiths, and Helen Tiffin, *The Empire Writes Back: Theory and Practice in Post-Colonial Literatures* (London and New York: Routledge, 1989).

35. The colonization of Canada's "French-Other," Quebec, by a decidedly North American (here meant to include Anglo-Canadian and mainstream U.S.) culture has been touched on by Robert Schwartzwald in his essay "Fear of Federasty: Quebec's Invented Fictions," in *Comparative American Identities: Race, Sex, and Nationality in the Modern Text,* ed. Hortense Spillers (New York: Routledge, 1991), 181. Fung's Asian queer community can be understood as another "Other-Canada" that experiences a cultural colonization under the sign of North America.

36. Antonio Benítez-Rojo, *The Repeating Island: The Caribbean and the Postmodern Perspective,* trans. James E. Maranisis (Durham, N.C.: Duke University Press, 1992), 11.

37. Fung's videos are available through Video Data Bank, School of the Art Institute of Chicago, 112 South Michigan Avenue, Suite 312, Chicago, IL 60603 (telephone: 312-345-3550).

Taboo Memories and Diasporic Visions: Columbus, Palestine, and Arab-Jews

Ella Shohat

Dr. Solomon Schechter [Cambridge expert in Hebrew documents a century ago] agreed to look at them, but chiefly out of politeness, for he was still skeptical about the value of the "Egyptian fragments." But it so happened that he was taken completely by surprise. One of the documents immediately caught his interest, and next morning, after examining . . . he realized that he had stumbled upon a sensational discovery. . . . the discovery has so excited Schechter that he had already begun thinking of traveling to Cairo to acquire whatever remained of the documents. . . . Schechter was fortunate that Cromer [the British administrator of Egypt] himself took interest in the success of his mission. The precise details of what transpired between Schechter and British officialdom and the leaders of the Cairo's Jewish community are hazy, but soon enough . . . they granted him permission to remove everything he wanted from the Geniza [a synagogue chamber where the community books, papers, and documents were kept for centuries], every last paper and parchment, without condition or payment. It has sometimes been suggested that Schechter succeeded so easily in his mission because the custodians of the Synagogue of Ben Ezra had no idea of the real value of the Geniza documents—a species of argument that was widely used in the nineteenth century to justify the acquisition of historical artifacts by colonial powers. . . . [C]onsidering that there had been an active and lucrative trade in Geniza documents . . . and impoverished as they were, it is hard to believe that they would willingly have parted with a treasure which was, after all, the last remaining asset left to them by their ancestors. In all likelihood the decision was taken for them by the leaders of their community, and they

were left with no alternative but acquiescence. As for those leaders . . .
like the elites of so many other groups in the colonized world, they evi-
dently decided to seize the main chance at a time when the balance of
power—the ships and the guns—lay overwhelmingly with England. . . .
Schechter . . . filled out about thirty sacks and boxes with the materials
and with the help of the British embassy in Cairo he shipped them off
to Cambridge. A few months later he returned himself—laden . . .
"with spoils of the Egyptians."
—From Amitav Ghosh, In an Antique Land[1]

I begin my essay with a quotation from Amitav Ghosh's remarkable account
of the emptying out of the Jewish-Egyptian Geniza archive, which by World
War I was stripped of all its documents. The contents of the archive were
then distributed to Europe and America, with a large part of the documents
going into private collections. There is nothing unusual about such a colonial raid of the archive—in this case a very literal archive indeed. What is
unusual, however, are the ways the two groups of coreligionists, the European Ashkenazi Jews and the Sephardic Arab-Jews, fell out on opposite sides
of the colonial divide. European Jews' closeness to Western powers permitted the dispossession of Arab-Jews, even before the advent of Zionism as a
national project.

In this historical episode, the culture of the Egyptian Jewish community
was partially "disappeared" through the confiscation of its most sacred documents. At the moment of the Geniza removal, two years after its "discovery"
in 1896, Egyptian Jews had been for millennia a symbiotic part of the geocultural landscape of the region. The British Jewish scholars, like their non-
Jewish compatriots, cast a similarly imperial gaze at the Egyptian Jews, the
very people who produced and sustained the Geniza for almost a thousand
years, and whose remarkable achievement these scholars were engaging in
appropriating, but whom the scholars describe as "aborigines," "scoundrels,"
whose religious leaders have the "unpleasant" habit of kissing other men "on
the mouth."[2] In a traumatic turn of events, the diasporization of the Geniza
anticipated by half a century the exiling of its owners. In the wake of the
Israeli-Arab conflict, especially after the British withdrawal from Palestine,
and the establishment of the state of Israel in 1948, Arabs and Jews were
newly staged as enemy identities. If Ghosh's description vividly captures
a moment when Arab-Jews were still seen as simply "Arabs," colonized
subjects, with the partition of Palestine, Arab-Jews, in a historical shift, suddenly become simply "Jews."

The historical episode described by Ghosh and its aftermath suggest not
only that alliances and oppositions between communities evolve historically,

but also that they are narrativized differently according to the schemata and ideologies of the present. As certain strands in a cultural fabric become taboo, this narrativization involves destroying connections that once existed. The process of *constructing* a national historical memory also entails the *destruction* of a different, prior historical memory. The archive of the Geniza was largely written in Judeo-Arabic, a language my generation is the last to speak. Since the dispersal of its people from the Arab world, Judeo-Arab culture has been disdained as a sign of *galut* (diaspora)—a negative term within Euro-Israeli Zionist discourse. The European "discovery" and "rescue" of the Geniza from its producers had displaced a long tradition in which Ashkenazi Jewish religious scholars had corresponded and consulted with the Sephardi religious centers of the Judeo-Islamic world. But since the Enlightenment, Eurocentric norms of scholarship have established typically colonial relations that have taken a heavy toll on the representation of Arab-Jewish history and identity. In this essay, I will attempt to disentangle the complexities of Arab-Jewish identity by unsettling some of the borders erected by almost a century of Zionist and colonial historiography, with its fatal binarisms such as civilization versus savagery, modernity versus tradition, and West versus East.

Toward a Relational Approach to Identity

Recent postcolonial theory has at times shied away from grounding its writings in historical context and cultural specificity. Although innumerable poststructuralist essays elaborate abstract versions of "difference" and "alterity," few offer a communally participatory and politicized knowledge of non-European cultures. At the same time, however, the professionalized study of compartmentalized historical periods and geographic regions (as in Middle East studies and Latin American studies) has often resulted in an overly specific focus that overlooks the interconnectedness of histories, geographies, and cultural identities. In *Unthinking Eurocentrism,* Robert Stam and I argue for a relational approach to multicultural studies that does not segregate historical periods and geographic regions into neatly fenced-off areas of expertise, and that does not speak of communities in isolation, but rather "in relation."[3] Rather than pit a rotating chain of resisting communities against a Western dominant (a strategy that privileges the "West," if only as constant antagonist), we argue for stressing the horizontal and vertical links threading communities and histories together in a conflictual network. Analyzing the overlapping multiplicities of identities and affiliations that link diverse resistant discourses helps us transcend some of the politically debilitating effects of disciplinary and community boundaries.

The kind of connections we have in mind operate on a number of levels. First, it is important to make connections in temporal terms. Although postcolonial studies privilege the imperial era of the nineteenth and twentieth centuries, one might argue for grounding the discussion in a longer history of multiply located colonialisms and resistances, tracing the issues at least as far back as 1492. We propose connections in spatial/geographic terms, placing debates about identity and representation in a broader context that embraces the Americas, Asia, and Africa. We also argue for connections in disciplinary and conceptual terms, forging links between debates usually compartmentalized (at least in the United States): on the one hand, postcolonial theory associated with issues of colonial discourse, imperial imaginary, and national narrations, and, on the other, the diverse "ethnic studies," focusing on issues of "minorities," race, and multiculturalism. The point is to place the often ghettoized discourses about geographies ("here" versus "there") and about time ("now" versus "then") in illuminating dialogue. A relational approach, one that operates at once within, between, and beyond the nation-state framework, calls attention to the conflictual hybrid interplay of communities within and across borders.

My subtitle, "Columbus, Palestine, and Arab-Jews," already juxtaposes disparate entities to underline the ways in which nation-states have imposed a coherent sense of national identity precisely because of their fragile sense of cultural, even geographic, belonging. The formation of the postcolonial nation-state, especially in the wake of colonial partitions, often involved a double process of, on the one hand, joining diverse ethnicities and regions that had been separate under colonialism and, on the other, partitioning regions in a way that forced regional redefinitions (Iraq/Kuwait) or a cross-shuffling of populations (Pakistan/India, Israel/Palestine, in relation to Palestinians and Arab-Jews). Given the "minority"/"majority" battles "from within" and the war waged by border-crossers (refugees, exiles, immigrants) "from without," Eurocentric historiography has had a crucial role in handing out passports to its legitimate races, ethnicities, and nations. And in the words of the Palestinian Mahmoud Darwish's well-known poem, "Passport" ("Joowaz sufr"): "'ar min al ism, min al intima? fi tarba rabit'ha bilyadyn?" ("Stripped of my name, my identity? On a soil I nourished with my own hands?"). The same colonial logic that dismantled Palestine had already dismantled the "Turtle Island" of the Americas. Thus, the first illegal alien, Columbus,[4] remains a celebrated discoverer, while indigenous Mexicans "infiltrate" barbed borders every day to a homeland once theirs, while Native Americans are exiled in their own land.

Here, by way of demonstration of the "relational" method, I will focus on Sephardic Arab-Jewish (known in the Israeli context as Mizrahi) identity as it intersects with other communities and discourses in diverse contexts over time. I will take as a point of departure the 1992 quincentennial commemorations of the expulsions of Sephardic Jews from Spain to argue that any revisionist effort to articulate Arab-Jewish identity in a contemporary context that has posited Arab and Jew as antonyms can only be disentangled through a series of positionings vis-à-vis diverse communities and identities (Arab-Muslim, Arab-Christian, Palestinian, Euro-Israeli, Euro-American Jewish, indigenous American, African-American, Chicano/a), which would challenge the devastating consequences that the Zionist-Orientalist binarism of East versus West, Arab versus Jew has had for Arab-Jews (or Jewish-Arabs). Linking, delinking, and relinking, at once spatial and temporal, thus become part of adversary scholarship working against taboo formulations, policed identities, and censored affiliations.

Staging the Quincentenary

"Your Highnesses completed the war against the Moors," Columbus wrote in a letter addressed to the Spanish throne, "after having chased all the Jews . . . and sent me to the said regions of India in order to convert the people there to our Holy Faith."[5] In 1492, the defeat of the Muslims and the expulsion of Sephardi Jews from Spain converged with the conquest of what came to be called the New World. Although the celebrations of Columbus's voyages have provoked lively opposition (ranging from multicultural debates about the Eurocentric notion of "discovery" to satirical performances by Native Americans landing in Europe and claiming it as their discovered continent), the Eurocentric framing of the "other 1492" has not been questioned. Apart from some enthusiastic scholastic energy dedicated to the dubious pride in whether Columbus can once and for all be claimed as a (secret) Jew, expulsion events have been navigated within the calm seas of Old World paradigms. Furthermore, the two separate quincentenary commemorations, both taking place in the Americas, Europe, and the Middle East, have seldom acknowledged the historical and discursive linkages between these two constellations of events. To examine the relationship between contemporary discourses about the two "1492s" might therefore illuminate the role that scholarly and popular narratives of history play in nation-building myths and geopolitical alliances.

The Spanish-Christian war against Muslims and Jews was politically, economically, and ideologically linked to the caravels' arrival in Hispaniola. Triumphant over the Muslims, Spain invested in the project of Columbus, whose voyages were partly financed by wealth taken from the defeated

Muslims and confiscated from Jews through the Inquisition.[6] The *recon-quista's* policies of settling Christians in the newly (re)conquered areas of Spain, as well as the gradual institutionalization of expulsions, conversions, and killings of Muslims and Jews in Christian territories, prepared the grounds for similar *conquista* practices across the Atlantic. Under the marital-political union of Ferdinand (Aragon) and Isabella (Castile), victorious Christian Spain, soon to become an empire, strengthened its sense of nationhood, subjugating indigenous Americans and Africans. Discourses about Muslims and Jews during Spain's continental expansion crossed the Atlantic, arming the conquistadors with a ready-made "us versus them" ideology aimed at the regions of India, but in fact applied first toward the indigenous of the accidentally "discovered" continent. The colonial misrecognition inherent in the name "Indian" underlines the linked imaginaries of the East and West Indies. (Perhaps not coincidentally, Ridley Scott's film *1492: The Conquest of Paradise* [1992] has Orientalist "Ali Baba"-style music accompany the encounter with Caribbean "Indians.") India awaited its colonized turn with the arrival of Vasco da Gama (1498) and the Portuguese conquest of Goa (1510). If, in the fifteenth century, the only European hope for conquering the East—given the Muslim domination of the continental route—was via sailing to the West, the nineteenth-century consolidation of European imperialism in the East was facilitated by Europe's previous self-aggrandizing at the expense of the Americas and Africa. Thanks to its colonization of the Americas and Africa, Europe's modernization was made possible, finally allowing the colonization of North Africa (Maghreb) and the so-called Near East *(mashreq)*. "The Indian Ocean trade, and the Culture that supported it," writes Amitav Ghosh, "had long since been destroyed by European navies. Transcontinental trade was no longer a shared enterprise; the merchant shipping of the high seas was now entirely controlled by the naval powers of Europe." [7]

Although Moorish Spain testifies to syncretic multiculturalism *avant la lettre,* the *reconquista* ideology of *limpieza de sangre,* as an early exercise in European "self-purification," sought to expel, or forcibly convert, Muslims and Jews. The Crusades, which inaugurated "Europe" by reconquering the Mediterranean area, catalyzed Europeans' awareness of their own geocultural identity, and established the principle that wars conducted in the interests of the Holy Church were axiomatically just. The campaigns against Muslims and Jews as well as against other "agents of Satan," heretics, and witches, made available a mammoth apparatus of racism and sexism for recycling in the "new" continents. Anti-Semitism and anti-infidelism provided a conceptual and disciplinary framework that, after being turned against Europe's immediate or internal others, was then projected outward against Europe's distant or external others.[8] Prince Henry ("the Navigator"), the pioneer of Portuguese exploration, had himself been a crusader against the Moors at the battle of Ceuta. Amerigo Vespucci, writing about his voyages, similarly drew on the stock of Jewish and Muslim stereotypes to characterize the savage, the infidel, the indigenous man as a dangerous sexual omnivore and the indigenous woman as a luringly yielding nature.[9] In this sense, the metonymic links between Jews and Muslims—their literal neighboring and their shared histories—are turned into metaphoric and analogical links in relation to the peoples of the Americas.[10] The point is not that there is a complete equivalence between Europe's oppressive relations toward Jews and Muslims and toward indigenous peoples; the point is that European Christian demonology prefigured colonialist racism. Indeed, one can even discern a partial congruency between the phantasmic imagery projected onto the Jewish and Muslim "enemy" and onto the indigenous American and black African "savage," all imaged to various degrees as "blood drinkers," "cannibals," "sorcerers," "devils."[11]

One of the rare contemporary representations that expose ecclesiastical participation in genocidal measures, the Mexican film *El Santo Oficio* (The Holy Office, 1973) features the attempt by the Holy See to spread the Inquisition into the New World. Although the film focuses on the Sephardi *conversos*, it also shows that they are persecuted alongside heretics, witches, and indigenous infidels. Consumed by enthusiastic spectators, their burning at the stake is performed as a public spectacle of discipline and punishment, just as lynching was sometimes consumed as a popular entertainment by some whites in the United States. Screened at a Los Angeles ceremonial opening for a conference (organized by the International Committee— Sepharad '92) dedicated to the quincentennial expulsion of Sephardi Jews, *El Santo Oficio* provoked strong emotions. Its documentation of Sephardic-Jewish rituals practiced in secrecy, and its visual details of torture, rape, and massacre, were not received, however, in the spirit of the linkages I have charted here. The audience, consisting largely of Euro-American, Jewish, and a substantially smaller number of Sephardi-American educators, scholars, and community workers, was eager to consume the narrative evidence of the singular nature of the Jewish experience. To point out the links between the Inquisition and the genocide of the indigenous peoples of the Americas, between the Inquisition and the devastation of African peoples, would be tantamount to a promiscuous intermingling of the sacred with the profane. In the reception following the film, Chicano waiters catered food. The simplistic category of "them" (Spanish Christians), however, stood in remarkably ironic relation to the indigenous faces of the waiters; their presence suggested that the charting of Sephardi *conversos* history must be negotiated in relation to other *conversos*.

The importance of rupturing the boundaries of these histories becomes even clearer in the actual intersection of diverse histories of forced conversions in the Americas. For example, the case of Chicano and Mexican families of part Sephardic-Jewish origins suggests that at times the links are quite literal. Recent research by the Southwest Jewish Archives in the United States points out that Sephardic traditions remain alive in predominantly Roman Catholic Mexican-American families, although the family members are not always conscious of the origins of the rituals. They do not understand why, for example, their grandmothers make unleavened bread called *pan semita,* or Semite bread, and why their rural grandparents in New Mexico or Texas slaughter a lamb in the spring and smear its blood on the doorway. Revealing that some Chicanos and Mexicans are the descendants of secret Jews is a taboo that results in contemporary secrecy even among those who are aware of their ancestry.[12] The issue of forced conversions in the Americas and the consequent cultural syncretism implicates and challenges Jewish as well as Catholic Euro-indigenous institutions. The hybridity of Chicano and Mexican culture, however, does not necessarily facilitate the admission of another complex hybridity, one crossing Jewish-Catholic boundaries.

If the genocide of indigenous Americans and Africans is no more than a bit of historical marginalia, the linked persecutions in Iberia of Sephardi Jews and Muslims, of conversos, and *moriscos,*[13] are also submerged. The quincentennial elision of the Arab-Muslim part of the narrative was especially striking. During the centuries-long *reconquista,* not all Muslims and Jews withdrew with the Arab forces. Those Muslims who remained after the change of rule were known as *mudejars,* deriving from the Arabic *mudajjin,* "permitted to remain," with a suggestion of "tamed," "domesticated."[14] The Spanish Inquisition, institutionalized in 1478, did not pass over the Muslims. Apart from the 1492 expulsion of three million Muslims and three hundred thousand Sephardi Jews, in 1499 mass burnings of Islamic books and forced conversions took place, and in 1502 the Muslims of Granada were given the choice of baptism or exile. In 1525–26, Muslims of other provinces were also given the same choice. In 1566, there was a revival of anti-Muslim legislation, and between 1609 and 1614 came edicts of expulsions. In other words, the same inquisitional measures taken against the Jewish *conversos* who were found to be secretly practicing Judaism were taken against the *moriscos* found to be practicing Islam, measures culminating in edicts of expulsion addressed specifically to Muslims. As a result, many fled to North Africa, where, like Sephardi Jews, they maintained certain aspects of their Hispanicized Arab culture.

This well-documented history[15] found little echo in the events promoted by the International Committee—Sepharad '92, whose major funds came from the United States, Spain, and Israel. Spain, which still has to come to terms with its present-day racist immigration policies toward—among others—Arab North Africans, embraced its "golden age" after centuries of denial, while reserving a regrettable mea culpa only for the official spokespersons of "the Jews." As for all other representatives, including conservative upper-middle-class Zionist Sephardim, the elision of comparative discussions of the Muslim and Jewish (Sephardi) situations in Christian Spain was largely rooted in present-day Middle Eastern politics. The 1992 commemorations entailed a serious present-day battle over the representations of "Jewish identity" in terms of an East-West axis, a battle dating back to the nineteenth-century beginnings of Zionist nationalism.

The Trauma of Dismemberment

Zionist historiography, when it does refer to Islamic-Jewish history, consists of a morbidly selective "tracing the dots" from pogrom to pogrom. (The word *pogrom* itself derives from and is reflective of the Eastern European Jewish experience.)[16] Subordinated to a Eurocentric historiography, most quincentenary events lamented yet another tragic episode in a homogeneous, static history of relentless persecution. Not surprisingly, the screening of *El Santo Oficio* at the expulsion conference elicited such overheard remarks as "You think it's different today? That's also what the Nazis did to us. That's what the Arabs would do if they could." (A curious claim, since the Arab Muslims had a millennium-long opportunity to install an inquisition against Middle Eastern Jews—or against Christian minorities—but never did.) Such common remarks underline the commemorations' role as a stage for demonstrating (Euro-)Israeli nationalism as the only possible logical answer to horrific events in the history of Jews. The inquisition of Sephardi Jews is seen merely as a foreshadowing of the Jewish Holocaust. In this paradigm, the traumas left by Nazi genocidal practices are simplistically projected onto the experiences of Jews in Muslim countries, and onto the Israeli-Palestinian conflict.[17]

My point here is not to idealize the situation of the Jews of Islam, but rather to suggest that Zionist discourse has subsumed Islamic-Jewish history into a Christian-Jewish history, while also undermining comparative studies of Middle Eastern Jews in the context of diverse religious and ethnic minorities in the Middle East and North Africa. On the occasion of the quincentenary, the Zionist perspective privileged Sephardi-Jewish relations with European Christianity over those with Arab Islam, projecting Eurocentric maps of Christians and Jews as West and Muslims as East, and ignoring the fact that at the time of the expulsion, syncretic Jewish communities were flourishing all over the Islamic Middle East and North Africa. Quincentennial events not only rendered the interrelations between Jewish *conversos* and indigenous *conversos* invisible, but also undermined the Sephardic-Jewish and Muslim cultural symbiosis. The only Muslim country that received some quincentennial attention was Turkey, partly because of Sultan Beyazid II's ordering his governors in 1492 to receive the expelled Jews cordially. But no less important is Turkey's contemporary regional alliances, its national fissured identity between East and West. Unlike Arab Muslim countries, where expelled Sephardim also settled (Morocco, Tunisia, Egypt), Turkey has not participated in the Israeli-Arab conflict, nor in the nonallied embargo that has for decades regionally isolated Israel. Yet, even in the case of Turkey, the quincentennial emphasis was less on Muslim-Jewish relations than on the voyages of refuge, and on the Turkish (national) as opposed to the Ottoman Muslim (religious) shelter, an anachronistic framework given that the national/secular definition of Turkey is a twentieth-century development.

In this rewriting of history, present-day Muslim Arabs are merely one more "non-Jewish" obstacle to the Jewish-Israeli national trajectory. The idea of the unique, common victimization of all Jews at all times provides a crucial underpinning of official Israeli discourse. The notion of uniqueness precludes analogies and metonymies, thus producing a selective reading of "Jewish history," one that hijacks the Jews of Islam from their Judeo-Islamic geography and subordinates it to that of the European Ashkenazi shtetl. This double process entails the performance of commonalities among Jews in the public sphere so as to suggest a homogeneous national past, while silencing any deviant view of a more globalized and historicized narrative that would see Jews not simply through their religious commonalities, but also in relation to their contextual cultures, institutions, and practices. Given this approach, and given the Israeli-Arab conflict, no wonder that the Jews of Islam, and more specifically, Arab-Jews, have posed a challenge to any simplistic definition of Jewish identity, and particularly of the emergent Jewish Euro-Israeli identity.

The selective readings of Middle Eastern history, in other words, make two processes apparent: the rejection of an Arab and Muslim context for Jewish institutions, identity, and history, and their unproblematized subordination into a "universal" Jewish experience. In the Zionist "proof" of a single Jewish experience, there are no parallels or overlappings with other religious and ethnic communities, whether in terms of a Jewish hyphenated and syncretic culture or in terms of linked analogous oppressions. All Jews are defined as closer to each other than to the cultures of which they have been a part. Thus, the religious Jewish aspect of diverse intricated and interwoven Jewish identities has been given primacy, a categorization tantamount to dismembering the identity of a community. Indeed, the Euro-Israeli separation of the "Jewish" part from the "Middle Eastern" part, in the case of Middle Eastern Jews, has resulted in practically dismantling the Jewish communities of the Muslim world, as well as in pressures exerted on Mizrahim (Orientals) to realign their Jewish identity according to Zionist Euro-Israeli paradigms. Since the beginnings of European Zionism, the Jews of Islam have faced, for the first time in their history, the imposed dilemma of choosing between Jewishness and Arabness, in a geopolitical context that perpetuated the equation between Arabness and Middle Easternness and Islam, on the one hand, and between Jewishness and Europeanness and Westerness, on the other.[18]

The master narrative of universal Jewish victimization has been crucial for legitimizing an anomalous nationalist project of "ingathering of the Diaspora from the four corners of the globe," but which can also be defined as forcing displacements of peoples from such diverse geographies, languages, cultures, and histories, a project through which, in other words, a state created a nation. The claim of universal victimization has also been crucial for the claim that the "Jewish nation" faces a common "historical enemy"—the Muslim Arab—implying a double-edged amnesia with regard to both Judeo-Islamic history and the colonial partition of Palestine. False analogies between the Arabs and Nazis, and in 1992 with inquisitors, becomes not merely a staple of Zionist rhetoric, but also a symptom of a Jewish European nightmare projected onto the structurally distinct political dynamics of the Israeli-Palestinian conflict. In a historical context of Sephardi Jews experiencing an utterly distinct history within the Muslim world than that which haunted the European memories of Ashkenazi Jews, and in a context of the massacres and dispossession of Palestinian people, the conflation of the Muslim Arab with the archetypical (European) oppressors of Jew downplays the colonial-settler history of Euro-Israel itself.

The neat division of Israel as West and Palestine as East ignores some of the fundamental contradictions within Zionist discourse itself.[19] Central to Zionism is the notion of return to origins located in the Middle East.[20] Thus, Zionism often points to its linguistic return to Semitic Hebrew, and to its sustaining of a religious idiom intimately linked with the topography

"Laissez-passer." The author's parents Aziza and Sasson Shohat, Iraqi citizens displaced from their ancestral homeland with no possibility of return.

of the Middle East, as a "proof" of the Eastern origins of European Jews—a crucial aspect of the Zionist claim for the land. And although Jews have often been depicted in anti-Semitic discourse as an alien "Eastern" people within the West, the paradox of Israel is that it presumed to "end a diaspora," characterized by Jewish ritualistic nostalgia for the East, only to found a state whose ideological and geopolitical orientation has been almost exclusively toward the West. Theodor Herzl called for a Western-style capitalist-democratic miniature state, to be made possible by the grace of imperial patrons such as England or Germany, whereas David Ben-Gurion formulated his visionary utopia of Israel as that of a "Switzerland of the Middle East." Although European Jews have historically been the victims of anti-Semitic Orientalism, Israel as a state has become the perpetrator of Orientalist attitudes and actions whose consequences have been the dispossession of Palestinians. The ideological roots of Zionism can be traced to the conditions of nineteenth- and early twentieth-century Europe, not only as a reaction against anti-Semitism, but also to the rapid expansion of capitalism and of European empire building. In this sense, Israel has clearly been allied to First World imperialist interests, has deployed Eurocentric-inflected discourse, and has exercised colonialist policies toward the Palestinian land and people.

The question is further complicated by the socialist pretensions, and at times the socialist achievements, of Zionism. In nationalist Zionist discourse, the conflict between the socialist ideology of Zionism and the real praxis of Euro-Jewish colonization in Palestine was resolved through the reassuring thesis that the Arab masses, subjected to feudalism and exploited by their own countrymen, could only benefit from the emanation of Zionist praxis.[21] This presentation embodies the historically positive self-image of Israelis as involved in a noncolonial enterprise, and therefore morally superior in their aspirations. Furthermore, the hegemonic socialist-humanist discourse has hidden the negative dialectics of wealth and poverty between First and Third World Jews behind a mystifying facade of egalitarianism. The Zionist mission of ending the Jewish exile from the "Promised Land" was never the beneficent enterprise portrayed by official discourse, since from the first decade of the twentieth century, Arab-Jews were perceived as a source of cheap labor that could replace the dispossessed Palestinian fellahin.[22] The "Jews in the form of Arabs" thus could prevent any Palestinian declaration that the land belongs to those who work it, and contribute to the Jewish national demographic needs. [23] The Eurocentric projection of Middle Eastern Jews as coming to the "land of milk and honey" from desolate backwaters, from societies lacking all contact with scientific-technological civilization, once again set up an Orientalist rescue trope. Zionist discourse has cultivated the impression that Arab-Jewish culture prior to Zionism was static and passive, and, like the fallow land of Palestine, as suggested by Edward Said, was lying in wait for the impregnating infusion of European dynamism.[24] While presenting Palestine as an empty land to be transformed by Jewish labor, the Zionist "founding fathers" presented Arab-Jews as passive vessels to be shaped by the revivifying spirit of Promethean Zionism.

The Euro-Zionist problematic relation to the question of East and West has generated a deployment of opposing paradigms that often results in hysterical responses to any questioning of its projected "Western identity." Zionism viewed Europe both as ideal ego and as the signifier of ghettos, persecutions, and the Holocaust. Within this perspective, the "Diaspora Jew" was an extraterritorial rootless wanderer, someone living "outside of history." Posited in gendered language as the masculine redeemer of the passive Diaspora Jew, the mythologized sabra simultaneously signified the destruction of the diasporic Jewish entity. The prototypical newly emerging Jew in Palestine—physically strong, with blond hair and blue eyes, healthy-looking and cleansed of all "Jewish inferiority complexes," and a cultivator of the land—was conceived as an antithesis to the Zionist's virtually anti-Semitic image of the "Diaspora Jew." The sabra, which was modeled on the Romantic ideal, largely influenced by the German *Jugendkultur,* generated a culture in which any expression of weakness came to be disdained as *galuti*—that which belongs to the Diaspora. Zionism, in other words, viewed itself as an embodiment of European nationalist ideals to be realized outside of Europe, in the East, and in relation to the pariahs of Europe, the Jews. Thus, the sabra was celebrated as eternal youth devoid of parents, as though born from a spontaneous generation of nature, as in Moshe Shamir's key nationalist novel of the 1948 generation *Bemo Yadav* (In his own hands), which introduces the hero as follows: "Elik was born from the sea." In this paradoxical, idiosyncratic version of the Freudian *Familienroman,* euro-zionist parents raised their children to see themselves as historical foundlings worthy of more dignified, romantic, and powerful progenitors. Zionism posited itself as an extension of Europe in the Middle East, carrying its Enlightenment banner of the civilizing mission.

If the West has been viewed ambivalently as the place of oppression to be liberated from, as well as a kind of an object of desire to form a "normal" part of it, the East has also signified a contemporary ambivalence. On the one hand, it is a place associated with "backwardness," "underdevelopment," a land swamped, in the words of 1950s propaganda films, with "mosquitoes, scorpions, and Arabs." On the other hand, the East has symbolized solace, the return to geographic origins, and reunification with biblical history. The obsessive negation of the "Diaspora" that began with the Haskalah (European-Jewish Enlightenment) and the return to the homeland of Zion led, at times, to the exotic affirmation of Arab "primitiveness," as a desirable image to be appropriated by the native-born sabra. The Arab was projected as the incarnation of the ancient, the pre-exiled Jews, the Semitic not yet corrupted by wanderings in exile, and therefore, to a certain extent, as the authentic Jew. This construction of the Arab as presumably preserving archaic ways and rootedness in the land of the Bible, in contrast with the landless ghetto Jew, provoked a qualified identification with the Arab as a desired object of imitation for Zionist youth in Palestine/Israel, and as a reunification with the remnant of the free and proud ancient Hebrew.

This projection, however, coexisted with a simultaneous denial of Palestine. The role of archaeology in Israeli culture, it should be pointed out, has been crucial in disinterring of remnants of the biblical past of Palestine, at times enlisted in the political effort to demonstrate a historical right to the "land of Israel." In dramatic contrast to Jewish archaeology of the text,[25] this idea of physical archaeology as demonstrating a geography of identity carries with it the obverse notion of the physical homeland as text, to be allegorically read, within Zionist hermeneutics, as a "deed to the land." And corollary to this is the notion of historical "strata" within a political geology. The deep stratum, in the literal and the figurative sense, is associated with the Israeli Jews, while the surface level is associated with the Arabs, as a recent "superficial" historical element without millennial "roots." Since the Arabs are seen as "guests" in the land, their presence must be downplayed, much as the surface of the land has at times been "remodeled" to hide or bury remnants of Arab life, and Palestinian villages, in certain instances, have been replaced with Israeli ones, or completely erased. The linguistic, lexical expression of this digging into the land is the toponymic archaeology of place-names. Some Arabic names of villages, it was discovered, were close to or based on the biblical Hebrew names; in some cases, therefore, Arabic names were replaced with old-new Hebrew ones.

Parting Worlds, Subversive Returns

Yet, despite the importance of the idea of Return, it is no less important to see Zionist representation of Palestine in the context of other settlers' narratives. Palestine is linked to the Columbus narrative of the Americas in more ways than it would at first appear. The Columbus narrative prepared the ground for an enthusiastic reception of Zionist discourse within Euro-America. The Israeli-Palestinian conflict as a whole touches, I would argue, on some sensitive historical nerves within "America" itself. As a product of schizophrenic master narratives, colonial-settler state on the one hand, and anticolonial republic on the other, "America" has been subliminally more attuned to the Zionist than to the Palestinian nationalist discourse. Zionist discourse contains a liberatory narrative vis-à-vis Europe that in many ways is pertinent to the Puritans. The New World of the Middle East, like the New World of America, was concerned with creating a New Man. The image of the sabra as a new (Jewish) man evokes the American Adam. The American hero has been celebrated as prelapsarian Adam, as a New Man emancipated from history (i.e., European history), before whom all the world and time lay available, much as the sabra was conceived as the antithesis of the Old World European Jew. In this sense, one might suggest an analogy between the cultural discourse about the innocent national beginning of America and that of Israel. The American Adam and the sabra masculinist archetypes implied not only their status as creators, blessed with the divine prerogative of naming the elements of the scene about them, but also their fundamental innocence. The notions of an American Adam and an Israeli sabra elided a number of crucial facts, notably that there were other civilizations in the Promised Land; that the settlers were not creating "being from nothingness"; and that the settlers, in both cases, had scarcely jettisoned all their Old

World cultural baggage, their deeply ingrained Eurocentric attitudes and discourses. Here the gendered metaphor of the "virgin land," present in both Zionist and American pioneer discourses, suggests that the land is implicitly available for defloration and fecundation. Assumed to lack owners, it therefore becomes the property of its "discoverer" and cultivators who transform the wilderness into a garden, those who "make the desert bloom."

In the case of Zionist discourse, the concept of "return to the motherland," as I have pointed out, suggests a double relation to the land, having to do with an ambivalent relation to the "East" as the place of Judaic origins as well as the locus for implementing the "West." The sabra embodied the humanitarian and liberationist project of Zionism, carrying the same banner of the "civilizing mission" that European powers proclaimed during their surge into "found lands." The classical images of sabra pioneers as settlers on the Middle Eastern frontiers, fighting Indian-like Arabs, along with the reverberations of the early American biblical discourse encapsulated in such notions as "Adam," "(New) Canaan," and "Promised Land," have all facilitated the feeling of Israel as an extension of "us"—the U.S. Furthermore, both the United States and Israel fought against British colonialism, while also practicing colonial policies toward the indigenous peoples. Finally, I would argue for a triangular structural analogy by which the Palestinians represent the aboriginal "Indians" of Euro-Israeli discourse, while the Sephardim, as imported cheap labor, constitute the "blacks" of Israel.[26] (Taking their name from the American movement, the Israeli "Black Panthers," for example, sabotaged the myth of the "melting pot" by showing that there was in Israel not one but two Jewish communities—one white, one black.) The manifest Palestinian refusal to play the assigned role of the presumably doomed "Indians" of the transplanted (far) Western narrative has testified to an alternative narrative in whose narration Edward Said has been in the forefront. The story of Sephardim—as the Jewish victims of Zionism—also remains to be heard.[27]

The same historical process that dispossessed Palestinians of their property, lands, and national-political rights was intimately linked to the process that effected the dispossession of Arab-Jews from their property, lands, and rootedness in Arab countries, as well as their uprootedness from that history and culture within Israel itself.[28] But whereas Palestinians have fostered the collective militancy of nostalgia in exile (be it *fil dakhel*, under Israeli occupation, or *fil kharij*, under Syrian, Egyptian, and American passport or on the basis of laissez-passer), Sephardim, trapped in a no-exit situation, have been forbidden to nourish memories of at least partially belonging to the peoples across the river Jordan, across the mountains of Lebanon, and across

Yemeni Jews landing in Israel, October 1949.

the Sinai desert and Suez Canal. The pervasive notion of "one people" re-united in their ancient homeland actively disauthorizes any affectionate memory of life before the state of Israel. Quincentennial events luxuriated in the landscapes, sounds, and smells of the lost Andalusian home, but silence muffled an even longer historical imaginary in Cairo, Baghdad, Damascus, and hid an even more recent loss. For centuries, both Muslim and Jewish poets eulogized Andalusia, referring to the keys they persisted in carrying in exile. Yet, in contemporary Palestinian poetry, Andalusia is far from being only a closed chapter of Arab grandeur, for it allegorizes Palestine. In the words of Mahmoud Darwish's poem "Al Kamanjat" ("The Violins"):

> Al kamanjat tabki ma'a al ghjar al dhahibina ila al andalous
> al kamanjat tabki 'ala al 'arab al kharigin min al andalous
> al kamanjat tabki 'ala zaman daib la ya'ood
> al kamanjat tabki 'ala watan daib qad ya'ood.

> (The violins weep with the Gypsies heading for Andalusia
> the violins weep for the Arabs departing Andalusia.
> The violins weep for a lost epoch that will not return
> the violins weep for a lost homeland that could be regained.)

But the parallelism between Andalusia and Palestine stops precisely at the point of reclaiming a Palestinian future.

The 1992 discussions of expulsion brought out the "wandering Jew" motif of the Jews as perennially displaced people. But the Jews of the Middle East and North Africa, for the most part, had stable, "nonwandering" lives in the Islamic world. As splendidly captured in *In an Antique Land*, the Sephardim who have moved within the regions of Asia and Africa, from the Mediterranean to the Indian Ocean, did it more for commercial, religious, or scholarly purposes than for reasons of persecution. Ironically, the major traumatic displacement took place since 1948, when Arab-Jews were uprooted, dispossessed, and dislodged because of the collaboration between Israel and some of the Arab governments under the orchestration of Western colonial powers that termed their solution for the "question of Palestine" as a "population exchange."[29] That no one asked either the Palestinians or the Arab-Jews whether they wished to be exchanged is yet another typical narrative of Third World histories of partition. Sephardim who have managed to leave Israel, often in an (indirect) response to institutionalized racism there, have dislocated themselves yet again, this time to the United States, Europe, and Latin America. In a sudden historical twist, today it is to the Muslim Arab countries of their origins to which most Middle Eastern Jews cannot travel, let alone fantasize a return—the ultimate taboo.[30]

The commonalities between Middle Eastern Jews and Muslims is a thorny reminder of the Middle Eastern/North African character of the majority of Jews in Israel today. Not surprisingly, quincentenary events in Europe, the Middle East, and the Americas centered on the Spanishness of Sephardi culture (largely on Ladino or Judeo-Español language and music), while marginalizing the fact that Jews in Iberia formed part of a larger Judeo-Islamic culture of North Africa, the Middle East, and the European Balkan area of the Ottoman Empire. Major Sephardi texts in philosophy, linguistics, poetry, and medicine were written in Arabic and reflect specific Muslim influences as well as a strong sense of Jewish-Arab cultural identity, seen especially in the development of Judeo-Arab script, used in religious correspondence between Jewish scholars across the regions of Islam, as well as in some specific local Jewish-Arabic dialects.[31] The Jews of Iberia who had come from the East and South of the Mediterranean—some with the Romans, others largely with the Muslims—returned there when they fled the Inquisition. More than 70 percent returned to the Ottoman Empire regions, while the rest went to Western Europe and the Americas.[32] Thus, a historiography that speaks of a pan-Jewish culture is often the same historiography that speaks of "Arab versus Jew" without acknowledging Arab-Jewish existence.

The erasure of the Arab dimension of Sephardim-Mizrahim has been crucial to the Zionist perspective, since the Middle Easternness of Sephardi Jews questions the very definitions and boundaries of the Euro-Israeli national project. Euro-Israel has ended up in a paradoxical situation in which its "Orientals" have had closer cultural and historical links to the presumed enemy—the "Arab"—than to the Ashkenazi Jews with whom they were coaxed and coerced into nationhood. The taboo around the Arabness of Sephardi history and culture is clearly manifested in Israeli academic and media attacks on Sephardi intellectuals who refuse to define themselves simply as Israelis, and who dare to assert their Arabness in the public sphere.[33] The Ashkenazi anxiety around Sephardi-Mizrahi identity (expressed both by right and liberal left) underlines that Sephardi Jews have represented a problematic entity for Euro-Israeli hegemony. Although Zionism collapses the Sephardim and the Ashkenazim into a single people, at the same time the Sephardi difference has destabilized Zionist claims for representing a single Jewish people, premised not only on a common religious background, but also on common nationality. The strong cultural and historical links that Middle Eastern Jews have shared with the Arab Muslim world, stronger in many respects than those they shared with the European Jews, threatened the conception of a homogeneous nation on which European nationalist movements were based. As an integral part of the topography, language, culture, and history of the Middle East, Sephardim have also threatened the Euro-Israeli self-image, which sees itself as a prolongation of Europe, "in" the Middle East but not "of" it. Fearing an encroachment from the East upon the West, the Israeli establishment attempted to repress the Middle Easternness of Sephardic Jews as part of an effort to westernize the Israeli nation and to mark clear borders of identity between Jews as Westerners and Arabs as Easterners. Arabness and Orientalness have been consistently stigmatized as evils to be uprooted, creating a situation where Arab-Jews were urged to see Judaism and Zionism as synonyms, and Jewishness and Arabness as antonyms. Thus, Arab-Jews were prodded to choose between anti-Zionist Arabness and a pro-Zionist Jewishness for the first time in history. Distinguishing the "evil East" (the Muslim Arab) from the "good East" (the Jewish Arab), Israel has taken it upon itself to "cleanse" Arab-Jews of their Arabness and redeem them from their "primal sin" of belonging to the Orient. This conceptualization of East and West has important implications in this age of the "peace process," because it avoids the issue of the majority of the population within Israel being from the Middle East—Palestinians citizens of Israel as well as Mizrahi-Sephardi Jews; for peace as it is defined now does not entail a true democracy in terms of adequate representation of these populations, nor in terms of changing the educational, cultural, and political orientation within the state of Israel.

The leitmotif of Zionist texts was the cry to be a "normal civilized nation," without the presumably myriad "distortions" and forms of pariahdom typical of the *gola* (Diaspora), of the state of being a non-nation-state. The *Ostjuden,* perennially marginalized by Europe, realized their desire of becoming Europe, ironically, in the Middle East, this time on the back of their own *Ostjuden,* the Eastern Jews. The Israeli establishment, therefore, has made systematic efforts to suppress Sephardi-Mizrahi cultural identity. The Zionist establishment, since its early encounter with Palestinian (Sephardi) Jews, has systematically attempted to eradicate the Middle Easternness of those other Jews—for example, by marginalizing these histories in school curricula, and by rendering Mizrahi cultural production and grassroots political activities invisible in the media. Despite its obvious shifts since the partition of Palestine, however, Sephardi popular culture has clearly manifested its vibrant intertextual dialogue with Arab, Turkish, Iranian, and Indian popular cultures. Oriental-Arabic music produced by Sephardim—at times in collaboration with Israeli Palestinians—is consumed by Palestinians in Israel and across the borders in the Arab world, often without being labeled as originating in Israel. This creativity is partly nourished through an enthusiastic consumption of Jordanian, Lebanese, and Egyptian television programs, films, and Arabic video-music performances, which rupture the Euro-Israeli public sphere in a kind of subliminal transgression of a forbidden nostalgia. In fact, musical groups such as the Moroccan-Israeli Sfatayim (Lips) traveled back to Morocco to produce a music video sung in Moroccan Arabic against the scenery of the cities and villages that Moroccan Jews have left behind, just as Israeli-born Iraqi singers such as Ya'aqub Nishawi sing old and contemporary Iraqi music. This desire for "return of the Diaspora" is ironically underlined by what I would describe as a kind of a reversal of the biblical expression: "By the waters of Zion, where we sat down, and there we wept, when we remembered Babylon."[34]

Arab Muslim historiography, meanwhile, has ironically echoed the logic of Zionist paradigms, looking only superficially into the culture and identity of Arab-Jews both in the Arab world, and, more recently, within Israel. Thus, Ghosh, the visiting Indian anthropologist, notices what is otherwise unnoticeable: that in the Geniza's home country, Egypt,

> nobody took the slightest notice of its dispersal. In some profound sense, the Islamic high culture of Masr [Arabic for Egypt] has never really noticed, never found a place for the parallel history the Geniza represented, and its removal only confirmed a particular vision of the past. . . . Now it was Masr, which had sustained the Geniza for almost a Millennium, that was left with no traces of its riches: not a single scrap or shred of paper to remind her of the aspect of her past. It was as

though the borders that were to divide Palestine several decades later had already been drawn, through time rather than territory, to allocate a choice of Histories.[35]

The amnesia of this recent history in most contemporary Arab culture has fed into a Israeli and Arab refusal of the hybrid, the in-between. Even Israeli Arab-Jews, such as the Iraqi-Israeli writer Samir Naqash, who to this day writes his novels in Arabic, are "rejected" from membership in the Arab geocultural region, simply seen as "Israeli." The Jews of Islam thus today exist as part of a historiography in which our relations to the Arab Islamic world exist only in the past tense. Colonial partitions and nationalist ideologies have left little room for the inconvenient "minority" of Arab-Jews. Even the Geniza itself, presumably rescued from obscurity and decay at the hands of our own producers, has been used to support a nationalist narrative in which every text or fragmented document was deciphered for a Zionist transformation "megola le'geula" ("from Diaspora to redemption"). The historiographical work of Euro-Jewish scholars such as S. D. Goitein and E. Strauss might have facilitated the entry of an Indian anthropologist such as Ghosh into the Indian Ocean world of a twelfth-century Tunisian-Jewish trader, Abraham Ben-Yiju, who, unlike Ghosh, traveled in an era when "Europe" did not dominate the channels of scholarship and communication. But the Geniza scholarship was shaped and used within a context of Zionist Enlightenment readings of the otherized Jews of the Levant, the very same Jews whose cultural practices made possible the Geniza scholarship of Western academic institutions. Within these asymmetrical power relations, it is the work of Euro-Jewish scholars that infused the colonized history with national meaning and telos, while, ironically, at the same time, Arab-Jews were being displaced, and in Israel subject to a schooling system where Jewish history textbooks featured barely a single chapter on their history.

Today, Mizrahim inhabit the pages of Euro-Israeli sociological and anthropological accounts as maladjusted criminals and superstitious exotics, firmly detached from Arab history that looms only as deformed vestiges in the lives of Israelis of Asian and African origin. Sociology and anthropology detect such traces of underdevelopment, while national historiography tells the story of the past as a moral tale full of national purpose. Such scholarly bifurcation cannot possibly account for an Arab-Jewish identity that is at once past and present, here and there. Perhaps it is not a coincidence that the author of *In an Antique Land*—a hybrid of anthropology and history—ends up by splitting the subjects of ethnography and historiography, the first focusing on present-day Egyptian Muslims, and the second on past Arab-

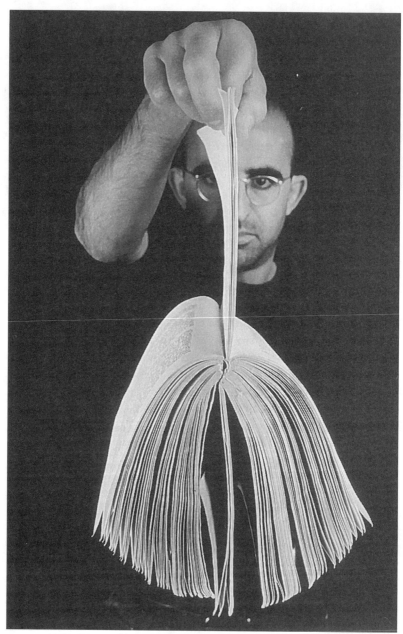

Meir Gal, "Nine Out of Four Hundred" (The West and the Rest), 1997.
The artist emphasizes the tiny proportion of pages assigned to Oriental-Jewish history in an Israeli history textbook. Used by permission of Meir Gal.

Jews. Ghosh, at the end of his book, stops his narrative at the very point where the subject of his historiography could have turned into a subject of his ethnography. Anthropological accounts of Ghosh's visits to Egypt are paralleled by his historiographical chronicle of the Judeo-Islamic world through the travels of Ben-Yiju. On Ghosh's final trip to Egypt, Ghosh notices Arab-Jewish pilgrims from Israel coming to Egypt to visit the tomb of the cabalistic mystic Sidi Abu-Hasira, a site holy for both Muslims and Jews, with many similar festivities. Yet, for one reason or another, he ends up never meeting them. Perhaps Ghosh's missed rendezvous, his packing up and leaving Egypt precisely as the Arab-Jews visit Abu-Hasira's holy site, is revelatory of the difficulties of representing a multidiasporic identity, the dangers of border crossing in the war zone. Thus, we Arab-Jews continue to travel in historical narratives as imbricated with a legendary Islamic civilization; but, as the postcolonial story began to unfold over the past decades, we suddenly cease to exist, as though we have reached our final destination—the state of Israel—and nothing more need be said.

In contrast to the negatively connoted term *Orientals* (in the United States), in Israel "Orientals" (Mizrahim) signifies radical politics, evoking a common experience shared by all Asian and African Jews in Israel, despite our different origins. On the part of radical Sephardi movements, it also suggests a resistant discourse that calls for linkages to the East, as opposed to the hegemonic discourse of "we of the West." The names of the 1980s movements East for Peace and the Oriental Front in Israel, Perspectives Judéo-Arabes in Paris, and the World Organization of Jews from Islamic Countries in New York point to the assertion of the historical and future interwovenness with the East. Mizrahim, along with Palestinians within Israel proper (Israeli Palestinians), compose the majority of the citizens of a state that has rigidly imposed an anti–Middle Eastern agenda. In a first-of-its-kind meeting between Mizrahim and Palestine Liberation Organization representatives held at the symbolic site of Toledo, Spain, in 1989, we insisted that a comprehensive peace would mean more than settling political borders, and would require the erasure of the East/West cultural borders between Israel and Palestine, and thus the remapping of national and ethnic-racial identities against the deep scars of colonizing partitions. A critical examination of national histories may thus open a cultural space for working against taboo memories and fostering diasporic visions.

Notes

Parts of this essay have appeared in preliminary form in *Middle East Report* 178 (September–October 1992) and *Third Text* 21 (winter 1992–93). An earlier version was included in

Cultural Identity and the Gravity of History: On the Work of Edward Said, ed. Keith Ansell-Pearson, Benita Parry, and Judith Squires (London: Lawrence and Wishart, 1997). I thank Meir Gal, Rachel Jones, and Tikva Parnass for their generosity and help with the images.

1. Amitav Ghosh, *In an Antique Land* (New York: Alfred A. Knopf, 1992), 89–94. Some of my comments here on the book were made in a CUNY Television conversation with Amitav Ghosh in March 1994. The conversation also included Tim Mitchell, and was organized and moderated by Kamala Visweswaran and Parag Amladi.

2. Ibid., 85, 93.

3. I thank Robert Stam for allowing me to use here some "shared territory" from our book *Unthinking Eurocentrism: Multiculturalism and the Media* (London: Routledge, 1994).

4. See, for example, "Green Card" artwork by Inigo Manglano-Ovalle.

5. Quoted in Jean Comby, "1492: Le choc des cultures et l'évagélisation du monde," *Dossiers de l'épiscopat français* 14 (October 1990): 14.

6. See Charles Duff, *The Truth about Columbus* (New York: Random House, 1936).

7. Ghosh, *In an Antique Land,* 81.

8. Jan Pieterse makes the more general point that many of the themes of European imperialism traced antecedents to the European and Mediterranean sphere. Thus, the theme of civilization against barbarism was a carryover from Greek and Roman antiquity, the theme of Christianity against pagans was the keynote of European expansion culminating in the Crusades, and the Christian theme of "mission" was fused with "civilization" in the *mission civilisatrice*. See Jan Pietersee, *Empire and Emancipation* (London: Pluto Press, 1990), 240.

9. For details, see Jan Carew, *Fulcrums of Change: Origins of Racism in the Americas and Other Essays* (Trenton, N.J.: Africa World Press, 1988).

10. The indigenous peoples of the Americas similarly were officially protected from massacres by the throne only once they converted to Christianity.

11. The presumed "godlessness" of the indigenous people became a pretext for enslavement and dispossession. Whereas Jews and Muslims were diabolized, the indigenous Americans were accused of devil worship. The brutalities practiced by official Christianity toward Jews and Muslims have to be seen, therefore, on the same continuum as the forced conversions of indigenous peoples of the Americas who, like the Jews and Muslims in Christian Spain, were obliged to feign allegiance to Catholicism.

12. Pat Kossan, "Jewish Roots of Hispanics—Delicate Topic," *Phoenix Gazette,* April 14, 1992, section C.

13. Moors converted to Christianity.

14. Spanish Muslim culture in Christian Spain, like Sephardi-Jewish culture, was expressed in Spanish as well.

15. See, for example, W. Montgomery Watt and Pierre Cachia, *A History of Islamic Spain* (Edinburgh: Edinburgh University Press, 1977); James T. Monroe, *Hispano-Arabic Poetry* (Berkeley: University of California Press, 1974).

16. This picture of an ageless and relentless oppression and humiliation ignores the

fact that, on the whole, Jews of Islam—a minority among several other religious and ethnic communities in the Middle East and North Africa—lived relatively comfortably within Arab Muslim society.

17. For a more complex analysis, see, for example, Ilan Halevi, *A History of the Jews: Ancient and Modern* (London: Zed Books, 1987); Maxime Rodinson, *Cult, Ghetto, and State: The Persistence of the Jewish Question* (London: Al Saqi Books, 1983).

18. See Ella Shohat, "Sephardim in Israel: Zionism from the Standpoint of Its Jewish Victims," *Social Text* 19–20 (fall 1988).

19. For more on the question of East and West in Zionist discourse, see Ella Shohat, *Israeli Cinema: East/West and the Politics of Representation* (Austin: University of Texas Press, 1989).

20. During the early days of Zionism, other "empty" territories were proposed for Jewish settlement; typically, they were located in the colonized world. However, one of Theodor Herzl's famous proposals for settlement—Uganda—created a crisis for the Zionist Congress, known as the Uganda crisis.

21. See Maxime Rodinson, *Israel: A Colonial-Settler State?* trans. David Thorstad (New York: Monad Press, 1973).

22. See Yoseff Meir, *Hatnua haTzionit veYehudei Teman (The Zionist Movement and the Jews of Yemen)* (Tel Aviv: Sifriat Afikim, 1982); G. N. Giladi, *Discord in Zion: Conflict between Ashkenazi and Sephardi Jews in Israel* (London: Scorpion Publishing, 1990).

23. The phrase "Jews in the form of Arabs" was used already during the first decade of the twentieth century by the early engineers (such as Shmuel Yaveneli) of "Aliya" of Jews from the regions of the Ottoman Empire. See Meir, *The Zionist Movement and the Jews of Yemen.*

24. See Edward Said, *The Question of Palestine* (New York: Times Books, 1979).

25. See, for example, Jacques Derrida, "Edmund Jabès and the Question of the Book," in *Writing and Difference,* trans. Alan Bass (Chicago: University of Chicago Press, 1978), 64–78; George Steiner, "Our Homeland, the Text," *Salmagundi* 66 (winter–spring 1985): 4–25.

26. In recent years, the term *sh'horim* (blacks) has also applied to the Orthodox religious Ashkenazi codes of dressing. I should point out that the sartorial codes favoring dark colors of centuries-ago Poland were never part of Sephardic-Arabic culture. Since the massive arrival in Israel of Ethiopian Jews in the 1980s, the pejorative term *blacks* or *kushim* has been used against Ethiopian Jews.

27. I specifically address the relationship between the Palestinian and the Sephardi-Mizrahi questions vis-à-vis Zionism in my essay on Sephardi identity in Israel, "Zionism from the Standpoint of Its Jewish Victims," a title referring to Said's essay "Zionism from the Standpoint of Its Victims" (*Social Text* 1 [1979]), also a chapter in Said's *The Question of Palestine.* Both have been republished in *Dangerous Liaisons: Gender, Nation, and Post-colonial Perspectives,* ed. Anne McClintock, Aamir Mufti, and Ella Shohat (Minneapolis: University of Minnesota Press, 1997).

28. Neither Palestinians nor Arab-Jews have been compensated for their lost property.

29. See, for example, Abbas Shiblak, *The Lure of Zion* (London: Al Saki Books, 1986); Gideon Giladi, *Discord in Zion* (London: Scorpion Publishing, 1990).

30. Thus, for example, when the Iraqi-Israeli writer Shimon Ballas wrote the novel *Vehu Aher (And He Is an Other)* (Tel Aviv: Zmora Bitan, 1991), which partially concerned an Iraqi Jew who remained in Iraq after the dislodging of his community and converts to Islam, he was vehemently attacked in a rush to censor the imaginary.

31. Jewish-Arabic language was written in Hebrew script, but the script resembles very little the Ashkenazi Hebrew script that became a lingua franca since the revival of modern Hebrew and its spread through Zionist institutions. Today, Sephardi prayer texts use the common Ashkenazi script, even when the prayer is in Judeo-Arabic, because the Ashkenazi script is better known to most younger-generation Mizrahim.

32. Most cultural expression of Jews in the Arab world, needless to say, was not in Ladino/Español but in Arabic (whether literary Arabic, Judeo Arabic, or other Arabic dialects). It was perhaps this misconception that led Bharathi Mukherjee to have her Iraqi Jewish protagonist, Alfie Judah, in *The Middleman* say that the "form of Spanish" we spoke in "old Baghdad" was "a good preparation for the Southwest" (i.e., of the United States).

33. Such attacks were made, for example, on Shimon Ballas after the publication of his novel *And He Is an Other,* as well as on myself after the Hebrew publication of my book *Israeli Cinema: East/West and the Politics of Representation* (published as *Hakolnoa halsraeli: Histpria veIdiologia* [Israeli cinema: history and ideology; Tel Aviv: Breirot, 1991]).

34. See Ella Shohat, "Dislocated Identities: Reflections of an Arab-Jew," *Movement Research: Performance Journal* 5 (fall–winter 1992).

35. Ghosh, *In an Antique Land,* 95.

Part II Urban Hybridities

The Anatomy Contraption

Tony Birch

I

Inside the Museum of Anatomy
we may discover bloodless surety
no distracting heartbeat
or fluctuating temperatures
no function life exists
behind the glass doors
of anatomy

for anatomy—
once sawbones
part apothecary
barely a station above the butcher—
became a precise science
so exact, it could not be said
to be a mere skill

within the glass cubes
rows of cabinets
in the numbering and labeling
within the
descriptive catalogue
of the specimens
in this museum
treasures come together
to form a completed text—
the body

II

the museum is guarded
by a guilded-framed
shades of grey portrait of
the long-dead
Professor Wood Johns
forever gazing pensively
through the stream of
tiled-corridor-light
toward the meaningless
of outside life

before entry we
commence instruction—
this is a
PRIVATE ANATOMY MUSEUM
(for)
ANATOMY STUDENTS ONLY
the collection
is protected by
RULES GOVERNING THE USE
OF THE MUSEUM:

(for instance)

Only students currently enrolled
in this university for courses of
instruction in anatomy have the
right to use the museum. All
others who desire to use it
should apply to the inquiry office—
level 7

Any breakages should be reported
immediately to inquiry office—
level 7

(We desire this museum so we enter.)

III

Inside, sweet silence
but for the irritation of
the nagging repetitive ticking
of a black-faced clock

the hooded microscopes
wait attentively
to be touched by soft young hands
blinds are drawn, natural light prohibited
fingerprints of life denied entry

no dirt exists here
the skins of glass
soup-bowl half-skulls
empty wastebins
waxed wood benches
have been vacuumed of identity:

no. 1-2-1.
A superficial dissection of
the side of the head showing
the parotid gland, facial nerve,
cutaneous nerves of the scalp
and the musculature of the
face, scalp, and auricle

no. 4-4-8
Dissections of three infant hearts
each showing a patent ductus arteriosus
(the work of Dr. S. Scofield, 1962)

IV

In the museum
there is
NO SMOKING
NO EATING ALLOWED
(obviously)
DO NOT REMOVE SPECIMENS
FROM THE CABINETS
(but please observe)
THE VARIOUS ARTICULATIONS
OF THE BASE OF THE SKULL:

Dog

Lemur

Sheep

Old World Monkey

Orangutan

Chimpanzee

Man

an understanding
and acceptance of
the chain of being
is a necessary prerequisite
for instruction in this museum

any dissenting views
will be transfered
to level 7

V

The museum is a menagerie of
ABNORMALITIES OF THE
ARTERIES OF THE LEG
a one-eyed man returning
a wink through the opaque haze
lines of partial faces
an athlete's knee
a pair of nicotined lungs

(which after being photographed here
went on to make their debut
on an antismoking poster
that traveled the city
on the side of a tram
the commuters ignored
the blackened images of death
and lit up regardless
coughing up phlegm
in a show of defiance)

this is *the* panopticon
created from slices, splices
bits and pieces,
X rays, windpipes,
spinal cords and a
SMALL BOWEL STUDY—
(note the tube in the
duodenum outlining its typical C shape)

In the museum of Man—
of dead men and the

occasional woman
there is no Other
these bodies are not to be
exoticized, celebrated, or denigrated

they are unknown aged
white-skinned benign old men
petrified, gasping forever
a final silent breath

they are men—sleeping
behind long soft lashes
they are men—forever unshaven
with dark traces of a pre-ozone-depleted-sun
on the backs of their wrinkled necks

they are tired old men—
without faces, without bodies
right-side lateral men with
heads shaved clean like billiard balls
a pair of shoulders worn out by life
variations of bone and wrist
an outstretched arm, a calloused hand
digits snipped clean in half
with garden shears

and behind them
in a corner of the room
there is "art"—a painting
of nineteenth-century surgeons
hovering over a body
opened to a shaft of light
decending from Heaven
the painting was a gift to
this institution from
another:
KOL. GERMAIDE GALERIE
den Haag, no. 1.

VI

Question:

Explain the absence of the midline aorta?

Observe:

Sagittal section of a monkey embryo

Question:

Describe the development of the
submandibular gland?

Observe:

Monkey heart corresponding to a
human fetus at 10 weeks' gestation.

(all will be revealed)

follow the course of the left vagus nerve
over the arch of the aorta
and the left superior supercostal vein
later passing to the left
posterior pulmonary plexus
you will then clearly note
the left phrenic nerve
superficial to the scalenus anterior
and passing anterior
to the internal thoracic artery

466
467
468
469

4 fetal skeletons
4 escapees from a
science-fiction movie

In 1959 Dr. I. A. Penn peeled back a
lower leg for us to observe.
No. 338 is his
posterior tibial artery and nerve.
Please observe.

VII

In the museum
there is the odd fabrication
a rubberized newborn boy
lies garroted
in a baize-lined draw

he was fashioned
by Monsieur Tramond of Paris

who has left his mark
on the boy's forearm
it is inscripted—
Tramond of Paris

a sound is detected
young "med students"
already suited in white-coated props
furiously put pencil to paper
while hovering over Tramond's baby

note:
A lower jaw—before birth—
at birth—two years—about four
years—twelve years

note:
Section A
thyroid
heart
liver
mesonephros

note:
no. 542
sartorium-rectus fem.-capsule-
lat. cut. n.-gl. med-cl. min-
lat. fem. circ.-tensor f. 1.

note:
in the upper specimen the ribs are free

VIII

"ANATOMIE OSTÉOLOGIE SCIENCES NATURELLES"

glass and mahogany cabinets house
the skeletal frames of
natural man
but man cannot stand alone
the bones are fused together
with alloy nuts and bolts
manufactured by the migrant workers
of the Sidcrome Company

wire springs and
copper-weaved sheets

hold man upright
the fabricated
the artificial unnatural
creates natural man

a team of four skeletons
stands here bemused
bodies in a void
one is smiling slightly

a long-dead student?
or a cleaner perhaps?
once discovered an opening
a way in
and slipped him
a now faded note
"quiet I am loafing"
it reads

no. 321 informs
that we are witnessing
the development of the cranium
but do not be deceived
nothing ever develops here
all the components
have "passed away"
but still the cranium at 10 weeks
is presented
in a progressive stage of life:

occipital bone
temporal bone
semicircular canal
cochlea
Meckel's cartilage
sphenoid bone
pharynx
foranen caecum

(the list
begs only one question—
who was Meckel?)

IX

no. 371
"fetus at 20 weeks"
was put to rest by
Dr. L. S. Coles
on a summer morning
in 1960

he had toast and tea
for breakfast
kissed his wife
on the cheek
and jumped into his
two-tone two-ton
Studebaker

driving away from suburban obscurity
into the vitality of
the Anatomy Department

there he checked the quality
of the teeth of his saw
the sharpness of his boning knife
and went to work
(such information is unavailable
to those who visit
the museum)

24 years on
the baby remains
in a beautiful sleep
in a mother's womb
they are joined
on a brightly fluoro-lit
glass wall by others
the embryonic, the newborn
and children

the bodies of women
are presented
only as vessels
containers within containers
housing the yet-to-be-born
no knowledge of these women
is presented or required

(do these images haunt?—
there is a child here
who does not exist
below the neck
she smiles softly at me
while looking over her shoulder
at the vivisector
and his tray of sterile instruments
her face rests against the glass

this is the one
I will return to life
so I imagine her face
about to surface
in a shallow rock pool
on a Bunnarong coastline—
only we know this)

in the museum
there are no histories
no stories
anonymity in anatomy
there is the aged grain of the wood
but it does not speak
there are only the dates and names
of the men who acted
so efficiently

the bodies were given up
by their families, themselves
and the State
their purpose in death
is to serve a higher purpose—
knowledge and medicine?
above all to serve
the museum itself

we have reached
the pinnacle
there is nothing here
the only tale to be told
is one of imperial cannibalism
anatomy creates, devours,
and regurgitates itself

the purpose of any collection
is in the collecting itself

the purpose of the display
is in its inaccessibility

the locked door completes
any collection

RULE 4-8-4 section 2.1.:
DO NOT PUT A NAME TO A FACE
DIRECT ALL SUCH IMAGININGS TO
LEVEL 7.

X

(ON LEAVING THE MUSEUM)

WARNING

the equipment in this building is
the property of the university

Any person found removing any item
or found in possession of any item
who has not been duly authorized in
writing to remove such an item
may be prosecuted

container nos.
68-139-361-
429 and 532
ARE NO LONGER
ON DISPLAY

(rumor has it that they
were removed from display
as they closely resembled
the body parts of past
actual living people. For instance
students began to note the
similarities between no. 361
"the dissection of the left palm"
and the waving hand of
a dead prime minister once viewed
in a *Cinetone* newsreel.)

this resulted in the following
WARNING:

Any person found in the possession
of knowledge of any item which
is not included in the catalogue shall
be deemed to be in possession of
unauthorized knowledge and shall
report to level 7
where they will be
required to present themselves before
the Board of Directors
of the School of Medicine
and submit themselves for
further examination

From Pastiche to Macaroni

Celeste Olalquiaga

Imán is a beautiful young Latino gay with whom I occasionally party, switching back and forth between the gaps of his second-generation Spanish and my schooled English. Until recently, we had a common ground in that comfortable linguistic mélange where our very opposite experiences of Latino-American and Latin American cultures met, him being a native English speaker with a Latin legacy, me a Latin American brought up speaking English.[1] But the other night that ground shifted right from under me when he greeted me warmly in something that sounded familiar, but of which I could only make out the word *honey*. I thought drugs had done him in, but as things turned out, I was the one out of it: Imán had added a new layer to his Spanglish, that of black and Latino drag balls. It all came together when someone finally explained that he had joined the House of Xtravaganza.

Imán's verbal crossing of not only two cultures, but also, perhaps more important, at least two subcultures, is emblematic of the intricate web of codings that constitute cosmopolitan experience. His baroque glossolalia renders obsolete all notions of identity based on ethnic or sexual essentialisms, going far beyond the simple multiplication of disparate cultural traits implied in multiculturalism; for his polyvalence is not the mechanical addition of separate identities that schizophrenically coexist along one another as in Sybil, the woman with seventeen personalities; and his resilience stands in glaring contrast to the melting-pot generations, whose cultural plurality evaporated in a slow but relentless boil that whitewashed them of all their vitality. Imán's uniqueness resides in having absorbed all the registers

Counterinvasion paranoia at its best: The Chrysler building is claustrophobically walled in by the perceived Babel of multiculturalism. Cover drawing "I ♥ Babel" by Edward Sorel, copyright 1995 The New Yorker Magazine, Inc. All rights reserved. Reprinted by permission.

in which he was either inscribed or chose to inscribe himself, allowing each one to reshape him all over again until he became much more than the sum of his parts.

Although for some, Imán's androgyny makes him a freak of nature and his polyglotism a worthy descendant of the builders of the Tower of Babel, for others his skill for camouflage and change is only the sophisticated (and, in a world where subcultures are expanding by the minute, legitimate) version of instinctive survival strategies that enable him to live his difference with relatively few repressions. This infinite ductility and constant shifting of styles are characteristic of postmodernity, and, as such, they are often downplayed as superficial and arbitrary: superficial, because postmodern metamorphosis refuses a centered and systematic line of thought that would grant it historical depth and continuity, anchoring it to the fatigued hierarchies of class, gender, and race; arbitrary, because postmodern versatility moves freely between multifarious discourses and styles, unapologetically choosing eclecticism over consistency. Yet, it is precisely this mobility and heterogeneity that have burst open the binding strictures of ideological constructs at their seams, enabling the overflow of all that had been outcast as bizarre and distorted.

Imán's newfound patter is one among myriad dialects and slangs in that Fourth World of homeless, exiles, immigrants, transvestites, punks, single mothers, and other urban displaced. It is the product of a time when the artificial boundaries of nations and cities have collapsed under the weight of a diversity that could no longer be bound by uniform languages or monological discourses. It is the oral equivalent of the polysemantic clutteredness of Chinatown, Fourteenth Street, and Times Square, whose shrewd merchants, Chinese, Arab, or Jewish, transit fluidly between English, Spanish, Chinese, Hebrew, and Arabic—a macaronic verbality perfectly suited to a pastiched visuality. It is the vehicle of simulation and impersonation in a culture where fantasy and reality have become indistinguishable, and where abandoning the self to become another is among the most valued forms of gratification. It is profane, irreverent, and illegal because it flourishes in the cracks of a mainstream culture determined to annihilate, by integration or eradication, anything different from itself.

Imán's Xtravagantic Spanglish is his home, a symbolic place where he can safely unravel the complexity of his urban persona without being attacked, despised, or made fun of. Like most slang, it transforms divergence into distinction, rejection into validation, awkwardness into style. An outermost expression of intimate vulnerability, it is both a weapon and a shield, protecting with mystification the fragile territory of marginal belongings.

Constructing and deconstructing Babel: Perfectly illustrating the linguistic puzzle, this sixteenth-century image of an unfinished Babel also can be understood as

But, in contrast to those codings where exclusiveness is granted by a blatant inaccessibility, Imán's lingo is so similar to common speech that it easily passes for it, in the same way that the members of his adoptive drag family infiltrate the regimented roles of straight society. What is spoken is a make-believe language that feigns the syntax and cadence of regular talk, while surreptitiously establishing its own universe of references and network of tacit

NEW! THE TOWER OF BABEL. Signed and dated 1563, this painting by Pieter Bruegel the Elder is based on the book of Genesis II, in which there is an attempt to build a "tower whose top may reach unto heaven". The builders are struck by the heavens with a language barrier that ends construction of the tower, and forms the many languages of the world. Meticulously rendered is a magnificent structure with ramps, a multitude of workmen with King Nimrod commanding them, and vast building implements. Bruegel's understanding of construction appears in the enormity of this imaginary project. Our 9000-piece jigsaw measures a giant $54\frac{1}{4}$" x $75\frac{1}{2}$." **#03-J3507.** $99.95

depicting the tower in ruins. From *Bits & Pieces: The Great International Puzzle Collection* catalog (Holiday 1995).

alliances. In so doing, it perpendicularly traverses the ritual formalities of business and professional exchange without antagonizing them, and further expands the already elastic boundaries of quotidian jargon.

This ability to ride on linguistic conventions while simultaneously proposing an alternative discourse adds a metaphoric dimension to Imán's particular brand of cityspeak. Its polytonality, hodgepodge vocabulary, and veiled allusions endow it with the lyricism and evocation often praised as the most achieved forms of poetry. And, like those remnants of vulgar Latin that, inscribed on the walls of ancient Rome as the first graffiti, provided an invaluable documentation of Latin into the Romance languages, so Imán's vernacular parlance manifests the extreme flexibility with which popular culture absorbs and converts institutionalized norms and regulations, ultimately outlasting what is otherwise fated to the sure death of stagnation.

In the rudimentary anti-postmodern arithmetic that officially advocates for a unitary identity with many satellite cultures adorning its deflated crown, Imán's mutability and fragmentation do not add up to a round number, his ambiguity and transience undeserving of his being counted as a full person. But, in the infinite exchanges that conform daily urban life, Imán has won as many places as he can vogue himself into: he can be many more people than he was born to be, an indisputable advantage over being stuck with one same life for the rest of existence.

Notes

1. There is very little Latin in Latin America, as Dan Quayle found out, much to his embarrassment and our amusement, when visiting South America and complaining that nobody spoke Latin. In the nineteenth century, the term *Hispanoamérica,* which emphasized the difference between Spanish-speaking countries and Brazil, was preferred, but since then the more encompassing *Latinoamérica* has prevailed. Somewhat following this chronology, the term *Hispanic* was first adopted in the United States to distinguish the ethnicity of the immigrants from Central and South America and the Spanish-speaking Caribbean, but later abandoned for *Latin* or its Spanish versions of *Latino* and *Latina.* To complicate matters further, no one in Latin America claims to speak Spanish; instead, we correctly refer to our language as Castilian, because the variety of languages spoken in the different regions of Spain precludes the notion of a single, homogeneous, "Spanish." As a consequence of this misunderstanding, Latinos are sometimes called "Spanish," a cultural confusion that erases Latin America from the map. "From Pastiche to Macaroni" was originally published in Exit Art's catalog *The Hybrid State,* New York City, 1992. The illustrations were added by the author for its publication in this book.

Afro-Kitsch

Manthia Diawara

The title for this essay comes from Donald John Cosentino, who wrote an article on Afro-kitsch, applying it to African art.[1] I am using it in respect to African-American art and, specifically, in respect to the discourses of Afro-centricity and the kind of work I do myself—literary theory and film theory.

The word *kitsch* is often applied to objects that mark signs of indeterminacy: "Is it art or is it kitsch?" Kitsch connotes the banal, the inauthentic, the cheap imitation. Kitsch art is often accused of cutting loose old forms from their social networks and redeploying them in utterly new contexts. In addition, kitsch art functions to reinforce identification and to promote consumption of the object thus put forth; it requires an unmediated emotional response. Finally, kitsch art is said to be a murderer of authentic art.

This definition seems untenable today—we are well aware of the post-structuralist celebration of difference, hybridity, creolization, and the carnivalesque. Questions of textuality are no longer so simple. In fact, the definition of kitsch art, which I have adopted here from Herman Bloch, seems conservative today. It positions the high and rarefied over the low and popular. But I want to retain kitsch, nonetheless, in order to address such related matters as national style, mass conversion, and nostalgia. I am concerned that forums such as these have become sites of temporary feel-good, spaces for mass conversions that cover our wounds without healing them, or redeeming us. Revolutionary traditions are invoked only to be co-opted in these cathartic moments. And generic Pan-African symbols increasingly seem the preferred style for that mode of uplifting.

Spike Lee's *Do the Right Thing* is a good example of the ambivalent situation for which kitsch art is known. In 1989, the year *Do the Right Thing* was made, there was a ban on realism. Hollywood produced mostly sequels and remakes. We had one more *Indiana Jones, Star Trek,* and *Superman.* And amid this nostalgia for old glory, the attempt to recover what America "used to be," *Do the Right Thing* seemed authentic. After all, the Reagan–Bush administration was returning us to glorious America, and this was not so glorious for black people.

But by what means do we measure *Do the Right Thing*'s authenticity? Wahneema Lubiano reminds us that the authenticity of the representation of the black community in films such as *Do the Right Thing* depends more on films by other black directors than on some essentialist notion of the black community.[2] *Do the Right Thing* produced mass identification in at least three directions (and this is why it is kitsch): black neonationalists saw it as an emblem of their call; whites identified negatively in the form of their denial; and feminists recreated a martyrdom in its discourse. Is it art or is it kitsch?

As if that was not enough, John Sayles created his version of *Do the Right Thing* in *City of Hope.* And there we have it—repetitions, sequels, imitations. Certainly, if Spike Lee can speak for black people, John Sayles can speak for white and black liberals. Is it art or is it kitsch? Art or racism?

I turn now to James Brown to further address the murkiness of kitsch art. I am concerned here with the new in kitsch. In other words, can kitsch make new? And can a new discourse be cutting-edge, grounded in the material conditions of a people, combining politics and culture in order to liberate us? I am going to give the authentic me at this point.

In 1965, Radio Mali advertised a concert by Junior Wells and his All-Star Band at the Omnisport in Bamako. The ads promised that the Chicago group would electrify the audience with tunes from such stars as Otis Redding, Wilson Pickett, and James Brown. I was very excited because I had records by Junior Walker, and to me, at that time, with my limited English, Junior Wells and Junior Walker were one and the same. (That still happens to me, by the way.) It was a little disappointing that we could not have James Brown in person. I had heard that Anglophone countries such as Ghana, Liberia, and Nigeria were luckier. They could see James Brown on television, and they even had concerts with Tyrone Davis, Aretha Franklin, and Wilson Pickett.

Sure enough, the concert was electrifying. Junior Wells and his All-Star Band played "My Girl," "I've Been Loving You Too Long," "It's a Man's World," "There Was a Time," "I Can't Stand Myself," "Papa's Got a Brand-New Bag," "Respect," "Midnight Hour," and, of course, "Say It Loud (I'm Black and I'm Proud)." During the break, some of us were allowed to talk with the musicians and to ask for autographs. Our translator was a white guy from the United States Information Agency. I remember distinguishing myself by going past the translator and asking one of the musicians the following question: "What is your name?" His eyes lit up, and he told me his name and asked for mine. I said, "My name is Manthia, but my friends call me J. B." He said something about James Brown, and I said something else. By that time, everybody else was quiet, watching us. I had only two years of junior-high-school English and the three-month summer vacations I had spent in Liberia to assist me. I got the nickname J. B. from my James Brown records.

The next day the news traveled all over Bamako that I spoke English like an American. This was tremendous in a Francophone country where one acquired subjecthood through recourse to *francité* (thinking through French grammar and logic). Our master thinker was Jean-Paul Sartre. We were also living in awe, a form of silence, thinking that to be Francophone subjects, we had to master *francité* like Léopold Sédar Senghor, who spoke French better than French people. Considered as one who spoke English like Americans and who had a fluent conversation with star musicians, I was acquiring a new type of subjecthood that put me perhaps above my comrades, who knew by heart their *Les Chemins de la liberté* by Sartre. I was on the cutting edge—the front line of the revolution.

For me, then, and for many of my friends, to be liberated was to be exposed to more R&B songs and to be au courant of the latest exploits of Muhammad Ali, George Jackson, Angela Davis, Malcolm X, and Martin Luther King Jr. These were becoming an alternative cultural capital for the African youth—imparting to us new structures of feeling and enabling us to subvert the hegemony of *francité* after independence.

I want to use this personal anecdote to make a few comments about the discourse of blackness and of Afrocentricity, which I call the "kitsch of blackness"—hence, Afro-kitsch. I have placed the music of James Brown and others at the cutting edge to make some remarks about the academic front line.

Words and phrases such as *revolution, subversion,* and *transformation of society* are no longer permitted in Marxist theory, feminist theory, or deconstruction. (I name these only because I work inside of them.) In my opinion, feminism lost the cutting edge when it turned its back on the subversion of patriarchal systems and concentrated instead on the empowerment of a few women. One can appropriately label the present state of feminism as "essentialist," because it no longer looks for the social constructions that oppress women. It has become a grand narrative with a beginning, a middle, and an end. Marxism, too, lost the cutting edge when its best theorists abandoned the revolution and was co-opted by structuralist analyses of hegemonic texts. Finally, deconstruction reached a dead end when it ran out of texts to deconstruct and became a theory about difference with a capital "D." As Stuart Hall said, some differences might not make any difference at all.

One might say that James Brown lost the cutting edge when he was co-opted by disco music in the seventies. We had to look to George Clinton and the Parliament Funkadelic to determine whether or not James Brown had eluded co-optation. Deconstructivists, feminists, and Marxists no longer have texts with which to theorize their subversive views; they have turned their backs on the material conditions of their discourses. They turn to themselves, cite themselves, and repeat themselves. Meanwhile, like every bourgeoisie, their rank and file keeps growing and their critique of the system grows less and less subversive. It is this intellectual self-fashioning and self-promotion, in the name of a theory that bears the appearance of subversion (and yet only shapes the career of the theorist), that led me to title my essay "Afro-Kitsch."

Afrocentrists, having learned the rules of the game from feminists, Marxists, and deconstructivists, have turned their backs to texts. By *texts,* I mean the lived experiences of black people in New York, Detroit, Lagos, and Dakar. Afrocentrists have re-created Egypt, the old African city, but their discourses, unlike James Brown's music in the sixties, do not serve the homeless in Philadelphia, let alone inspire revolution in South Africa. I submit that until Afrocentricity learns the language of black people in Detroit, Lingala in Zaire, and Bambara in Mali, and grounds itself in the material conditions of the people in question, it is nothing but a kitsch of blackness. It is nothing but an imitation of a discourse of liberation. Afrocentric academics fix blackness by reducing it to Egypt and kente cloths. Hence, like Judaism, Christianity, and Islam, Afrocentrism has become a religion, a camp movement, where one can find refuge from the material realities of being black in Washington, D.C., London, or Nairobi.

By placing James Brown on the cutting edge, and life on the front line, as Eddie Grant would say, I want to bring black cultural practitioners' attention to the precarious situation of kitsch theory. James Brown always risked the danger of co-optation, and once he was co-opted, he became a kitsch of himself, a cheap imitation. Feminism, deconstruction, and Afrocentricity are at the same impasse that James Brown met. They imitate themselves and refuse to look at new texts of oppression. They elevate intraclass rivalries to the rank of oppression against the homeless and the wretched of the earth. They co-opt oppression for themselves. One should not become as comfortable in blackness, or in feminism, as the happy men or women of religion. Blackness and feminism are not a discovery of a truth that lives with one ever after.

Elsewhere, I have defined blackness as a modernist metadiscourse on the condition of black peoples in the West and in areas under Western domination. Blackness is a compelling performance against the logic of slavery and colonialism by those people whose destinies have been inextricably linked to the advancement of the West, and who, therefore, have to learn the expressive techniques of modernity—writing, music, Christianity, industrialization—in order to become uncolonizable. Blackness, in the last instance, is a reflexive discourse, what W. E. B. Du Bois would have called "an afterthought of modernity," a critical theory on the cutting edge of modernity and modernism, a frontline discourse. Blackness is not removed from the material base of politics and theory. It always seeks to liberate spaces, to subvert orthodoxies, to give voice to the oppressed.

When blackness is conceived as a humanist metadiscourse on the condition of black peoples in the West and in areas under Western domination, it becomes easier to see how people in Africa appropriate its Western modes—Negritude, black consciousness—to sing their right to independence. The formulation of blackness in the West also empowers them with Africanism: African tradition, history, language, and nomenclature. Blackness and Africanism depend on each other, feed on each other, though they are not always interchangeable.

Blackness, as a modernist metadiscourse on the West imbued with revolutionary potential, is always enabling as a model to other repressed discourses such as feminism, gay and lesbian rights, and minority cultures in totalitarian systems. The Chinese students and workers in Tiananmen Square sang "We Shall Overcome"—a black song signaling a challenge to the logic of authoritarianism through Christianity. Blackness itself is challenged in the hands of its postcolonial and postmodern subjects. By focusing on such zones of ambivalence as identity formation, sexual politics, and hybridization, the postmodern subjects of blackness attempt to prevent it from falling into the same essentialist trap as whiteness.

Notes

1. Donald John Cosentino, "Afrokitsch," in *Africa Explores: Twentieth Century African Art,* ed. Susan Vogel (New York: Center for African Art, 1991), 240–55.

2. Wahneema Lubiano, "But Compared to What? Reading Realism, Representation, and Essentialism in *School Daze, Do the Right Thing,* and the Spike Lee Discourse," *Black American Literature Forum* 25:2 (summer 1991): 253.

"Barricades of Ideas": Latino Culture, Site-Specific Installation, and the U.S. Art Museum

Chon A. Noriega

A powerful idea, waved before the world at the proper time, can stop a squadron of iron-clad ships, like the mystical flag of the Last Judgment.

—José Martí, 1891

Re-placing Latino Identity

Caught between the ironclad ships of two empires, one in decline (Spain), the other emergent (the United States), José Martí codified the culture of imperialism, locating the point of resistance to it in the indigenous, mestizo, and African-descent peoples and cultures of "Our America."[1] Written in 1891, Martí's essay is a call to Latin America to become "one in spirit and intent" in the face of both continued imperialism and the impact of "imported methods and ideas" for governance in the newly independent nations. Although Martí died in 1895 fighting Spanish armies in Cuba, his idea persists that anti-imperialism in the Americas requires a pan-national "American" identity in order "to fit liberty to the body of those who rebelled and conquered for it."

Martí's predicament and solution provide the basis on which to rethink contemporary U.S. Latino identity and cultural expression in general, and Latino installation art in particular. I examine the latter because it enacts many of dilemmas of the former, while also being somewhat self-reflexive about its location within social space: installation refers at once to a new genre of art whose display is about display (rather than edification-cum-market value), and to the very practice of museum exhibition whereby art is installed within a designated space to serve a specific function. A closer examination of Martí's essay "Our America" provides terms with which to situate contemporary "identity" discourses within the paradox central to Martí's own project.

If Martí critiqued national, racial, and class hierarchies, he also mobilized them as he attempted to locate identity across local, national, and international domains. He did so by locating its desired effects across these domains: local knowledge became a cultural resource, state power (as an orchestration of local knowledges) defined national identity, and universal democracy existed as an international ideal that provided "space" for the new nations of Latin America. Thus, Martí made their interactions the basis for a different history, one that could include *our* America. But, by starting with Martí, I am also able to suggest another point of origin for installation art— an origin that grounds modernity and modern art within imperialism, rather than within a genealogy of aesthetic influences. Martí's articulation of identity within, between, and against two empires provides a model with which to understand how installation art speaks within and to the institution of art.

In considering "Our America" and other attempts to locate identity within geopolitical space, emphasis must be placed on the *style* in which such a space is imagined across competing discourses and temporalities.[2] Indeed, as an essayist, Martí has been understood in fairly straightforward terms as a political theorist and cultural critic. Little attention has been given to his prose style, even though his poetry is seen to anticipate and exceed Latin American modernism. Interestingly enough, that other dimension can be found in the religious metaphors that often provide a phantom structure for his writings. In "Our America," Martí's prophetic symbolism, which builds to a kaleidoscope of images and metaphors, mirrors the numbers, beasts, and other apocalyptic figures of the Book of Revelation, which closes the Christian Bible. Early in the essay, Martí makes repeated use of the biblical number seven to describe the opposition that exists both outside (seven-league boots) and inside (seven-month weaklings) the emergent nation. He then sets these against the forces of independence, which are figured as both body (a hundred apostles) and idea (Last Judgment). The end of the essay appeals to the reader's imagination for a "new America," but does so in the style of the Book of Revelation, with its evocation of a "new Earth" no longer torn by political strife. In this manner, Martí binds Revolution to Revelation in order to create the logic of an inevitable, yet evanescent, moment, a "proper time," when an idea will stop the ironclad ships and big sticks to the north.

The use of religious metaphors is a recurrent strategy in Martí's writings, one in which imperialism is pitted against itself, such that Christianity provides a metaphoric language for speaking against modernity. In an unfinished letter written the day before he was killed, Martí (who had spent the latter part of his life in the United States) claimed, "I have lived in the monster, and I know its entrails—and my slingshot is that of David."[3] But Martí's letter is not a simple expression of faith per se. In fact, Martí's belief was anything but simple, reflecting his contention that Latin American nations were formed in the "senseless struggle between the book and the lance, between reason and the processional candle." Thus, the religious metaphor must be seen as tactical insofar as the monster, "the giant with seven-league boots," proclaimed its actions in the name of reason, science, and progress, but placed its trust in God. If Martí wrote *against* modernity, he did not reject reason (he advocated secular education in the Americas), but rather placed its social consequences within an ethical discourse by way of biblical narratives.

More revelation than manifesto, Martí's essay incarnates an idea within the non-European body of Our America. But, if Martí incarnates a particular set of bodies, he also rejects the universalism of biblical revelation and its secular counterpart. As Ernesto Laclau observes, "The modern idea of a universal class and the various forms of Eurocentrism are nothing but distant historical effects of this logic of incarnation."[4] In other words, European imperialist expansion required the logic of incarnation in order to justify its project under the guise of a universal function (i.e., to civilize); but, in a crucial variation, European culture displaced or particularized the notion of a universal human essence, becoming itself the obscure object of (self-incarnation. "As a result," Laclau concludes, "the resistances of other cultures were presented not as struggles between particular identities and cultures, but as part of an all-embracing, epochal struggle between universality and particularisms—the notion of peoples without history expressing precisely their incapacity to represent the universal."[5] For Martí, however, incarnation does not produce a privileged agent, whether in the service of God or of History. It produces communities-in-relation. In order to understand this distinction, one must look first at the complex and contradictory way in which Martí figures the "people" of national communities.

In describing the body of those who fought for the independence of Our America, Martí refers to the *mestizo* (mixed race), *indio* (indigenous), and *negro* (black). Martí, however, wrote from the perspective of a *criollo* (Creole) ruling class. Thus, although he promoted a mixed-race ideal *(mestizaje),* he also manifested (and utilized) the conflicted notions of race in Latin America, where "race" functions on a number of levels other than that of color: cultural resource, class identification, and index of the nation *(la raza).*

Martí speaks about specific races (as cultural resources), yet privileges a mixed norm (as national ideal), all from an implied *criollo* or "white" position (as ruling class or state formation). Then, turning to the international arena, he denies race altogether: "There can be no racial animosity, because there are no races." Here, racial difference becomes an effect of nations, but it is rejected as the basis for *inter*national relations and replaced by the "universal identity" of humanity. For Martí, however, such "universal identity" is the product of nature, not reason, and "springs forth from triumphant love and the turbulent hunger for life." Its violation is a "sin." Such statements are more than the last gasps of Romantic idealism. Rather, within his layered discourse, Romantic idealism functions as a tactical element (as do race and faith), not as the predominant paradigm, wherein Martí sought to articulate a national identity within the context of hemispheric and global politics.

In talking about the nation, then, Martí necessarily imagines the hemispheric community necessary to dislodge the imperialist claims of Europe and the United States. It is not *a* nation. One nation could not stand against the United States; and, if it could, it would merely replace it as the universal. Instead, Martí invokes the idea of a class of nations, in order to establish a lateral ("democratic") relationship within the Americas as well as within the Western Hemisphere. "If democracy *is* possible," Laclau argues, "it is because the universal does not have any necessary body, any necessary content. Instead, different groups compete to give their particular aims a temporary function of universal representation."[6] Whereas Laclau writes about democracy within the nation, Martí applies this process both within and among nations. In the former, race structures the nation; in the latter, a supraracial "universal identity" places nations in an ethical relationship to one another. Such an approach shifts the predominant terms of national discourse from a spatial framework—of territorial boundaries and center-margin relations unfolding in linear time—to a temporal one. Thus, in his simultaneous appeal to ideas, actions, and the Last Judgment, Martí steps outside the time frame of modernism, because its notion of linear progress conspires against Our America, and instead he suggests the "proper time" of an apocalypse. But it is a repeatable apocalypse that signals not so much the "end of history" as a thwarting action against the "universal" history of the West.

In *Nation and Narration*, Homi K. Bhabha describes a "double time" of the nation, in which the people are represented as both pedagogical object ("an *a priori* historical presence") and performative subject ("that continual process by which the national life is redeemed").[7] What makes Martí's narrative different, however, is that it is pan-national, rather than national, and its double time is torn between the present and the future, rather than the past and the present. Furthermore, while Benedict Anderson's analysis of nationalism leads him to ask why nations "celebrate their hoariness, not their astonishing youth,"[8] Martí celebrates the newness of Our America when compared to the hoariness of the United States and France: "Never in history have such advanced and united nations been forged in so short a time from such [disparate] elements." This sense of a social formation rooted in violence-become-hybridity often divides the pedagogical objects of Latin American national identities between the archaeological and the propositional, the residual and the emergent, the past and the future.

Martí, then, initiates a future-tense performative discourse for Latin American politics, one that asserts the power of the idea over the object, because, in fact, the object-as-referent does not yet exist, nor will it come into existence without the expression of the idea. Besides, as Martí knew all too well, the object is evanescent in a way that the idea is not: "Barricades of ideas are worth more than barricades of stone."

Performing an Ineffable History

In contemporary U.S. Latino political discourse and artistic expression, one can see many of the same features found in the writings of José Martí: the search for indigenous, or autochthonous, knowledges, articulated by an intelligentsia using the very language of "the West" itself (as a *part* of "the West"), and played out against the ubiquitous power of the United States. In these contradictions, U.S. Latino narratives perform a "national" identity in which the stable categories of Western thought are fractured and reset into creative functional mixtures. The resultant rhetorical gestures, hybrid forms, and ephemeral objects speak to a future that will bridge the rupture between the past and present: pre-Conquest and postcolonial. The present, then, becomes the site of performance where two ineffable histories (one residual, the other emergent) are installed, producing a provisional context or space within which to imagine Latino communities and cultures.

It is for these reasons that Latino artists often engage in strategies of collective memory, archaeology, and cultural reclamation. In this respect, Latino art represents a collective process that permeates the borders of institutional space, not to achieve some naive "postmodern" dissolution of traditional categories, but to continue Martí's project to "remap" America.[9] But this process is easily misconstrued as the discrete appearance of the "political" and "folk" within the art museum; or, in terms of institutional motivation, dismissed as an appeal to demographic shifts and as a concession to political pressures. Rather than engage the work itself, critics write about the contextual factors that make close visual analysis unnecessary—that make "Latino" and "art" irreducible terms. Thus, if Latino art remaps America, it does so precisely within this contested terrain wherein funding sources, public exhibitions, art collection, and critical discourse determine the proper name for art.

I am especially interested in Latino art that works within an ephemeral or evanescent format, an "installation," insofar as the histories and practices that are given "voice" do not at the same time acquire the usual "object" or commodity status within the museum/art market. Given its placement within the "white cube" of the museum or gallery, certain questions arise about the historical parameters for installation art. For all the sound and fury over its political content and market ramifications, installation art has yet to become the focus of sustained critical or historical analysis.[10] Its precursors tend to be found in the theatrical aspects of pop art, especially the "happenings" of the 1960s, so that installation art becomes identified as a "new genre" (sometimes of the 1970s, sometimes of the 1980s) grounded in the divide between modernism and postmodernism in the arts. Such a history—which is more often implied than stated—is little more than the history of the museum or gallery itself, in which the history of a form begins (and ends) with its arrival in an art space. If, for example, the authors of *Installation Art* argue that "installation, as a hybrid activity, is made up of multiple histories" defined by the modernist "impulse to establish some equivalence" between aesthetic and social spaces,[11] *their* history nonetheless remains contained within a discourse of art for art history's sake.

To be fair, installation presents itself, somewhat disingenuously, as an art form that exists in opposition to museum practices and the art market: it is "unsalable," labor-intensive, and short-term. Moreover, installations can be quite critical of their location. Documentation becomes their displaced product; the installations themselves are dismantled and either recycled in some other form or thrown away. What is central, then, is the experience of the installation within a specific time and place. Documentation becomes the poor—if at times expensive—substitute for the residue of revelation within the body of the viewer. Of course, site-specific installations have been bought and sold, not to mention traveled to other sites, so we are left with an apparent contradiction.

But if we follow a genealogy of forms across multiple spaces, another history emerges, one in which, for Latinos at least, the art installation owes as much to the baroque and its synthesis with the indigenous practices and rituals of Our America as it does to the avant-garde and postmodern. Thus, in following an installation practice such as the Latino altar as it traverses the church, home, community *centro,* museum, and public sphere, one goes beyond the provincial history of aesthetic influences, charting instead the production of social space around sacrificial elements of Latino expressive culture. Such an approach reveals not just hybrid formations geared toward shifting notions of cultural affirmation, maintenance, and resistance,[12] but the fundamental role of gender within cultural politics. The home altar becomes an access point for a female discourse that initiates a movement from one institutional space (church) to another (museum), but makes these part of a trajectory through the intimate space (home) and public space (centro cultural) of a lived community. All of this is quite different from suggesting that the Latino home altar is postmodern avant la lettre because it collapses traditional categories: New and Old World belief systems, the sacred and the profane, high art and popular culture, patriarchal and matriarchal, America and América. Rather, in being more attentive to space, one can see how Latino artists participate in the circulation and transformation of cultural traditions and collective practices, from the archaeological to the contemporary, within the contexts of home, community, and museum.[13]

In her work as a curator, writer, and artist, Amalia Mesa-Bains exemplifies the history and process by which the Latino home altar (as a form of what she calls "intimate space") extended its reach into the Latino community as well as the art museum. As a curator and writer, Mesa-Bains has played a central role in defining Chicano and Latino art in terms of vernacular forms.[14] In the traveling exhibition Ceremony of Memory (1989–91), for example, she proposes a Latino genre based on the secular transformations of ceremonial or spiritual art forms found in the everyday life of Hispanic communities.[15] Concurrent with the cultural politics of their curatorial premise, Mesa-Bains's exhibitions also represent a significant entry point into the art museum for Latino artists.[16]

Mesa-Bains's own career as an artist begins with home altars produced for Chicano art spaces and university museums. Although Mesa-Bains apprenticed under traditional altar-maker Yolanda Garfias-Woo in 1975, she relocates the altar from private to public setting, from domestic worship to secular exhibition, while retaining the altar's ritual function as a female auxiliary to the patriarchal institution of the Catholic church.[17] Mesa-Bains's altars often celebrate Mexican and Chicana women who have acquired iconic status within the national imaginary (whether of Mexico or of the United States), albeit at the expense of their gender, sexuality, or ethnicity: Frida Kahlo (1977, 1978, 1987), Sor Juana Inés de la Cruz (1981), and Dolores del Rio (1983, 1987, 1989–90, 1990–93). By expressing difference through national icons, the altars become what Jennifer González calls a "museum of the self" that is at once personal and social, private and public, self-representation and cultural commentary.[18]

In the 1990s, Mesa-Bain's work became increasingly site-specific; often situated within entire rooms, and composed of interactive pieces. In addition, the "altar" shifted from being the predominant form to being a functional element within a broader attempt to bring Euro-American and Our American cultures, histories, and aesthetics into direct relationship. Her first installation to mark this shift, "Emblems of the Decade: Numbers and Borders" (1990), borrowed its format from the seventeenth-century Mexican emblem—with its interplay between *inscriptio* (title), *subscriptio* (message), and *pintura* (visual image). Mesa-Bains juxtaposed two sites within her installation: "Numbers," which presented statistical data on Latinos; and "Borders," a domestic tableau complete with altar, relics, and mementos. In doing so, she commented on the Decade of the Hispanic in which social equity was argued for and against on the basis of numbers: voter registration, disposable income, immigration rates, and health statistics. In introducing the Latino home under the sign of "Borders," Mesa-Bains produces the liminal referent that remains abstracted from these policy debates.[19] But she does so in a radically different way than in her altar installations. Whereas her altars migrated from home to museum, keeping these spaces noncontiguous while the work itself bore the weight of two irreducible contexts, Mesa-Bains's new work created a layered space within the installation itself. In "Emblems of the Decade," for example, she situates the altar within a domestic tableau and sets this "ethnographic" display against a "scientific" one. What allows her to bring these two nonart forms into relationship with each other and into the *art* museum is the larger aesthetic context of the installation. The final irony, however, is that Mesa-Bains defines her installation by way of a premodern art form, the didactic emblem, returning her once again to the auxiliary religious domain of the home altar and of the origins of the art museum itself.

In contrast to Mesa-Bains, María Brito takes a more personal approach that eschews overtly political or "ethnic" references, but neither does it deny these registers.[20] Instead, the personal dimension, represented almost as a "return of the repressed," becomes the starting point toward social interpretations. Like Mesa-Bains, Brito works with domestic space, although in a more fragmentary way that seeks less to re-present the home and domestic practices than it does to invert and expose its symbol-laden rooms and objects. In "El Patio de Mi Casa" (1991), the patio—that part of the home that is open to and faces the public—is an unusually short bed with high headboards that straddles what appears to be two tectonic plates mapped onto the floor. In the center of the bed is a box out of which a bare, treelike spire emerges. These troubling fragments of domestic space are at once metonymic of the home and family, and metaphoric of other spatial contexts: the unconscious, the community, the nation, and—as suggested by the map—the lasting legacy of the conquest of the Americas. Brito reveals that what is the most private thing about *her* home is also its most public, making the woman's body, sense of self, and state-sanctioned sexuality into a complex metaphor that straddles both private-public spheres and nations.[21]

In contrast to these "domestic" installations, I would like to end by briefly considering and comparing the work of two artists who play with language and situation: Daniel J. Martinez and Celia Alvarez Muñoz.[22] Martinez draws on situationist, Constructivist, and Fluxus concepts about art and social intervention.[23] His work tends to be confrontational and is designed to generate a visceral response and media discourse. As such, Martinez uses the idiom and icons of popular culture itself. Whereas Martinez deconstructs the dominant language, Muñoz works within the space between cultures and languages. Rather than elicit an open confrontation, Muñoz prefers the *indirecta* (innuendo), bilingual pun, and structured absence, modes of address that Muñoz uses to work on the viewer from behind a sentimental and nostalgic facade.[24] Muñoz's image-text installations also reference commercial photography and graphic arts—where, as with Andy Warhol, she began her career. It is in this juxtaposition of two languages and one image that Muñoz's work comments on what Bryan Wolf calls a twofold path—"the disappearance of the body and the rise of mass culture"—as part of her agenda "to render visible the processes of cultural invisibility."[25]

Despite their differences of generation, gender, and language usage, Martinez and Muñoz frame their address to the same museum audience. In a telling exception to Grant Kester's insightful indictment of the alternative arts sector, their work does not conjure up an "implied viewer" whose absence further confirms the beliefs of the actual ("politically correct") viewer.[26] Indeed, more often than not, the Latino artist is acutely aware of the audience and exhibition contexts that frame the very possibilities for his or her art. When, for example, Martinez used the museum tags to proclaim "I Can't Imagine Ever Wanting to Be White" at the 1993 Whitney Biennial, there could be no implied audience: everyone was implicated. The text itself was fragmented across five color-coded tags:

(1) "I CAN'T"
(2) "IMAGINE"
(3) "EVER WANTING"
(4) "TO BE"
(5) "WHITE."

On a sixth tag, the entire sentence appeared. Each audience member was given one of the tags at random, so that the phrase had to be reconstructed through social interaction with other audience members.

In order to show what is at stake in such a direct and interactive address, I will consider Martinez's performative installation in more detail. First, in typical fashion, Martinez's title for the piece drew on "dominant" rather than "minority" discourses: "Museum Tags: Second Movement (Overture) or Overture con Claque—Overture with Hired Audience Members." This time, however, rather than parody the mass culture of popular television advertisements, Martinez parodied the elite culture of the opera house or symphony hall. This shift worked not just in terms of the Whitney Museum's status as elite institution, but also in terms of its main ritual, the three openings that precede the actual exhibition. These openings are by "invitation only," and are limited, for the most part, to the cultural elite and art critics who sustain the art world. As an "overture"—or an instrumental introduction to an extended musical work—Martinez's museum tags made the opening audience itself into the players or instruments, drawing attention to their role in establishing the critical and commercial framework for the exhibition.

But, in confronting the cultural politics of an exhibition that was dubbed the "Multicultural Biennial," Martinez also puns on the word *overture*, which can also mean a first offer or proposal, providing a critical allusion to the lauded political "openings" taking place in other countries, from *apertura* to *perestroika*. In his use of the word *overture*, Martinez draws attention to the fact that "openings" are first offered or proposed by the system that has kept various freedoms closed. In effect, Martinez questions whether the underlying assumptions about cultural capital and racial difference have changed; that is, whether the aesthetic overture is congruent with the social one.

Despite his explanatory title, Martinez's work was read at face value as an instance of a reactive otherness. How, then, are we to read Martinez's tags? To be blunt, one could argue that Daniel Martinez is white. But to do so throws the whole black-white dualism that underpins racial politics in the United States into question. Such an approach makes Martinez's work that much more complex, because when one looks at the criticism of the Whitney Biennial, *everyone* assumes that Martinez is *not* white. Thus, Martinez plays it both ways, asserting himself as white and nonwhite in the same statement. In a reductive fashion, one could swing back and forth between these two positions:

1. Martinez is of Mexican descent, so he is not white.
2. He is light-skinned and does not speak Spanish, so he is white.
3. He is an artist who is politically committed to the goals of the Chicano movement, so he is not white.
4. He is as "American" as anyone who was raised by the television-cum-babysitter, so he is white.

In the end, he exposes "whiteness" as a cultural construct, one that is inadequate to mapping the social coordinates of identity, politics, and culture. But it is not just that critics missed the point, or failed to get the joke; it is that there is not a language for talking about Latino (and other racial minority) artists outside of a discourse of otherness. After all, most curators operate under this assumption, whether in the naive belief in the power of a simple reversal of terms (the glib postcolonial aphorism that the margin is now the center), or in the calculated use of "minorities" within national cultural politics.

But, in either case, critics should read the formal clues, something that did not happen very much in the criticism of the exhibition. As a "performance," the museum tag fragmented the statement, and transformed museum attendance into a random semiotic chain in which each word (or person) acquired meaning through its relationship to other words (or people). The first thing that should have been noticed is that the phrase "I CAN'T" reads two ways: (1) as the declaration of a will to resist ("I REFUSE"), and (2) as the internalization of a societal prohibition ("I AM NOT ALLOWED"). There is no single position for Martinez to occupy.

Un americano / Un-American

What are the possibilities, then, for the exhibition and critical evaluation of works that engage such multiple references and spaces? To date, Chicano, Puerto Rican, Cuban-American, and other Latino works of art are not considered part of "American" art or of the U.S. national culture. The major "American" museums and galleries have resisted the necessary shift toward a curatorial agenda that embraces the diverse cultural practices within the United States.[27] Consequently, Latino artists are excluded from "American" exhibitions, or included at the "affirmative" level, without a significant reorientation of central concepts and aesthetic criteria. Given that dynamic, a more troubling trend has been the brokering of Latino artists into U.S. museums by way of exhibitions of Latin American art. What could otherwise be a provocative exploration of pan-national aesthetics, of Our America, becomes another form of the denial of citizenship.

Latino artists today face the same dilemma Martí did a century earlier: the need to imagine an inclusive context—Our America—in contradistinction to America (the United States). Unlike the exile Martí, however, Latinos-cum-citizens cannot claim to be within the "monster" without also being one of its constituent parts; that is, although the pan-national point of identification may be the same (Our America), the national context is its antithesis (America). After all, Latinos *are* U.S. citizens. Framed in this way, the constitution of a differential Latino identity becomes contingent on the simultaneous achievement of universal access and rights within a national context. Laclau sees this contingency as a paradox in which "the price to be paid for total victory *within that context* is total integration within it."[28] But Laclau's formulation, like the assimilation paradigm, assumes an ahistorical and inflexible context unmarked by difference. Clearly, the failure of that national context to assimilate racial minorities suggests that total integration cannot occur without also changing the context, especially insofar as that "context" depends on the exclusion of racial minorities.

Latino cultural expressions have been for the most part constituted as the other side of what passes for the "critical distance" of modern or postmodern belonging. Latino artists are seen as too "sincere"; and, as such, there is assumed to be no mediation or attention to the signifier in their cultural expressions. But sincerity is no simple matter, because, like irony, it is asserted in the face of multiple contexts; as such, both are hybrid discourses. Tellingly, Martí's last book of poetry, *Versos Sencillos* (*Simple Verses,* 1891), written at the same time as "Our America," begins with the famous line, "Yo soy un hombre sincero" (I am a sincere man). But the simplicity and sincerity of these poems is misleading if taken at face value. Thus, when Martí, el hombre sincero, proclaims "Our America," irony becomes a matter of faith—as Tomás Ybarra-Frausto has noted about Latino art—rather than a calculated, distanced, intellectual pose.[29] More quixotic than Brechtian, Martí engages in a future-tense performative discourse, in which a pan-national "American" identity and its context are sincerely proposed against an ironic awareness of present-day realities. There are, then, two sets of contexts—the present and the future; the national and the pan-national—and a differential identity constitutes itself as the negotiation between these two sets of points.

Two observations need to be stressed about such a differential identity. First, Latino art *is* a cultural, political, aesthetic, and market phenomenon. For better or worse, it does exist. But, given the different registers within which it is produced, exhibited, spoken about, and acquired, Latino art cannot add up to one thing or remain entirely distinct from other aesthetic categories. Making matters more difficult, neither exhibition history nor scholarship provides the basis for understanding "Latino" art as an aesthetics-in-process that has critical mass, intertextual associations, internal complexity, and, above all, considerable range that overlaps with other types of art. Therefore, rather than start with the premise of cultural or racial otherness (that is, posit Latino art as a genre equivalent to its exclusion), I want to propose that we sometimes start with general questions about an *art* genre, where the consequent analysis will not be so bound by ethnicity, but neither will it deny cultural and social determinants. In a survey of Latino installation artists, for example, one cannot help but be struck by the complex and contradictory nature of the work, whether charted within an individual career or across categories of aesthetics, ethnicity, and national origin. In fact, in this instance, it may not make sense to foreground ethnicity as much as genre, although such subtleties are lost on many in the art world, where Chicanos, Puerto Ricans, Cubans, and other Latinos—despite their cultural differences from each other and aesthetic similarities with installation artists more generally—share a history of being excluded that is as persistent as it is unspoken.

Second, Latino-identified artists break the rules of two cultures, two traditions, without at the same time blurring the boundaries between them. Instead, their iconic overlays and hybrid forms are always made with an eye toward the unequal power relations that exist between and within cultures. In this sense, their art reveals the need, not for an essential truth, an underlying coherence, but rather to sustain contradictory images, shapes, languages, and frames of reference—all within the evanescent moment of the installation. The paradox of my essay, of course, is that I have been making declarative and definitive statements about what Latino artists do—all the while insisting that what they do is *undo* declarative and definitive statements in order to remap social space by performing hybridity. As such, everything I have written is misplaced.

Notes

An earlier version of this essay appears in the exhibition catalog *Revelaciones/Revelations: Hispanic Art of Evanascence* (Ithaca, N.Y.: Hispanic American Studies Program, Cornell University, 1993).

1. José Martí, "Our America," *Our America: Writings on Latin America and the Struggle for Cuban Independence,* trans. Elinor Randall, ed. Philip Foner (New York: Monthly Review Press, 1977), 84. Unless otherwise noted, subsequent quotations of Martí are from this essay.

2. As Benedict Anderson argues, "communities are to be distinguished, not by

their falsity/genuineness, but by the style in which they are imagined" (*Imagined Communities: Reflections on the Origin and Spread of Nationalism*, rev. ed. [London: Verso, 1991], 6). I discuss this in relation to contemporary Latino political discourse in "El hilo latino: Representation, Identity, and National Culture," *Jump Cut* 38 (June 1993): 45–50.

3. Letter to Manuel Mercado, May 18, 1895, in José Martí, *Obras Completas*, vol. 4 (Havana: Editorial Nacional de Cuba, 1963), 168; my translation.

4. Ernesto Laclau, "Universalism, Particularism, and the Question of Identity," *October* 61 (summer 1992): 85. Reprinted in *Emancipation(s)* (London: Verso, 1996), 20–35.

5. Ibid., 86.

6. Ibid., 90.

7. Homi K. Bhabha, "DissemiNation: Time, Narrative, and the Margins of the Modern Nation," *Nation and Narration*, ed. Homi K. Bhabha (London: Routledge, 1990), 291–322.

8. Quoted in ibid., 293.

9. On the remapping of "America" as part of a Latino social movement, see Juan Flores and George Yúdice, "Living Borders/Buscando América: Languages of Latino Self-Formation," *Social Text* 24 (1990): 57–84.

10. For the first book-length study, see Nicolas de Oliveira, Nicola Oxley, and Michael Petry, *Installation Art* (Washington, D.C.: Smithsonian Institution Press, 1994).

11. Ibid., 7, 11.

12. See Shifra M. Goldman and Tomás Ybarra-Frausto, *Arte Chicano: A Comprehensive Annotated Bibliography of Chicano Art, 1965–1981* (Berkeley: Chicano Studies Publication Unit/University of California, 1985), 3–55.

13. In the early 1990s, culminating in the 1993 Whitney Biennial, installation-based exhibitions became the target of popular criticism based on their reputed "PC" identity politics. There was more at stake, however, insofar as these installations openly called into question the relationship of the art museum to all those spaces it stands against: laboratory, ethnographic display, fun house, peep show, movie theater, video store, public library, and the home.

14. See, for example, Amalia Mesa-Bains's essays "Contemporary Chicano and Latino Art," *Visions* (fall 1989): 14–19, and "El Mundo Femenino: Chicana Artists of the Movement—A Commentary on Development and Production," in Richard Griswold del Castillo, Teresa McKenna, and Yvonne Yarbro-Bejarano, eds., *Chicano Art: Resistance and Affirmation, 1965–1985* (Los Angeles: UCLA Wight Art Gallery, 1991), 131–40.

15. See Amalia Mesa-Bains, *Ceremony of Memory: New Expressions in Spirituality among Contemporary Hispanic Artists* (Santa Fe, N. Mex.: Center for Contemporary Arts of Santa Fe, 1988).

16. For other exhibitions curated by Mesa-Bains, see her *Ceremony of Spirit: Nature and Memory in Contemporary Latino Art* (San Francisco: The Mexican Museum, 1993); and René H. Arceo-Frutos, Juana Guzmán, and Amalia Mesa-Bains, *Art of the Other Mexico: Sources and Meanings* (Chicago: Mexican Fine Arts Center Museum, 1993).

17. See Kay F. Turner, "Mexican American Women's Home Altars: The Art of Relationship," Ph.D. diss., University of Texas at Austin, 1990.

18. Jennifer A. González, "Rhetoric of the Object: Material Memory and the Artwork of Amalia Mesa-Bains," *Visual Anthropology Review* 9.1 (spring 1993): 82–91.

19. See Julia P. Herzberg, "Re-Membering Identity: Visions of Connections," in *The Decade Show: Framework of Identity in the 1980s* (New York: Museum of Contemporary Hispanic Art, New Museum of Contemporary Art, and the Studio Museum in Harlem), 54–56.

20. For a sense of the complexity of such a position, see the group interview of Cuban-American artists by Jenni Lukac in *Art Papers* 17.1 (January–February 1993): 17–19.

21. If, in her earlier work, Brito inverted and exposed domestic spaces, in "Merely a Player" (1993), she created her first enclosed installation, turning the home into an autobiographical labyrinth. See the exhibition catalog, *Revelaciones/Revelations: Hispanic Art of Evanescence* (Ithaca, N.Y.: Hispanic American Studies Program, Cornell University, 1993), and the documentary of the same title (available through the Cinema Guild). For earlier critical work on Brito, see Ricardo Pau-Llosa, "The Dreamt Objectivities of María Brito-Avellana," *Dreamworks* 5.2 (1986–87): 98–104; and Lynette M. F. Bosch, "A Renaissance Art Historian Looks at Cuban American Art," unpublished manuscript, 1993.

22. Interestingly, whereas Mesa-Bains and Brito appeared in the alternative exhibition *The Decade Show,* Muñoz and Martinez were among the first Chicanos, or Latinos, included in a Whitney Biennial (1991 and 1993, respectively).

23. For an overview, see Martinez's artist book *The Things You See When You Don't Have a Grenade!* (Santa Monica: Smart Art Press, 1996), which includes essays by Coco Fusco, Mary Jane Jacobs, Susan Otto, and others.

24. Karin Lipson, "Making It to the Show," *New York Newsday,* April 19, 1991, 66–67; Anita Creamer, "An Artist of Two Worlds: Contradiction Is Inspiration for Celia Muñoz," *Dallas Life Magazine,* January 22, 1989, 8–12, 18–19.

25. Bryan Wolf, "The Responsibility to Dream," *Profession* 95 (1995): 19, 20–21. Wolf examines Muñoz's mixed-media piece, "Which Came First? Enlightenment Series #4" (1982).

26. Grant Kester, "Rhetorical Questions: The Alternative Arts Sector and the Imaginary Public," *Afterimage* (January 1993): 10–16.

27. For a critical overview of Latino and Latin American exhibitions, see Mari Carmen Ramírez, "Beyond the 'Fantastic': Framing Identity in U.S. Exhibitions of Latin American Art," *Art Journal* (winter 1992): 60–68; reprinted in Gerardo Mosquera, ed., *Beyond the Fantastic: Contemporary Art Criticism from Latin America* (Cambridge: MIT Press, 1996), 229–46.

28. Laclau, "Universalism, Particularism, and the Question of Identity," 88–89.

29. Tomás Ybarra-Frausto, conversation with the author.

Lincoln Highway

Sikivu Hutchinson

It is a city that is driven through, shuttled past in blazing light and shadow, prey to the tongue of the speedometer. Past the slanting tease of the church steeple, past the gazebo, the barber shop, the faded pomp of town hall, the settlement grid of stop-on-a-dime houses, the motel, awaiting fresh blood. It is a fragment of lost languages, an eternal space of reckoning, the quiet incantation in the lullaby of post–New Deal public policy.

It is a body that is driven through, unraced, aware of its own peculiar circuit of time; at once within and without the fiction of the linear, the days that slowly unravel on strip malls and in diners, in pool halls and trailer parks, and the corridors of the American Legion, violently inscrutable.

Reading the text of the Lincoln Highway—the phallogocentric subtext of which is all too apparent in its evocation of the early American interstate driver, intoxicated by speed on the mythic highway—I would like to suggest a tale of desire, embodiment, public works and private enterprise. Throughout this essay I will use transit as a site of historical and critical inquiry, enfolding the figure of black women's journey to the North (in departure from the traditionally masculine figuration of the journey) with that of the ensuing presidential race of 1996; steaming through the iconic citadels of small town Americana, perpetually Main Street bound, in search of the European immigrant's journey to whiteness. "This is America—a town of a few thousand, in a region of wheat and corn and dairies and little groves. The town is, in our tale, called Manchester, New Hampshire. But its Main Street is the continuation of Main Streets everywhere."[1]

Driving, her eyes leaving the road for a moment, she finds that the map of small-town, iconic America, of Main Street USA, unravels before her again and again, in bloodred relief, its body just barely visible. Leaving the kitchens of Jackson, Mississippi, and the tenant farms of Pine Bluff, Arkansas, in trains segregated well past the Mason-Dixon Line, in cars that shuttled past motels whose signs flipped "vacancy" in the neon dead of night, black women workers became a vital part of the "Great Migration," journeying to Northern cities in search of better jobs and more humane living conditions. The Great Migration occurred roughly between 1915 and 1960, when the American city experienced a sea change in transportation development.[2] Spanning the dawn of the auto age, the collapse of the electric railway industry, and the rise of the interstate highway system, the migration era would see the wholesale othering of urban public space. Whereas the centered, streetcar-dependent industrial city was informed by the marriage of modernism, social Darwinism, and the fiction of bootstraps white immigrant mobility, the decentered, migration-era city would build on this legacy of white redemption, riding the highway of New Deal entitlements toward spatial apartheid.

The nineteenth-century industrial city was assailed by urban planners as a breeding ground for moral corruption and sloth. Viewed as a site of crucible for the European immigrant's assimilation of such proverbial American values as individualism, "hard work," and thrift, the city was traditionally counterpoised with the iconic figure of the small town. The advent of the electric railway in the late nineteenth century made the white European immigrant dream of escape from the urban center possible by pushing the boundaries of the central city.[3]

When the first black women migrants reached Chicago and New York, in response to the *Chicago Defender*'s clarion call to join the "northern drive" to the "Promised Land," the figure of the American city still retained its dual identity as bastion of immorality and Enlightenment values.[4] One would be hard-pressed to re-member her movement, its unauthorized language of desire, within the official record of odysseys and family separations. The "crazy willen workin' women" who filled the pages of Northern newspapers with testimonials of the city joined the swollen ranks of "reckless" Negroes who took to the road in the shadow of World War I.[5] In newspaper accounts on going North during the teens and twenties, many writers allude to the paradoxically "American" tenor of the journey.[6] For example, in their landmark study *Black Metropolis*, St. Clair Drake and Horace Cayton link the migration to the masculine odyssey to the western frontier. "When the Negro, responding to the cultural hopes of his time, leaves the South and comes to the cold, industrial North, he is acting upon the same impulses that made them of the West great. The Negro can do no less; he shares all the glorious hopes of the West, all of its anxieties, its corruptions, its psychological maladies."[7]

Often portrayed as the baptismal in the black migrant's quest for the right of democracy, the northern drive was inevitably compared to the European immigrant's journey to America.[8] The fiction of the West, the road, and the "parallel" example of the immigrant resonated within many portrayals of the migration. It was widely believed that the North would allow the black migrant to achieve full rights of citizenship. Despite this optimism, however, the migrant's view was informed by the consciousness that "immigrant populations . . . understood their 'Americanness' as an opposition to the resident black population."[9] This confluence of "racial polarization and immigration" (what critic M. Patricia Fernandez-Kelly has characterized as "the two great American dramas")[10] would redefine the racial frontier of the American city in the dawn of the auto age.

During this period, the second generation of Model T's and A's had only just begun to roll out of production. Because it was still largely a plaything of the wealthy, the automobile was widely dismissed as a flash in the pan by the electric railway and railroad industries.[11] Most interstate travel was done by train, and those who did choose to travel by car were forced to navigate a haphazard network of often treacherously unpaved roads. For most migrants, traveling cross-country through the heart of Main Street USA during the Jim Crow era involved a variety of detours courtesy of the "Green Book," a guide to lodgings open to blacks.

During the teens and early twenties, car owners, petroleum makers, and Main Street merchants organized lobbies called highway associations for improved roads. The highway associations attempted to advance the cause of road building by outlining potential highway routes that would span from coast to coast. In 1913, an association lead by the Packard Motor Car Company devised a plan for a route dubbed the Lincoln Highway, which would run from Jersey City to San Francisco, looping through smaller communities in the Midwest. Lacking the resources to build the highway itself, the association improved a mile of road midway between two towns on the proposed route. Here, "local motorists would struggle through the mud and bumps to the new highway, whiz along at 30 or 40 miles . . . and, once intoxicated by the speed and smoothness of the ride, nearby communities [would] raise the funds to extend Main Street out to the seedling mile."[12]

The highway associations and the seedling mile schemes of the early twentieth century foreshadowed the limitless horizon of the modern interstate. Foreshadowing the voracious drive for space and vast outlays of federal monies that fueled the development of the interstate highway system, the good roads movement of the teens was an extension of the frontier drive, which would eventually anoint the suburb as *spiritual* heir to the legacy of Main Street. Thus, although private enterprise initially propelled the movement for improved roads, the Federal Aid Road Acts of 1916 and 1921 institutionalized the project of road building within the national agenda.[13] As a reinscription of the fantasy of boundlessness *and* finitude symbolized by the frontier society, the Federal Aid Road Acts articulated the narrative of surpassing temporality (that is, the triumph of time over space). It is my contention that this narrative is powerfully reflected in the way that the shift to privatized transit during the 1940s informs the contemporary ontology of immigrant identity, race, and public space in the United States.[14]

The ten Republican candidates have converged here in Manchester in gas-guzzling posses, virgins for the stump, fresh from the haunted assembly lines of Flint and Dearborn, having traced the spectral path of the Grand Old Party on the Lincoln Highway and arrived in consensus to find Main Street awaiting, untouched, save for the unmentioned 30 percent white working class on welfare. Manchester's buildings, its streets, still bear the marks of the railroad companies that molded them with federal land grants in the late 1800s, one town to every station.[15]

At the rubicon of the 1996 presidential race, the demonization of the federal government has finally come full circle from its Civil War–era states' rights heritage. Across the United States, antigovernment tirades, from the terrorist bombing in Oklahoma City and the railroad sabotage in Arizona, to the terrorist attacks of freshman Republican senators (for whom welfare recipients are "wolves" and the Environmental Protection Agency is the "Gestapo of government"), have cast big government as the new Red menace.

Perhaps the most consistently reviled target in this line of rhetoric has been the urban public sphere. In riding the crest of rightward politics and gutting New Deal–era entitlement programs such as AFDC, the Clinton administration fatally undermined the relationship between cities and the federal government. This relationship has been twofold. While massive federal funding for highways and the racist practices of such organizations as the Federal Housing Administration (FHA) contributed to the decline of the "inner city," the implementation of entitlement programs during the 1930s has proven to be the most significant means of providing the urban poor with some degree of protection from the "social stagnation" and "hinterland" bias of state government.[16] As Mark Gelfend explains, "The New Deal marked a new epoch in American urban history," for, "overlooked by the

Constitution and ignored in a century-and-a-half of national legislation," the social-service needs of urban areas were finally recognized as being of national concern.[17]

Thus, in the scheme of the post–New Deal, post–Cold War era, the urban public sphere has become the new site of cathexis for all the hysteria the states' rights lobby can muster. In Los Angeles alone, massive cutbacks in state and federal funding to county health, welfare, and emergency medical services have health officials scrambling to procure funding from such unlikely sources as the bloated and embattled Los Angeles Metropolitan Transit Authority (LAMTA).[18] In 1996, the nation's severely underfunded public housing system was dealt a fatal blow by President Bill Clinton's failure to increase provisions for new housing subsidies in the federal housing appropriations bill.[19]

Such developments are the legacy of a generation in which urban public space has been figured as "other." Although this phenomenon reached its fruition with the Great Migration, the roots of antiurbanism lie in the "problem" of nineteenth-century European immigrant identity.[20] In order to grasp the way urban public space has been figured as other, it is necessary to return to Main Street as icon and ideal, where the "octopus" and the auto age converged in the Anglicization of the European immigrant.[21] Lurking on the map of Americana unfurled on the road to states' rights is the frontier economy of Main Street, a place where "common goals could be reconciled with rugged individualism."[22] As the first centers of trade, commerce, and social life in both the frontier towns of the Midwest and the colonies of the East, Main Street is valorized as icon of a lost ideal of Anglo-American community. In the Midwest, some of the first white settlements on the so-called frontier lands were the direct result of advertisements from railroad companies such as the Illinois Central and the Northern Pacific, which encouraged newly arrived European immigrants in New York and New England to come where "land was cheap, property was constantly increasing in value, and every man had a voice in government."[23]

The telos of progress that informed the immigration of mostly Protestant, Western European settlers to the Midwest in the 1800s is powerfully represented in the figure of Main Street USA. As "shorthand" for American values, Main Street symbolizes the transcendence of time and space that underlies the Anglo-American paradigm of whiteness and American imperial identity. An identity position predicated on the surpassing of racial difference, the beingness of whiteness derives from its ability to *escape* the very category of race. As critic Adolph Reed notes: "'Whiteness' in fact, evolved as a generically meaningful status only gradually over the 19th and early

20th centuries . . . with the incorporation of immigrant populations into an evolving system of social, political, and economic hierarchy. Whiteness became increasingly significant as a kind of safety net, providing a baseline of eligibility to rights, opportunities and minimal social position."[24] Here, the category of whiteness was broadened to include non-Anglo European immigrants, who had traditionally been excluded from some aspects of white privilege by virtue of ethnicity and religion. Whiteness transcended the very category of race itself.[25] The "expansion of whiteness as a generic category" within which formerly stigmatized ethnic groups such as Irish and Polish immigrants were "homogenized as white" attended the push toward the frontier (officially declared "closed" in 1890) of the western "territories," and the pushing of the frontier of the industrial cities of the East.[26] In this respect, the assimilation of the European immigrant into the iconic space of Main Street was a path of transit beyond the nineteenth-century frontier of race and the scourge of city life.

Pushing ever westward, the telos of progress and the ontology of transiting that informed the frontier economy's fury of land speculation, terrorism, and dispossession of Native Americans stands as the iconic narrative and defining metaphor for European immigration. In this sense, Main Street becomes the site of the primal scene of American whiteness, its inaugural site; it signifies the white subject's transcendence of cultural and racial difference, and the surpassing of body that served as the transformation of the non-Anglo European immigrant in the United States.

Within the *urban* narrative of European immigrant communities, this ontology of transiting is compellingly illustrated in the role the subway played in conferring the rights of bourgeois democracy on European immigrants in Lower Manhattan. Before the advent of underground transit, the Lower East Side was hazardously congested and overpopulated, rife with infectious diseases and unlivable housing. Along with areas such as Hell's Kitchen, Greenwich Village, and Yorkville, the Lower East Side was portrayed by progressive reformers of the early twentieth century as a hindrance to immigrant assimilation.[27] As subway historian Clifton Hood observes, "In their view, the Lower East Side, Hell's Kitchen (et al.) . . . amounted to foreign colonies that encouraged newcomers to cling to their native languages, religions and folkways rather than assimilating with American culture."[28] By moving significant numbers of these populations into outlying areas such as Washington Heights and the Bronx, the subway helped to efface the ethnic differences of non-Anglo immigrants, thereby allowing them access to the privileges of bourgeois democracy.

The advent of the New York subway system in 1904 firmly established suburban enclaves that functioned as safe havens "embodying the small town ideal: clean . . . prosperous and conducive to voting, home ownership and acculturation."[29] The formation of these enclaves was a big transition for many European immigrant communities. Their assimilation of mainstream American values was achieved at the behest of New Deal institutions such as the Federal Housing Administration.[30] One of the most significant influences on the landscape of urban and suburban America, the FHA simultaneously facilitated the provision of low-cost mortgages to white suburban homeowners and enforced restrictive covenants preventing black residents from settling in white areas.[31] Such practices became the backbone of residential segregation in the urban North. It is from this legacy that the figure of the inner city was conflated with blackness and the specter of black pathology, such that "the black settlement or 'black ghetto' has been textually and visually represented as being a 'slum' . . . binary oppositions define[s] black settlement space as irrational . . . and immoral and white settlement space as ordered, rational, beautiful, pure and moral."[32]

In the postindustrial era, "the single family residence, private ownership of land, and individualized transportation in preference to public spaces" are all the hallmarks of this immigrant odyssey through Main Street and urban America, the frontiers of white subjectivity.[33] It is this heritage that contemporary Anglo-American political discourse struggles to reassemble in the shadow of the United States' eclipse as the dominant player within the global economy. It is here that urban public space is marked as other, as the ground on which whiteness is the invisible frontier.

Taking to the road, on Capitol Hill, on the floor of the Senate, in the klieg lights that glare over the passing motorcade and the dog and pony show turning into the public square of historic New Hampshire, she wields her itinerary and turns her gaze to that route into the phallic imaginary, the place where the white body disappears, and the body of the city is written as virus and abject: disease and betrayal. It is the question of the body that she poses—after the demise of the horse-drawn carriage and the twenty-year reign of the electric interurban on Main Street, when the hurtling pulse of the first family Packards of 1916 have gained sway and the rhythm of visuality has shifted, making "each tiny motorized . . . vehicle . . . an alternative, not only to the railroad, but to the cinema."[34]

The roadside cinema of billboard merchandising that sprang up in the wake of Main Street is littered with carcasses: phantoms of origin that mark the divide between public and private space, the mythos of the Great Migration as read against the westward expansion of European immigrant towns and the immigrant's "redemption" from the city. Crossing the Mason-Dixon

Line to Chicago, faking the line out, going east to Boston, New York (where black women migrants outnumbered black men), black women answered the wartime demand for female workers, entering "the mainstream of the American labor force" as metalworkers, upholsterers, clerks and bookkeepers, social workers, and dentists.[35] In the city, Harlem journalist Elise McDougal observed, black women were "free[d] from the cruder handicaps of primitive household hardships and the grosser forms of sex and race subjugation."[36] In the city, having shifted from the economy of Jim Crow to that of de facto segregation, black women would stand once again at the forefront of the wartime female labor force, working for much lower pay at jobs that had been vacated by European immigrant women.

This historic redefinition of the American workforce would profoundly alter the shape of the United States' teleology of progress, disrupting the rigid boundaries that separated the public sphere from the domestic. It would temporarily throw the circumscription of white femininity into relief, while highlighting the intersection of race, gender, and class oppression that had informed the structure of black women's work since slavery.

The experiences of black women workers in the North reinforced the historical inscription of black femininity under slavery as hybrid space, between public and private, double to the ideal of private domestic space that white femininity signifies within Western discourse. As Paula Giddings notes in her history of black women, "The satisfaction Black women received working in the mainstream of labor was tempered by their having to perform the dirtiest and most difficult tasks. The historical stereotypes assigned to Black women were largely responsible for this."[37]

Thus, this question of the body, posed in the disjunctive time of the urban city, suggests the familiar odor of the othering of black women from the very category of the female. Again, black women are othered, as workers, as breeders within the slave economy that aided the rise of the frontier towns that round out the protectionist rants of Patrick Buchanan and the anti-immigrant creed of the downsized American worker.

Main Street lies here, the lack at the heart of origin, mise-en-scène of the white family, as that path between the stations that the railroad company laid, where she disembarks, her hand on the steering wheel.

Notes

1. Sinclair Lewis, *Main Street* (New York: Harcourt, Brace and Howe, 1920).

2. The term "Great Migration" has been used by some historians to refer to the mass black migration that occurred during the World War I period of 1915 to 1921, while others have used the term in a broader sense to refer to migrations from World War I

to the postwar era. For further elaboration see Malaika Adero, ed., *Up South: Stories, Studies and Letters Of This Century's Black Migrations* (New York: New Press, 1993); Nicholas Lemann, *The Promised Land* (New York: Alfred A. Knopf, 1991).

3. For further discussion, see Mark Foster, *From Streetcar to Superhighway: American City Planners and Urban Transportation, 1900–1940* (Philadelphia: Temple University Press, 1981).

4. Adero, *Up South,* xii; John Jeffries, "Toward a Redefinition of the Urban," in *Black Popular Culture,* ed. Gina Dent (Seattle: Bay Press, 1992), 157–58.

5. Paula Giddings, *When and Where I Enter: The Impact of Black Women on Race and Sex in America* (New York: Bantam Books, 1984), 140–42; Adero, *Up South,* 77, 88.

6. Adero, *Up South,* 50.

7. St. Clair Drake and Horace Cayton, *Black Metropolis: A Study of Negro Life in a Northern City* (New York: Harper and Row, 1945), xxv.

8. See Adero, *Up South.*

9. Toni Morrison, *Playing in the Dark: Whiteness and the Literary Imagination* (Cambridge: Harvard University Press, 1992), 47.

10. M. Patricia Fernandez-Kelly, "Migration, Race and Ethnicity in the Design of the American City," in *Urban Revisions: Current Projects for the Public Realm,* ed. Russell Ferguson (Cambridge: MIT Press, 1994), 22.

11. For further discussion on the assumptions of the railroad and railway industries vis-à-vis the automobile, see Foster, *From Streetcar to Superhighway.*

12. Chester Liebs, *From Main Street to Miracle Mile: American Roadside Architecture* (Boston: Little, Brown, 1985), 18.

13. Ibid., 19.

14. I use the word *ontology* with respect to the metaphysics of presence that undergirds the dyadic relationship between blackness and whiteness in the formation of white identity.

15. Lewis Atherton, *Main Street on the Middle Border* (Bloomington: Indiana University Press, 1958), 5.

16. Mark I. Gelfend, *A Nation of Cities: The Federal Government and Urban America, 1933–1965* (New York: Oxford University Press, 1975), 66.

17. Ibid., 65.

18. The LAMTA has been charged by city officials and community transit advocates with misuse of funds. In 1996, it became the subject of a U.S. Senate subcommittee investigation into its handling of a controversial fixed-rail project.

19. Jason DeParle, "Slamming the Door," *New York Times Magazine,* October 20, 1996.

20. For an excellent discussion on the trajectory of antiurbanism, see Thomas Angotti, *Metropolis 2000: Planning, Poverty and Politics* (London: Routledge, 1993).

21. During the nineteenth-century, the railroad monopoly was branded the "octopus" by progressive reformers in protest over its corrupt sway over the U.S. economy.

22. Sam Roberts, "Yes, a Small Town Is Different," *New York Times,* August 30, 1995.

23. Atherton, *Main Street on the Middle Border,* 5.

24. Adolph Reed, "The Fiction of Race," *Village Voice,* September 24, 1996, 22.

25. See Morrison, *Playing in the Dark.*

26. Reed, "The Fiction of Race," 22.

27. Clifton Hood, *722 Miles: The Building of the New York Subways and How They Transformed New York* (New York: Simon and Schuster, 1993), 127.

28. Ibid.

29. Ibid., 128.

30. Reed, "The Fiction of Race," 22; Fernandez-Kelly, "Migration, Race and Ethnicity in the Design of the American City," 16–25; Richard B. Sherman, *The Negro in the City* (Englewood Cliffs, N.J.: Prentice Hall, 1970), 29–30.

31. Fernandez-Kelly, "Migration, Race and Ethnicity in the Design of the American City."

32. Stephen Nathan Haymes, *Race, Culture, and the City: A Pedagogy for Black Urban Struggle* (Albany: State University of New York Press), 72.

33. Jere Stuart French, *Urban Space: A Brief History of the City Square* (Iowa City: Kendall Hunt Publishing, 1978), 98.

34. Liebs, *From Main Street to Miracle Mile,* 4.

35. Giddings, *When and Where I Enter,* 143.

36. Quoted in ibid.

37. Ibid., 144.

Hybrid Genres, Performed Subjectivities: The Revoicing of Public Oratory in the Moroccan Marketplace

Deborah A. Kapchan

Imagine someone . . . who abolishes within himself all barriers, all classes, all exclusions, not by syncretism but by simple discard of that old specter: logical contradiction; *who mixes every language, even those said to be incompatible; who silently accepts every charge of illogicity, of incongruity; who remains passive in the face of Socratic irony (leading the interlocutor to the supreme disgrace:* self-contradiction*) and legal terrorism (how much penal evidence is based on a psychology of consistency!). Such a man would be the mockery of our society: court, asylum, polite conversation would cast him out: who endures contradiction without shame? Now this anti-hero exists; . . . the confusion of tongues is no longer a punishment, the subject gains access to bliss by the cohabitation of languages working side by side:* the text of pleasure is a sanctioned Babel.
— Roland Barthes, The Pleasure of the Text

It would seem necessary to invent a new, historically reflexive, way of using categories, such as those of genre.
— Fredric Jameson, The Political Unconscious: Narrative as a Socially Symbolic Art

Unlike their counterparts in West Africa and South America, female vendors and orators do not have a long history in the Moroccan marketplace. Clifford Geertz asserted that "overall, the bazaar is an emphatically male realm, and so far as Sefrou is concerned there is not a single woman of any real importance in either the trade or the artisan worlds" (1979, 240). When Jean-François Troin noted the increasing participation of women in the markets of the Jbala region of northern Morocco in 1975, he referred to women's gradual "whittling" at "certain sectors of the commercial sector, usually reserved for men" (1975, 64). Although these analyses do not represent the whole of market practices in Morocco, it is clear that the division of labor in the open-air marketplace has changed considerably since the 1980s. Not

only are women sellers of contraband—a recent category of vendor in my research site of Beni Mellal—but they are becoming orators in the *halqa,* the
performance area of the market; this role is historically unprecedented in all
of the markets that I have researched.

By examining the relations of intertextuality in women's performance of
marketplace oratory in Beni Mellal, Morocco, one can better understand the
changes they are effecting in both the poetic and the public spheres. In this
essay, I will argue that women have a highly ambiguous, deliberately polysemic relationship to this performative genre—a relationship that is ultimately hybrid in nature. The strategic revoicings of this primarily male speech
genre are carving out new positions for women in the marketplace writ large.

The subject of genre is receiving renewed attention from literary scholars
and anthropologists alike.[1] Feminists have compared generic convention to
Jacques Lacan's "law of the father"—a pervasive and ultimately hegemonic
structure that must be challenged by a return of the repressed (Benstock
1991; Irigaray 1991). Social critics following in Bakhtin's wake view genre
as a particular worldview, one in which alternate realities and rules may be
constructed to challenge and sometimes overturn the classical, the high, the
status quo (Bakhtin 1981, 1986; cf. Briggs 1992; Hanks 1987). What seems
certain is that while some are proclaiming the death of genre, or at least its
transfiguration beyond identifiable bounds, others—particularly subaltern
groups such as lesbians and other minorities—are creating genres (some
quite conventional) in a project of "strategic essentialism" (Spivak 1993) that
carves out a recognizable identity in the public sphere.

Despite a plethora of new and hybrid genres, or perhaps because of this
proliferation, questions concerning the limits of genre continue to be of
concern. Although it is accepted wisdom that postmodernism is characterized by mixed and blended forms that efface and perpetually redefine
boundaries, the blurring of genres that Geertz referred to in 1983 has not
been sufficiently theorized. What are the implications for such a radical
destabilization of categories? And why resurrect the category of genre?

Discourses about genres are discourses about boundaries—interpretive,
stylistic, and pragmatic.[2] As Fredric Jameson notes, genres are institutions,
social contracts imbued with ideology. Our use of genre is thus a political, if
not always conscious, choice. This is because all generic expression bears an
indexical relation to "prior discourse" (Bakhtin 1981, 342). Genres contain
the sediment of the past (Jameson 1981, 140–41); they are built on the
words of others. Whether a speaker establishes connection with that past,
thereby upholding "tradition" and its inherent authority, or whether she
changes the indexical relations of words, space, and performer to construct

difference, has important consequences for social change (Briggs and Bauman 1992). In the latter case, such generic reorientations, or "revoicings," leave their impress on the larger social imaginary (Kapchan 1996). The extent to which expressive hybridizations effect social transformation depends on the density of their performativity—that is, on the degree to which they are appropriated into a public culture as icons of difference and change.[3]

Performed genres are particularly significant in creating new and hybrid identities, as actors use them to maintain, reinforce, or revise the social imagination according to their interests. As a discursive field where the traditional past meets the contemporary invention of tradition, genre is a crossroads—of time and space, of convention and creativity, encoding history and determining the future. This is particularly true of speech genres, which, despite their ephemerality, maintain a deep rootedness to their context of enunciation. Insofar as genres are hybridized, then, so are worlds and worldviews—and this largely through the media of performance (performed mediation). What do these inherently ambiguous and self-reflexive forms accomplish? And how are they generated?

The genre of women's public oratory in the Moroccan marketplace provides an example of how a speech genre can be appropriated and hybridized—with the result that historically dominant conceptions of "public" and "private," "male" and "female" are put into question. In articulating a verbal genre historically practiced by men, Moroccan women orators challenge the moral and political canon that associates feminine performance with the private realm *(ad-dakhel)*. Although the establishment of feminine authority in the public realm requires alignment with dominant discourses, the feminine revoicing of public oratory also inscribes a feminine presence into a formerly male domain, thereby expanding discursive space (Fraser 1992, 124). This expansion is mediated by both the genre of marketplace oratory *(al-hadra dyal suq)* and the marketplace itself. Not only does this analysis diverge from the traditional mapping of gender and genre in the Middle East and North Africa, but it locates verbal art in a context of hetereogeneity wherein discourses of religion, morality, and kinship vie with those of self-interest, capitalism, and commodification.[4] Although women's emergence into the discursive domain of the market requires their complicity to the laws of genre, it is their expressive hybridization that ultimately transforms the larger public sphere.

A Carnival of Voices

The speech genre that might be referrred to as either oratory, artful selling, spiel making, or doomsaying in Euro-American analyses is not delineated in

Moroccan terminology except under the heading of *al-hadra,* "talk."
Al-hadra in the context of the marketplace is a form of discourse that embodies many speech genres, much as a novel embodies several literary genres
(Bakhtin 1986, 61–62). What is more, marketplace oratory is characterized
by its relation to the carnivalesque—not only in the limited definition of
this term (namely, the combining of high and low categories and their inversion), but also in the idea that neither a genre nor a subject can be circumscribed or fixed, that both are always in a state of "unfinalized transition"
(ibid., 164). That women are gaining artistic prominence in this public
speech genre adds yet another voice to the carnival. Women orators in the
Moroccan marketplace take advantage of an already hybrid discourse to further hybridize the public sphere.

An herbalist sits under a large sun umbrella outside the western wall of a
marketplace at the foot of the Middle Atlas Mountains in Morocco. Before
her are piles of minerals and herbs, including dried sea urchins, some roots,
and a blue fluorescent rock that is chipped for use. It is market day and she
has come to do business. She is selling *tabkhira,* an unblended assortment of
plants, herbs, roots, and minerals with a touch of sulfur *(kabrit)* added for
dramatic effect. This odiferous combination is wrapped in newspaper and
taken home to be ground with mortar and pestle and then thrown on a hot
brazier, causing the sulfur to ignite. The act is thought to be sufficient to
release someone who has been bewitched from the hold of a spell.

This woman is also a self-proclaimed *majduba,* a disciple or "entranced
one" of the saint Moulay Ibrahim, whose tomb and pilgrimage center are located outside of Marrakech.[5] She wears large plastic sunglasses rarely found in
this region, tucking the frames behind her ears and under her head scarf. Her
jellaba is faded and frayed, displaying an appearance of poverty and a disregard
for decorum. The *majduba* employs Moroccan Arabic (the primary language
of the marketplace), mixing it with some sentences in Berber, and drawing occasionally on religious quotation in classical Arabic. Her musical intonation is
made up of long litanies of similarly stressed syllables. With a deep and commanding voice that ranges from loud to screaming, she competes with other
herbalists in the vicinity, most of them men with microphones:[6]

"Every one of these [packets] has a piece of each one of these [herbs], as
if you prayed to the Prophet. Who will trust in God with me? And whoever
says there's no such thing as magic, go up to the tomb of my grandfather
Moulay Brahim, and my father Hamid. And go up to [the tomb of] my father Omarr. And see how many women and men are shackled by chains by
the work of Satan! And how many brides, *lalla,* they leave them abandoned.

Transaction in the marketplace.

She's shackled, poor thing, and she says, 'I'm begging your protection, oh Omarr.'"

"Ahh, *lalla!*" a squatting woman sighed.

"'They burned me with fire, oh Omarr!'"

"Come here, *lalla,* let me tell you."

"'I'm begging your protection, oh Moulay Ibrahim!'"

"I want to tell you about one girl," began the client.

"Pray on behalf of the Messenger of God *[sali 'la rasul-allah],*" said the *majduba.*

"She's engaged and she has her marriage certificate."

"*Ayya, lalla.*"

"And she's married and he took someone else who's stuck to him."

"*Aywa.* Why? That mother of the other one is awake and you, her mother, are asleep, poor thing! Pray to the Prophet."

"Until the act fell and everything and he took someone else!"

"Listen to me, *lalla,* pray to the Prophet. *Ayaaaaaah!* Pure Soussis!"[7]

"She doesn't want him anymore."

"God, God be with you, our grandfather Moulay Ibrahim. No, no, listen to me. Of course, she doesn't want him anymore, because the others have turned around him [with magic]. We women are hard!:

If they love you, they'll feed you
and if they hate you, they'll bewitch you."

"She's the first," the client said.

"*He who enters the women's souk, beware!"* the *majduba* quoted,

"They'll show you a ton of profit,
and make you lose your salary!
The ruses of women are their own.
From their ruses come and escape!
Oh, the women belted with snakes
and those wrapped with scorpions!

Pray on behalf of the Messenger of God. *Ayya,* oh woman, whoever is a woman, never hold a[nother] woman dear."

The *majduba* goes on to instruct her client what incense to use, how to mix and burn them with the dirt from underneath the sole of the abandoned bride, and what to expect from the process. She then assures her client that she will be available at several markets in the region for future consultation.

"*Ayya,* lalla, aaaaaah, ayya, ayya. *There's no might or power except with God, the High, the Great. There's no God but God and Muhammed is his Prophet* [classical Arabic]. Here, my dear."

This fragment of oratory is characteristic of the marketplace, a composite of oaths, formulas, axiomatic sayings, and, in this case, feminine testimony. The hybrid quality of marketplace genres (the intertextual and intergeneric borrowings between religious quotation, bargaining, hawking, swearing, storytelling, and divining) sets them apart from the more intimate, monosexual, and ritualized speech events of the private domain.

Revoicing Genre

In the speech event above, several distinct oral genres are appropriated and revoiced. For reasons of space, I concentrate here on only two—religious scripture and the recorded "wisdoms" *(hikam)* of Sidi Abderahman al-Majdub—

in order to illuminate how feminine subjectivities emerge in new generic contexts and in the space of the open-air marketplace, a discursive site that has long been coded as a masculine domain in this area of central Morocco.

Religious Aphorisms, Mixing Codes, and the Performance of Authority

When the *majduba* quotes religious text in classical Arabic, she is demonstrating her competence not only in religious doctrine, but in another linguistic register as well. Despite the fact that these religious phrases in classical Arabic are now part of the oral tradition (not dependent on book literacy), they are nonetheless marked as a special form of speech because of the fact that they are not spoken in Moroccan dialect.[8]

> la hawla wa la quweta ila b-llah al-'ali al-'azim.
> (There's no might or power except with God, the High, the Great.)

> la ilaha lilla allah, sayd-na mohamed rasulu-llah.
> (There's no God but God [and] Mohamed is his Prophet.)

The first of these phrases comes from the Qur'an. The second is the *shahada*, the profession of faith required of all Muslims. Although common, the repetition of these phrases in a public setting by a woman has special significance. By speaking these words, the *majduba* draws on religious traditions of Quranic education as well as a folk ethic that attributes religious texts with mystical power that may be harnessed to effectuate changes in personal circumstance (to keep a husband from wandering or to make children successful in their studies, for example). The *majduba* sells incense, she does not write charms like many male clerics (*fqih*, sing; *fqaha*, pl.); yet, her performance of religious text in the "higher" register of classical Arabic sets her in the same role in many respects—that of religious counselor. The fact that she refers to herself as a *majduba* means that her life is oriented around the communication of a religious ethic, whether in language or by embodying the role of a renouncer.

These religious aphorisms are by no means arcane; they are often memorized by children in Quranic preschool, a religious nursery school run by a *fqih*, where children spend the mornings chanting and memorizing Quranic verses. But the women gathered around the *majduba* are not repeating the phrases; in all likelihood they are quite familiar with them, if only from listening to their children recite them. The significance of these phrases in the *majduba*'s discourse comes from their performative context. Although these aphorisms are in the verbal repertoire of the majority of Moroccans, only those with authority can and do *perform* them in front of a formal audience.[9] Their pronouncement procures social authority and power for the speaker by invoking official ideologies and associations of literacy. By demonstrating her textual knowledge (acquired aurally), the *majduba* partakes of the status accorded those, such as clerics or professional reciters of the Qur'an *(tolba),* who understand the power of words and how to use this power.

The *majduba*'s discourse is a religious one; she is a saint venerator, a self-proclaimed renouncer. Yet, the validation of marketplace presence through religious index is not particular to religious figures. Directives such as "Pray on behalf of the Prophet" are common market fare, a way of sacralizing the secularity of buy-and-sell relations. When someone directs an audience to "Pray on behalf of the Messenger of God" *(sali 'la rasul-allah)* in Morocco, the proper response is "May God's prayers be on you, [oh] messenger of God" *(allahuma sali 'l-ik ar-rasul-allah).* In this case, the response remained unvocalized. Nonetheless, the evocation of such "inner speech" (Volosinov 1973) connects the audience to a religious ethic. A shared moral ground is immediately called up by the repetition of conventional religious formulas.

Pronouns and Metapragmatics

Religious verses are plentiful in the larger text of the *majduba*'s performance and in marketplace oratory generally. They refer to a belief system in which there is a salient canon of appropriate public behavior. Within this system, the expression of weakness, especially in regard to matters of male-female relations, is less than honorable. But the *majduba* must elicit such personal narratives in order to fulfill her role as counselor and to sell her remedial incense. She accomplishes this without losing face by distancing herself from the shameful utterances, using direct reported speech:

"She's shackled, poor thing, and she says, 'I'm begging your protection, oh Omarr!'"

"'They burned me with fire, oh Omarr!'"

"'I'm begging your protection, oh Moulay Ibrahim!'"

The direct quoted speech is spoken in the voice of an abandoned bride soliciting the aid of saints (and by implication, that of the *majduba*). The *majduba* embodies this voice of need. In playing the role of someone who has been "burned," she clears a space for audience identification and participation while distancing herself from the expressed vulnerability, creating intertextual distance between the quoted speech and her own voice (Briggs and Bauman 1992). The "I" in this utterance is a "quoted I," a self-conscious performance of otherness (Urban 1989). The *majduba* is giving voice to the private discourse of another in a public space. The "I" in "I'm begging your protection, oh Moulay Ibrahim" is an "I" in need of spiritual counsel and magical incense, an "I" that belongs to the "they" of the audience. In her use of reported speech, the *majduba* creates a discursive space wherein many voices are audible, while, at the same time, her multivocal performance establishes her own verbal competency, her ability to author public discourse.

Hikam: *The Reported "Wisdoms" of Sidi Abderahman al-Majdub*

The *majduba*'s use of *unmarked* reported speech is more problematic. She quotes a succession of "wisdoms" or counsels *(hikam)* authored by Sidi Abderahman al-Majdub, a Sufi teacher during the sixteenth-century reign of Sultan Moulay Ismail. Sidi Abderahman became known for his poetic sagacity during a historical period when religious leaders (marabouts) had considerable political influence (see Eickelman 1976). The *majduba* appropriates three of Sidi Abderahman's counsels in succession, virtually bombarding the audience with rhyming words that have been set apart in the Moroccan verbal canon. This stacking of the words of another produces an affect of heady eloquence; it is a strong assertion of competence in the oeuvre of Sidi Abderahman, an appropriation of his linguistic expertise. The *majduba* says nothing to indicate that these words are not her own; yet, these texts are in the verbal repertoire. Not all people know their author, but most would recognize them as frequently quoted sayings. By *not* framing these words as reported speech, however, the pronouns become porous to many identities, they shift. Whereas the *majduba* begins her litany with "We women are hard," this "we" quickly becomes the third person plural, "they":

"We women are hard!:

If they love you, they'll feed you
and if they hate you, they'll bewitch you."

"She's the first," the client said.

"*He who enters the women's souk, beware!*" the *majduba* quoted,

"*They'll show you a ton of profit,*
and make you lose your salary!
The ruses of women are their own.
From their ruses come and escape!
Oh, the women belted with snakes
and those wrapped with scorpions!

Pray on behalf of the Messenger of God. *Ayya,* oh woman, whoever is a woman, never hold a[nother] woman dear."

The *majduba's* voice enters into the quoted words here because they are unmarked for either direct or indirect reported speech, yet they are also renowned as the words of a historical male figure. This does not exempt the *majduba* from responsibility, but it does add an element of ambiguity to the encoded message. Is she *revoicing* Sidi Abderahman's words? Is she adding an element of irony to his slander against women, confirming the power of women that Sidi Abderahman acknowledged in the negative by restatement in positive sarcasm? Or is she simply quoting him? And is there anything "simple" about such a quote?[10]

By speaking these words, the *majduba* indexes the spiritual authority of a man whose tradition she continues. Although part of oral tradition, its history is easily traced: one need only buy a cheap copy of Sidi Abderahman's sayings at a nearby used-book tent. Sidi Abderahman is not known for his progressive views on women. In another axiom, he says, "Women are fleeting vessels / Whose passengers are doomed to destruction."[11] These sayings, more like warnings, are often used in cynical contexts—spoken by one male friend to another in order to cure the latter of the "blindness" of romantic love and longing, for example.

The *majduba* is not embodying a male voice when she says, "We women are hard!" And yet, when she quotes the counsels of Sidi Abderahman al-Majdub, women become "they," a marked category. This shifting of pronominal referent is significant because the *majduba* is indexing a belief system that is subaltern and illicit (magic). By quoting someone else's words, the *majduba* distances herself from the dishonorableness and social stigma of feminine magic. Whereas magical agency is unproblematically projected onto women in male oratory of this kind, the *majduba's* appropriation of male discursive strategies casts aspersions on her own sex, and, by extension, on herself. Because women are the clientele for such magical activity, they become their own "other" in the discourse of the *majduba.* Yet, the theatricality of the event—determined, to a large extent, by the density of reported speech employed, but also by the *majduba's* screaming intonation and free use of intimidation—puts the voice and intent of the discourse into question. There is a basic irony here: the *majduba* is a main participant in the "women's souk" *(suq an-nisa')* against which her words caution. Yet, her words, like her near-comical (because unusual) sunglasses, seem to wink at us. Her use of *hikam* is decidedly different than that of the sixteenth-century male Sufi leader who authored them. Such traditional words in the mouth of a woman and in the context of the marketplace produce a transformation of this genre from a didactic one to a subtly parodic one. By revoicing these utterances, the *majduba* critiques the worldview embodied in them by putting it on hyperbolic display.

The *majduba* continues to employ poetic speech that describes women as "belted with snakes" and "wrapped with scorpions." The segment culminates with advice: "Whoever is a woman, never hold a[nother] woman dear." Women should not trust other women. This sets up a linguistic paradox (Bateson 1972), for the *majduba* is a woman who requires the trust of her audience in order to do her business. In the final analysis, the *majduba* manages to circumvent this paradox. She does not directly say "trust me" (although she does go a long way in order to convince her audience that she is trustworthy); rather, she asks, "Who will trust in God with me?" Trust is required, but the *majduba* channels it toward God, thus making hers an enterprise in league with God's. If you trust God, then you will buy this incense and it will work for you. Trust in God equals trust in the efficacy of the incense equals trust in the seller of the goods. The result is money in the *majduba*'s pocket. This creation of co-identity in the face of contradiction and through the confluence of categories is very subtle and thus successful.

We are still left with the disturbing associations of the recontextualized discourse, however, and the apparent contradictions that these recycled utterances create between the openness of the *majduba*'s poetics and the restricted interpretations that are inherent in the traditional and generic speech that she employs. These words have traditionally been in the mouths of men, but when a woman calls down women in the manner of men, in the public context of the marketplace, there is reason for suspicion. She is metapragmatically calling attention to her own use of stereotypes, employing them and creating distance from them. Only members of an in-group have this license. Calling attention to stereotypes says, in effect, "Women, who are you? Are you this, what 'they' say you are?" Even if the *majduba* affirms that, yes, women are "hard," she is also noting the schisms in the feminine community, providing a social critique of the competition and lack of cohesion that exist there, and—insofar as she acknowledges that the consequences are detrimental (which she does)—condemning both.

The *majduba* does not announce her citations as reported speech, but the absence of marked quotation is conspicuous, as several of the aphorisms she uses were said by Sidi Abderahman al-Majdub, an important cultural figure whose life still remains in social memory. Despite the fact that the words are not her own, nor are they socially recognized as her own, the *majduba* "possesses" them by not calling attention to their reported status, thereby governing the interpretative frame more directly.[12] This does not solidify the boundaries of the utterance so much as it opens them to different interpretative frames, making possible the implicit metacommunicative commentary of the *majduba*. Volosinov refers to this process as one of infiltration: "Language devises means for infiltrating reported speech with authorial retort and commentary in deft and subtle ways. The reporting context strives to break down the self-contained compactness of the reported speech, to resolve it, to obliterate its boundaries" (Volosinov 1973, 120–21). The dissolution of authorial boundaries allows the *majduba* to revoice an utterance with an established interpretation. In this sense, reported speech, although seeming to bid for closure and monologic status, actually opens the interpretative possibilities of discourse, renegotiating the circumstance and position of its speakers. Whereas the quotation of authoritative language may be an explicit strategy to establish intertextual proximity with prior discourse, the *majduba*'s revoicing of these quotes leaves this relation ambiguous. She neither identifies with these words nor critiques them explicitly; implicitly, she does both simultaneously.

Because these quotes are not framed as quotes, their interpretation is open-ended, their parodic value always slightly veiled. Instead of delimiting these voices, the *majduba* allows the *hikam* to resonate in the diverse consciousnesses of the now mixed-gender marketplace. The multifunctionality of the pronouns she employs, their ability to simultaneously reference multiple selves, is also an index to the changing functions of women as representations of the marked gender in contemporary Moroccan society. At issue here are not necessarily definitions of selfhood, who "I" am, but definitions of gender, who "we" are.[13] By carefully, though not necessarily consciously, manipulating the words of others (via reported speech and the appropriation of traditional genres of speech) and infusing these words with her own voices, the *majduba* calls the hegemony of any one voice into question.

The *majduba*'s speech is more than literal, it is pragmatically overdetermined; its meaning depends on its situatedness in any one of a number of possible interpretative frames. In marketplace speech, these frames are various and constantly shifting. "Trust God and don't trust others" is one of the messages. "Be cunning" is another. Mix genres, appropriate language, turn categories on their heads. "He [or, in this case, she] who enters the women's souk *[radd bal-ak]*, beware!" This is one of the only consistent messages of the *majduba*'s discourse: pay attention, beware, and be wary in a market of mixed messages.

A Moroccan herbalist orating to her audience.

Transgression and the Revoicing of Gender

In another example of women's marketplace oratory—the discourse of an *'ashshaba,* or "herbalist"—we find a direct confrontation of codes of honor and linguistic appropriateness. Like the *majduba,* the *'ashshaba* uses religious aphorisms to temper her sales spiel, including quoted scripture in the high register of classical Arabic. She is also selling a commodity that purports to rid the client of spells perpetrated by women, although her goods must be ingested, not just burned as incense. Unlike the *majduba,* the *'ashshaba* uses very explicit language in her attempts at persuasion, broaching topics that, until recently, have only been spoken about in monosexual gatherings. She is talking to thirty-four men and twelve women about problems of induced impotency, magical agency, and spiritual and sexual worth (see photo). Her language is bawdy and humorous. She is not talking to individuals, however, but rather to gender categories—you [men], we women. It is, in effect, these categories that are in the process of discursive negotiation in her speech:

> God gave you [men] five liters of blood and us [women] seven liters of blood—the blood of menstruation and the blood of childbirth. Why are you [men] beautiful with three [appetites] and we're beautiful with four? Why has God given you [men] one desire and us ninety-nine? You just have one desire. If it's gone, you won't have honor in your house anymore. The man will appear like a donkey next to his wife. You see,

nothing enables or honors you except desire *[nafs]*. If it goes so far as to be lacking, you can count your soul *[ruh]* as having no value. Even religion and medicine are not ashamed [to address these issues]!

The *'ashshaba's* mention of the blood of childbirth and menstruation in a public and mixed-sex gathering is unequivocally shameful. Perhaps more important than her daring, however, is her discursive construction of metaphysical assumption. In Muslim religious thought there is a consistent duality between the carnal self *(nafs)* and the transcendent soul *(ruh)*. *Nafs,* or desire life, is considered the beast to be subdued in the process of the Sufi's purification of soul, for example (see Anderson 1985, 1982; Mills 1991, 248–49; Rosen 1978; Schimmel 1975). In the *'ashshaba's* discourse, however, the value of the soul *(ruh)* is predicated on an active desire life *(nafs)*. The link between the mind and the body is bridged in her ideology.

This is a convenient philosophy for someone who is selling an herbal remedy that counters spell-induced impotence, as it asserts that honor is only accessible through restoring carnal desire, first by buying the *'ashshaba's* herbs, then by embracing women. But this is more than a sales strategy. To assert that honor is only accessible via sexuality is not new, but women in the *'ashshaba's* discourse are not passive vehicles through which men construct their honor; rather, women have the power both to take away a man's honor (by casting spells of impotence) and to constitute a man's honor and their own. The attribution of such agency to women in public oratory spoken *by a woman* to and about men is significant; the *'ashshaba* embraces the stereotype of women's active sexuality (Mernissi 1987) and uses it both to express her power and to sell her herbs.

The *'ashshaba's* speech is a self-conscious breaking with social conventions of honor. The herbalist acknowledges the shameful *(hashuma)* quality of her speech by justifying it—she says that both religion and medicine (literally "pain," *derr*) also address these important topics publicly and with impunity, thus putting herself in the same category as a spiritual adviser or a medical doctor (customarily both men who are free to discuss these issues).[14] She also defends her right to speak the taboo: *U Allah, ma-nhasham had-ak,* she declares in another segment ("By God, I won't be ashamed before you!"). This declaration "keys" the entire discursive scene as one that self-consciously flaunts social convention (Bauman 1977; Hymes 1974). Despite the fact that similar things have been spoken in the marketplace before, they have always been spoken by men to men. The *'ashshaba* is calling attention to the taboo of mentioning these topics in public and heterogeneous company, while asserting her intention to break the rules. Although she appears to adhere to thematic models of male-female relations, she rhetorically violates the rules for mixed-gender interaction and appropriate speech.

Like the *majduba,* the *'ashshaba* calls on religious aphorism, direct reported speech, and quotation of scripture in classical Arabic to establish authority and credibility with her audience. Yet, it is often difficult to distinguish what and whose voice is being asserted. For example, the *'ashshaba* states:

> Be careful you're not deceived by a woman. And she'll tell you, "All right, you're my husband and are dear to me and if you died tonight I would mourn for you." Don't trust [it]! By God, we're being hypocrites about that! Because these four, they eat and don't get full. Count with me: One, the eye eats and it doesn't get tired of its seeing. Two, the ear eats and it doesn't get tired of hearing news. Three, the earth eats and isn't content with water and rain. And the fourth . . . finish it with your mind, God give you honor and respect, sirs and men.

In this passage, we again encounter the disturbing voice of a woman calling down her own sex by using stereotypes that are only too facile. But once again, a paradox is presented; for, although the *'ashshaba*'s use of direct quoted speech serves to distinguish the narrator's voice from the narrated voice (see Bauman 1986, following Roman Jakobson), that distance is immediately spanned when the *'ashshaba* follows the quote with "Don't trust [it]! By God, *we*'re being hypocrites about that!" (emphasis added). The irony here is that the *'ashshaba* is dressed in mourning clothes (consisting of a white djellaba, white *belga* shoes, white socks, and a white scarf draped around her head and tied under her chin). She informs the audience later in her discourse that her husband has just died and that her father died a month before him. Therefore, either she is mourning her husband, providing a counterexample to her assertion that women are hypocrites, or she is acting outside the canon of honor, in which case she undermines her own discourse ("Be careful you're not deceived by a woman")! Moreover, although she will assert that she is about to go to Mecca, she is now in the marketplace doing business, clearly in breach of the prohibition for mourning women to have social intercourse (verbal exchange or even eye contact) with men during the four months and ten days following their husbands' death.

The *'ashshaba*'s presence in the marketplace in mourning clothes alerts us to women's transition from the private "feminine" realm to the public, working, and "masculine" one, for men are not required to mourn their wives, but are expected to continue in their public life with no visible reminder of mourning. They do not thereby suffer dishonor: "God give you honor and respect, sirs and men," the *'ashshaba* asserts, as if to ensure her own.

There are contradictory logics at work in this discourse that reflect the ambivalent status of women who, in their appropriation of a male role and an often mysogynist oratory, are also voicing a feminine presence in the public sphere. The privileging of any one interpretation over another is determined by one's social position and gender. Whether or not one notices the subtle winks, the pragmatic undermining of genres, or the disharmony between what is said and who is saying it, however, there is one reaction that is common to the *'ashshaba*'s marketplace oratory: *a wily, hashuma hadek shi,* "damnation, that's shameful!"

Embodied Hybridization

The pragmatic revoicing of genre is intricately related to the increasing visibility of women in the material economy. Women's physical presence in the marketplace grounds them in a new domain of discourse, while their speech indexes their emergent status in the public realm (cf. Hanks 1990). Such revoicings change the shape of recontextualized speech by introducing a different time-space orientation to genres that carry their own historical associations into the present (Bakhtin 1986; see also Ben-Amos 1976). The sayings *(hikam)* of Sidi Abderahman al-Majdub, for example, express a certain social ethic (characterized by chauvinism) that is in the process of being challenged in some realms of contemporary Moroccan thought and practice. The relation between genre and gender here is clear: stereotypical notions of gender find expression in a genre such as *hikam,* while novel expressions of gender (exemplified in women's presence in the market) appropriate and transform genres by altering the habitual relation between context and utterance, content and form. Such subversions make genre itself a salient category and medium of social (ex)change, while performance becomes a measure of authority. Women verbal artists in the marketplace make the politics of difference palpable by infusing tradition with a newly gendered poetics. Their embodiment and revoicing of public speech genres make their audience experience what is usually only recognized—or misrecognized: the power of words to effect social change.

The carnival ambience of the marketplace allows for the relaxation of interactional norms that reign in the more private segments of life, providing a fertile ground for the emergent expression of new social identities. But the marketplace is not an all-out carnival. Not all rules are suspended, but all may be contested. The very law of marketplace genres is the breaking of the law of combination—genres that, separately, have an indexical relation to the serious (such as scripture and oaths), the transcendent (proverb, axioms), or even the comic (curses and playful speech), produce a different pragmatic effect when juxtaposed, mixed together, or revoiced by a woman (see Kapchan 1996). Thus, notions of genre as well as notions of subject are fractured, ideals of wholeness and impermeability destroyed. The significance of this carnivalized genre extends beyond its immediate function of selling incense, however. Analysis of the process of expressive hybridization illuminates how genres, considered as social practice, infiltrate and transform each other in ways that have historical and political consequences (Hanks 1987).

As defined near the beginning of this essay, genre bears a necessary relation to past discourse, whether imitating tradition or asserting maximal distance from convention (see Briggs and Bauman 1992 for an elaboration of this theory). The examples discussed here suggest that any quoted utterance may contain multiple voices, whether these "words of others" are marked or unmarked for reported speech, announced or silently usurped. By playing with the polysemy of generic expression, marketplace women bring the excess of semantic and pragmatic association to the surface, testing the limits of genre as well as categories of gender. If they sometimes employ negative stereotypes of feminine gender, it is in order to situate themselves in a domain that has always been inhabited by men. Yet, although their speech draws on categories of masculine authority, it also undermines all that is closed, compartmentalized, and impermeable. The presence of women in the marketplace puts traditional definitions of womanhood into question, and everything is subject to question in their language. They are the anti-heros, the liminars, the sanctioners of Babel.

Notes

1. See Abu-Lughod 1986, 1993; Bauman 1992; Behar 1990; Besnier 1989; Briggs 1988; Briggs and Bauman 1992; Caton 1990; Feld 1995; Gal 1990; Hanks 1987; Haring 1992a, 1992b; Kirshenblatt-Gimblett 1989; Perloff 1992; Sherzer 1987; Stewart 1991; Todorov 1990.

2. Genres may often be defined by their linguistic "style": as Briggs and Bauman note, "Genre styles . . . are constellations of co-occurrent formal elements and structures that define or characterize particular classes of utterances. The constituent elements of genre styles may figure in other speech styles as well, establishing indexical resonances between them" (1992, 141). Transformation in genre is indexical of larger social transformation. Thus, "a subset of diacritical generic features may be combined with those that characterize another genre to effect an interpretive transformation of genre, a phenomenon that Dell Hymes (1974) terms 'metaphrasis'" (Briggs and Bauman, 1992; cf. Urban 1984).

3. As repositories of history, genres take on particular importance in times of

political upheaval or socioemotional change (Hanks 1987; Haring 1992); they are the site of historicization in the dialogue between past and present, between ideology and practice.

4. The study of verbal genres in the Middle East has produced a rich literature that explores the construction of both personal and community identities and the relation of expressive life to issues of political economy, gender construction, and cultural ethics. These studies have demonstrated the role of speech genres in mediating conflict (Caton 1990; Meeker 1979), encoding affect (Abu-Lughod 1990; Grima 1992), voicing dissent (Abu-Lughod 1986; Joseph 1980; Mills 1991), and creating community and tradition (Webber 1991; see also Abu-Lughod 1993; Beeman 1986). All these genres are associated with one gender or the other and help to constitute the definition of gender for the larger community; many are contextualized in homogeneous social settings and most assume a single moral economy or two complimentary and gendered systems of value.

5. The worship of saints, or marabouts, is the main defining characteristic of North African Islam. According to Eickelman (1976, 6–7), marabouts are "persons, living or dead, to whom is attributed a special relation toward God which makes them particularly well placed to serve as intermediaries with the supernatural and to communicate God's grace *(baraka)* to their clients. On the basis of this conception, marabouts in the past have played key religious, political, and economic roles in North African society, particularly in Morocco." A *majdub* (masculine) is someone who has a supernatural magnetism, and thus a certain authority, in regard to the world of the spirit; in contemporary Morocco, it refers to someone who has lost care of (and sometimes control over) worldly existence *(dunya)*. The *majduba* in our study is a disciple of the marabout Moulay Ibrahim. The word *majdub* has now become synonymous with a social outcast, reflecting a lower estimation of roles that do not profit or directly participate in the current capitalist modes of production.

6. There are four other Moroccan women listening to the *majduba's* spiel. Three are standing about half a meter away and one, the woman who will tell the *majduba* her tale of woe, is squatting at the very edge of the *majduba's* display of incense ingredients, under the shade of the umbrella. There is also a boy, about twelve years old, to the left of the women in the audience. My research assistant, Si Mohamed, and I are standing to the right, very much a part of the small semicircle.

7. The Soussi Berbers are known for their expertise in magic.

8. See Eickelman 1992; Spratt 1992; and Wagner 1993 on the symbolic value of literacy in Morocco.

9. The exception to this is children's often halting recitation in Quranic school.

10. Reported speech plays an essential role in Islamic theology and exegesis, especially as far as the *hadith* is concerned. *Hadith,* which literally means "report" or "narrative," refers to the oral record (now transcribed) of the utterances and deeds of the Prophet (see Hourani 1991, 70–71). Three types of hadith are recognized: (1) true narrative *(hadith assahih),* (2) good narrative *(hadith hassan),* and (3) weak narrative *(hadith za'if).* The first is actually attributable to the Prophet through a traceable lineage; the second depends on a lineage that has a few links missing; and the third is unreliable (though

not necessarily dismissable) because its genealogy is faulty. These chains are less reliant on the degree of harmony between the texts than they are on whether or not the links in the chain actually knew and spoke to one another—the importance of oral transmission is primary.

11. Fatima Mernissi (1987, 43) translated this axiom from the book *Les Quatrains du Mejdoub le Sarcastique: poète Maghrébin du XVIème siècle,* collected and translated by Scelles-Millie and Khelifa (1966, 161).

12. "The question of how much of the other's meaning I will permit to get through when I surround his words with my own is a question about the governance of meaning, about who presides over it, and about how much of it is shared" (Clark and Holquist 1984, 237).

13. See Singer (1989) and Urban (1989) on pronoun use and conceptions of the self in linguistic analysis.

14. The expression often cited in this regard is "there's no timidity in religion" (*La hya f-d-din* [Moroccan Arabic], *La haya'a fi ad-dini* [classical Arabic]), meaning that religious discourse does not hesitate to speak about topics that are otherwise taboo.

Works Cited

Abu-Lughod, Lila. 1986. *Veiled Sentiments: Honor and Poetry in a Bedouin Society.* Berkeley: University of California Press.

____. 1990. "Shifting Politics in Bedouin Love Poetry." In Catherine Lutz and Lila Abu-Lughod, eds. *Language and the Politics of Emotion.* New York: Cambridge University Press.

____. 1993. *Writing Women's Worlds: Bedouin Stories.* Berkeley and Los Angeles: University of California Press.

Anderson, Jon W. 1982. "Social Structure and the Veil: Comportment and the Composition of Interaction in Afghanistan." *Anthropos* 77: 397–420.

____. 1985. "Sentimental Ambivalence and the Exegesis of 'Self' in Afghanistan." In *Self and Society in the Middle East: Anthropological Quarterly* (special issue), ed. W. Anderson and D. F. Eickelman, 203–11. Washington, D.C.: Catholic University of America.

Bakhtin, M. M. 1981. *The Dialogic Imagination.* Trans. Caryl Emerson and Michael Holquist. Austin: University of Texas Press.

____. 1986. *Speech Genres and Other Late Essays.* Trans. Vern W. McGee. Austin: University of Texas Press.

Barthes, Roland. 1975. *The Pleasure of the Text.* Trans. Richard Miller. New York: Hill and Wang.

Bateson, Gregory. 1972. *Steps to an Ecology of Mind.* New York: Ballantine Books.

Bauman, Richard. 1986. *Story, Performance, and Event.* Cambridge: Cambridge University Press.

____. 1992. "Contextualization, Tradition and the Dialogue of Genres: Icelandic Legends of the Kraftaskald." In *Rethinking Context,* ed. C. Goodwin and A. Duranti, 125–45. Cambridge: Cambridge University Press.

Bauman, Richard, ed. 1977. *Verbal Art as Performance*. Prospect Heights, Ill.: Waveland Press.

Bauman, Richard, and Charles L. Briggs. 1990. "Poetics and Performance as Critical Perspectives on Language and Social Life." *Annual Review of Anthropology* 19: 59–88.

Beeman, William O. 1986. *Language, Status, and Power in Iran*. Bloomington: Indiana University Press.

Behar, Ruth. 1990. "Rage and Redemption: Reading the Life Story of a Mexican Marketing Woman." *Feminist Studies* 16: 223–58.

Ben-Amos, Dan. 1976. "Analytic Categories and Ethnic Genres." In *Folklore Genres*, ed. Dan Ben-Amos, 215–42. Austin: University of Texas Press.

Benstock, S. 1991. *Textualizing the Feminine: On the Limits of Genre*. Norman: University of Oklahoma Press.

Besnier, Niko. 1989. "Information Withholding as a Manipulative and Collusive Strategy in Nukulaelae Gossip." *Language and Society* 18: 315–41.

Briggs, Charles L. 1988. *Competence in Performance: The Creativity of Tradition in Mexicano Verbal Art*. Philadelphia: University of Pennsylvania Press.

_____. 1992. "'Since I Am a Woman, I Will Chastise My Relatives': Gender, Reported Speech, and the Reproduction of Social Relations in Warao Ritual Wailing." *American Ethnologist* 19:2: 337–61.

Briggs, Charles L., and Richard Bauman. 1992. "Genre, Intertextuality and Social Power." *Journal of Linguistic Anthropology* 2:2: 131–72.

Caton, Steve C. 1990. *"Peaks of Yemen I Summon": Poetry as Cultural Practice in a North Yemeni Tribe*. Berkeley: University of California Press.

Clark, K., and M. Holquist. 1984. *Mikhail Bakhtin*. Cambridge: Harvard University Press.

Eickelman, Dale. 1976. *Moroccan Islam: Tradition and Society in a Pilgrimage Center*. Austin: University of Texas Press.

_____. 1992. "Mass Higher Education and the Religious Imagination in Contemporary Arab Societies." *American Ethnologist* 19:4: 643–55.

Feld, Steven. 1999. "From Schizophonia to Schismogenesis." In *Music Grooves*, ed. Steven Feld and C. Keil, Chicago: University of Chicago Press.

Fraser, Nancy. 1992. "Rethinking the Public Sphere: A Contribution to the Critique of Actually Existing Democracy." In *Habermas and the Public Sphere*, ed. C. Calhoun, 109–42. Cambridge and London: MIT Press.

Gal, Susan. 1990. "Between Speech and Silence: The Problematics of Research on Language and Gender." In *Toward a New Anthropology of Gender*, ed. DiLeonardo.

Geertz, Clifford. 1979. "Suq: The Bazaar Economy in Sefrou." In *Meaning and Order in Moroccan Society: Three Essays in Cultural Analysis*, ed. C. Geertz, H. Geertz, and L. Rosen, Cambridge: Cambridge University Press.

_____. 1983. "Blurred Genres: The Refiguration of Social Thought." In *Local Knowledge*, New York: Basic Books.

Grima, Benedicte. 1992. *"The Misfortunes Which Have Befallen Me": Paxtun Women's Life Stories*. Austin: University of Texas Press.

Hanks, William F. 1987. "Discourse Genres in a Theory of Practice." *American Ethnologist* 14:4: 668–92.

———. 1990. *Referential Practice: Language and Lived Space among the Maya.* Chicago and London: University of Chicago Press.

Hannerz, Ulf. 1987. "The World in Creolization." *Africa* 57:4: 546–59.

Haring, Lee. 1992a. "Parody and Imitation in West Indian Ocean Oral Literature." *Journal of Folklore Research* 29:3: 199–224.

———. 1992b. *Verbal Art in Madagascar: Performance in Historical Perspective.* Philadelphia: University of Pennsylvania Press.

Hourani, Albert. 1991. *A History of the Arab Peoples.* Cambridge: Belknap Press of Harvard University.

Hymes, Dell. 1971. "Introduction." In *Pidginization and Creolization of Languages,* ed. Dell Hymes, 65–90. Cambridge: Cambridge University Press.

———. 1974. *Foundations in Sociolinguistics: An Ethnographic Approach.* Philadelphia: University of Pennsylvania Press.

Irigaray, Luce. 1991. *The Irigaray Reader.* Cambridge, Mass.: Blackwell.

Jakobson, Roman. 1960. "Closing Statement: Linguistics and Poetics." In *Style in Language,* ed. Thomas A. Sebeok, 350–77. Cambridge: MIT Press.

———. 1971. "The Dominant." In *Readings in Russian Poetics: Formalist and Structuralist Views,* ed. L. Matejka and K. Pomorska, Cambridge: MIT Press.

Jameson, Fredric. 1981. *The Political Unconscious: Narrative as a Socially Symbolic Art.* Ithaca, N.Y.: Cornell University Press.

Joseph, Terri Brint. 1980. "Poetry as Strategy of Power: The Case of the Riffian Berber Women." *Signs* 5:3: 418–34.

Kapchan, Deborah A. 1993. "Hybridization and the Marketplace: Emerging Paradigms in Folkloristics." *Western Folklore* 52: 303–26.

———. 1996. *Gender on the Market: Moroccan Women and the Revoicing of Tradition.* Philadelphia: University of Pennsylvania Press.

Kirshenblatt-Gimblett, Barbara. 1989. "Authoring Lives." *Journal of Folklore Research* 26:2: 123–50.

Meeker, Michael. 1979. *Literature and Violence in Northern Arabia.* Cambridge and New York: Cambridge University Press.

Mills, Margaret A. 1991. *Rhetorics and Politics in Afghan Traditional Storytelling.* Philadelphia: University of Pennsylvania Press.

Perloff, Marjorie. 1992. *Postmodern Genres.* Norman: University of Oklahoma Press.

Rosen, Lawrence. 1978. *Bargaining for Reality: The Construction of Social Relations in a Muslim Community.* Chicago: University of Chicago Press.

Scelles-Millie, J. and B. Khelifa. 1966. *Les Quatrains de Mejdoub le Sarcastique: Poète Maghrébin du XVIème siecle.* Paris: G. P. Maisonneuve et Larose.

Schimmel, Anne-Marie. 1975. *Mystical Dimensions of Islam.* Chapel Hill: University of North Carolina Press.

Sherzer, Joel. 1987. "A Diversity of Voices: Men's and Women's Speech in Ethnographic Perspective." In *Language, Gender, and Sex in Comparative Perspective,* ed. Susan

Steele, and Christine Tanz, 95–120. Cambridge and New York: Cambridge University Press.

Singer, Milton. 1989. "Pronouns, Persons and the Semiotic Self." In *Semiotics, Self, and Society,* ed. Benjamin Lee and Greg Urban, 229–96. Berlin and New York: Mouton de Gruyter.

Spivak, Gayatri Chakravorty. 1993. *Outside in the Teaching Machine.* New York and London: Routledge.

Spratt, Jennifer E. 1992. "Women and Literacy in Morocco." *Annals of the American Academy of Political and Social Science* 520 (March): 54–65.

Stewart, Susan. 1991. *Crimes of Writing.* New York: Oxford University Press.

Todorov, Tzvetan. 1990. *Genres in Discourse.* Cambridge: Cambridge University Press.

Troin, Jean-François. 1975. *Les souks marocains: Marchés ruraux et organisation de l'espace dans la moitié nord du Maroc.* Aix-en-Provence: Edisud.

Turner, Victor. 1974. "Liminal to Liminard in Play, Flow, and Ritual: An Essay in Comparative Symbology." In Edward Norbeck, ed., *The Anthropology of Human Play.* Houston: Rice University Studies.

Urban, Greg. 1984. "The Semiotics of Two Speech Styles in Shokleng." In *Semiotic Mediation,* ed. E. Mertz and R. J. Parmentier, 311–29. Orlando, Fla.: Academic Press.

____. 1989. "The 'I' of Discourse." In *Semiotics, Self, and Society,* ed. Benjamin Lee and Greg Urban, 27–52. Berlin and New York: Mouton de Gruyter.

Volosinov, V. N. 1973. *Marxism and the Philosophy of Language.* Cambridge: Harvard University Press.

Wagner, Daniel A. 1993. *Literacy, Culture, and Development: Becoming Literate in Morocco.* Cambridge: Cambridge University Press.

Webber, Sabra J. 1991. *Romancing the Real: Folklore and Ethnographic Representation in North Africa.* Philadelphia: University of Pennsylvania Press.

Bridge and One:
Improvisations of the Public Sphere

Fred Moten

0

This essay exists only in the midst of an ongoing performance/ongoing audition of James Brown, the Godfather of Soul, and only as the expression of a mimetic, that accompanies and probably overwhelms an analytic, desire. But that's not quite right. Just trying to be like the Godfather, which is sad and rigorously ambitious and crazy and impossible, creates resonances that will appear as analytic, if soulful, breakdowns of some central oppositions: purity and hybridity, singularity and totality, and, yes, mimesis and analysis. Such resonances are inevitable because such an attempt at covering can't help but move in another understanding of rhythm and tone, where the one is not the one, where the one is held in a generative, anarchic, ensemblic cut that marks and opens the history and possibility of a descent, a lingering, and an action, the history and possibility of a revolutionary public. This cut or track, this recording of the livest of durative shows, bears the trace of an extended possession, the animation and inspiration of a tradition forged in the minute but unbridgeable, vast but embraceable, space between mimesis and analysis, the space or cut of improvisation, which Cecil Taylor calls self-analysis.[1]

The Godfather, one of our greatest theorists of that cut suspension, that breaking change or broken bridge where descent, lingering, and action would be imagined and would occur, moves in what could be called or what might appear as a funked-up postmodernism, the metacritical stance of the anar-ranger, improvising organization on the fly and then critiquing it: he's the one who, when he says keep it right there, don't turn it loose, 'cause it's a

mother or (to the funky drummer) don't solo but let us give you some, theo-
rizes for us the abundantly resistant or, more precisely, improvisational intervention that the cut/bridge can be rather than or in addition to or through
the unrationalized and un/dis/closing suture it is often thought in relation to
or thought to be—the site of a barren oscillation, a popular void, an apolitical fragment, no public space or sphere.

By way of the Godfather, I want to look at (1) the relation between political resistance and resistance in psychoanalysis (which means thinking the
relation between political resistance and transference, in particular that unprecedented but material transference that occurs in the rich and complex
tradition of what might be called black [self-]analytic discourse) that occurs,
for instance, in the fractured, excessive convergence of the ensemblic one
and the public sphere that is sounded in James Brown's music; (2) reformu-
lations and reemergences of the public sphere as the necessary and necessarily outer venue wherein the utopian force manifest in the creation of new
models of reality can be exerted precisely through the persistent and resonant resistance of those who will not be excluded—like, again, what's held
in the liberatory politics of form iconized in a certain anarchic ground,
empty center, or open rhythmic space that James Brown calls the one and
that is both manifest in all of its ambivalence and deftly and musically theorized (which is to say theorized by way of an alternative mode of organization) in booming bass and as the echo of an unheard scream, shaking the
signifier and breaking its law; (3) what we could call creative affect read
either as a sign of cultural resistance or a sign of a culturalist indifference to
resistance or, finally, a revolutionary improvisation of culture. I hope these
looks will make possible a reconstruction of resistance through modes of
organization akin to but before what has been thought in the name of a
proletarian public sphere, itself emerging out of a critique of the *bourgeois*
public sphere, inflected by something up ahead of what has been recently
thought in the name of a *black* public sphere, and its incomplete but suggestive indexing of an "impossible" *lumpen* public sphere.

So I begin by saying a bit about culturalist indifference to resistance and
the culturalist indifferentiation of cultural resistance in the formulation of
the public sphere given in the "Editorial Comment: On Thinking the Black
Public Sphere" written by Arjun Appadurai, Lauren Berlant, Carol A.
Breckenridge, and Manthia Diawara (aka the Black Public Sphere Collective) in *Public Culture* 15:

> The Black public sphere is post–Black nationalism, and includes the
> diaspora among its primary audiences. As the international market

continues to demonstrate, the transnational migration of signs and wares, narratives and archives generates Black life globally, and in many registers. . . . The objects of American Black public culture are not invested with magical black properties: the alterity of America here, like the Africa of *Roots,* confers imaginary value on the objects that circulate. Thus there is neither American nor African-Amerocentricity here. The commodities transport both nationality and racial signs: yet their value for a black diaspora is the possibility of a public sphere articulated around the circulation and possession of Black things.

The Black public sphere is thus not always a resistance aesthetic which defies modernity and finds comfort in the politics of identity and difference. To think the Black public sphere we have to be willing to rethink the relationship between markets and freedom, commodity and identity, property and pleasure. . . .

Resistance politics as usual shuns crossing over and selling out, which is why rhetorics of Black freedom have traditionally used languages of inclusive feeling—dignity, fairness—to describe a desired relation to the law and material life. To reach for audiences from the space of Black cultural production, as the Hip Hop generation, for example, has done, is to risk the violent commoditization of everyday capitalism. But in many emerging sites of pleasure, struggle and discourse, the Black public sphere wants to sell everything as long as it is paid in full.[2]

This is a vision of the black public sphere as hyped and accelerated bourgeois public sphere, as a form of publicity structured by what Karl Marx would call "bourgeois production in its most general and most embryonic form," wherein "the product takes the form of a commodity, or is produced directly for exchange."[3] Here, bourgeois exchange relations are conflated with a kind of postidentitarian ethos that is, I would argue, itself only the image of what would emerge, by way of resistance, as what C. L. R. James—more precisely than, because in excess of, Marx—envisions as the interinanimation of free association and universality, communism "(sexually) cut"[4] and, thereby, augmented by the work of the improvising ensemble. I want to try both to imagine and to describe the nature of this resistance, to understand how it enacts an iconic prefiguring and refiguring of communism even as it emerges from already existing productive modes. This is in order to argue that, on the one hand, the fetish character of the commodity (the mysticism it carries and emits) is not antithetical to resistance but is a fundamental aspect of its condition of possibility, and that, on the other hand, resistance is directed toward new organizations of production that are themselves the condition of possibility of stripping off the commodity's "mystical veil." The vision of the black public sphere articulated above requires the maintenance of that mystical veil, even as it purports to have uncovered its fundamentally nonmystical origins and operations. Again, such an uncovering comes only after the fact of resistance to already existing modes of production.

But resistance is surely neither that disavowal of the commodity that Diawara et al. rightly but too strenuously reject nor that seemingly ubiquitous "resistance" that we are led to believe turns out to have been always and everywhere embedded in production and in products, though certainly one must be attuned to the traces of a deeper though never fully activated resistance that animates already existing cultural production. I desire an understanding of how both conventional definitions and revisionary critiques of resistance, precisely at the nonconvergence of psychoanalytic and black proletarianizing discourses, are divided and abounded by a broken, resonant sound that holds within it the trace of a public sphere that is defined precisely by its originary position over the edge or in excess of conventional understandings of identity, interpretation, property, commodification, ethics, audition, aesthetics, politics, *freedom*. Again, the Black Public Sphere Collective is right to point out the necessity of a rethinking of the relationships between and among these by way of a critique of simplistically pathologizing discourses, especially when those discourses appear to be linked to idealistic moralizing condemnations of the production and exchange of commodities as such. But this rethinking requires not an abandonment of resistance and conversion but their revolutionary renaissance,[5] one that would understand that the secret the fetishized commodity still holds is that freedom which emerges not from a surrender to the alienated reduction of cultural work, cultural circulation, and human relation but from the radically excessive, sounding reach toward new, utopian, total representation as exemplified in the deep extremities of scream and boom. Such rethinking then holds the possibility of a formulation of the black public sphere as something other than either the replication of or incursion into the bourgeois public sphere. This is to say that such rethinking must exceed that hybridization of bourgeois exchange relations and postnationalist— postidentitarian—hybridity itself that structures the contemporary critical romance with transnationalism.

1

The bridge and the one are often conspicuous by their abundant presence in the work of the Godfather. They mark and structure sounds for a public sphere, for what is excluded along with or as absented sound and sounds for what is excluded in sound's valorization. But this bridge + one, this abundant rather than oscillational suspension, walks away or collapses. Or one is always a step or leap away from them. They evade or are invaded or are, as in another formulation of rhythm—that of Charles Mingus—encircled and avoided, danced around, ring(ed)—(shouted, scream[ed]/boom-edged). And something not adequately referred to by or in the constellation sexual cut/sexual difference/women/Woman animates—in a way not adequately theorized—this public sphere. This has to do with sight and sound, with sight and sound in a (black) (proletarian [and perhaps even its subversion and cut reconstruction by the lumpen) revolutionary public sphere, one embedded in culture but not culturalist and of another logic than that of the severe instrumentality that often marks the critique of resistance and/or revolution; similarly and oppositely, no unaffiliated, no unorganized, no unaestheticized resistance, though affiliation and organization and aestheticization are radically reformulated by this resistance, Lady's behind or waiting on a beat without center resistance, Ornette Mingus structure without center, one that is not a one, circle with a hole in the middle resistance, Aunt Hester's resistance: what I mean is, is, is, this: that and and and and how's that sound. Also: and most important, on the order of what Félix Guattari calls "grafts of transference"[6] yet to have been realized, on the order of the self-analysis of a black proletarian trace whose improvisation is what the public sphere woulda been, before all that, we gotta think through what is seductive in the signifier; which is what I meant, on the one hand, when I said don't look at me with that tone of voice as well as what I meant, on the other hand, when I was painting all of what that scream meant, hol' it right there, tol' you, boogie-woogie rumble, (rendezvous of) victory, as in "new coefficients of freedom,"[7] breaking, broken, augmented, augmentative rhythm and tone, novel abilities—emerging from disabilities—of representation, audiovisual publicity before the frame carved out by these four walls—black, bourgeois, proletarian, lumpen—publicity irruptive of the merely audiovisual's scope and hold. These new coefficients of freedom are shaped by slavery, by its conditions of life and labor, by certain transferential modes of the production of value, by new formulations of totality, all of which are somewhere before such notions of resistance as this:

> *Real* resistance, it is argued, is (a) organized, systematic, and cooperative, (b) principled or selfless, (c) has revolutionary consequences, and/or (d) embodies ideas or intentions that negate the basis of domination itself. Token, incidental, or epiphenomenal activities, by contrast, are (a) unorganized, unsystematic, and individual, (b) opportunistic and self-indulgent, (c) have no revolutionary consequences, and/or (d) imply, in their intention or meaning, an accommodation

with the system of domination. These distinctions are important for any analysis that has as its objective the attempt to delineate the various forms of resistance and to show how they are related to one another and to the form of domination in which they occur. My quarrel is with the contention that the latter forms are ultimately trivial or inconsequential, while only the former can be said to constitute real resistance. This position, in my view, fundamentally misconstrues the very basis of the economic and political struggle conducted daily by subordinate classes—not only slaves, but peasants and workers as well—in repressive settings. It is based on an ironic combination of both Leninist and bourgeois assumptions of what constitutes political action.[8]

Here, James C. Scott tries to show how what Samuel Beckett calls the spirit of system determines notions of political resistance that too easily exclude the often submerged, figurative, nonimmediate responses to domination employed by the dominated. Insofar as Scott allows an interpretative framework that fosters the recognition of everyday forms of subaltern political activity, his critique is valuable. Nevertheless, and in addition to *valorizing unorganized resistance in spite of its necessary ineffectiveness in the radical* transformation of power relations, his revision of the theory or definition of resistance is never not disconnected from a certain manifestation of authoritarian personality, *from* that personality's locus in the *tense,* transferential, *aspectual* suspension between the strong and the weak. In this sense, resistance and the theory or definition of resistance might be seen, in an Adornoesque fashion, as the impossible rationalization of a refusal or inability to resolve or *rupture* contradiction, a biphasic acceptance of its determinations and indeterminations. *The field being spoken here is that of the unhappy consciousness, theorized in cultural studies of race (and/or class, gender, sex, and sexuality) as tragic, the inescapability of its internal conflict virtually raising race to the ontological status it always strives for but can never have: thus the proliferation and valorization of critical modes that are arrested by ambivalence, that are embedded in and seek to advance and otherwise honor something in which they cannot now believe—a cultural-political tradition driven by the desire for a freedom at once improvisational and universalizing); thus the occultist faith in a certain deformation of the human—admittedly prompted by the long history of deformation to which they respond—rather than in the possibility of a nonexclusionary improvisation of the human. You might think this as the interruption of the dialectic as already figured, hiddenly, in Hegel. The rickety, rackety bridges that "cover" the interruptive chasm, that defer the irruption of what's in the dialectic's internal fissures (namely, ensemble, the ensemble, e.g., the James Brown Band) have a whole bunch of forms, any of which might have been called resistance, each of which is more properly known as the interminable labor of the negative.*

Yet, we can also show—by way of the transference, its interruption and what it interrupts: the interconnections of resistance and the end of neurosis; resistance and music—which is to say another organization, an anarchization of organization; resistance and conversion—which is to say revolution, which is to say repetition (with a difference and more + one), which is to say improvisation. And we can show the traces of a resistance whose implications include the re-formation of the public sphere as the ensemble wherein the oppositions of performative and interpretative, practical and theoretical, culturalist and conversionist, individual and collective, as well as the oppositional framework on which rests the theories of political resistance that Scott critiques and advocates, are situated. This showing becomes a possible thing, something lying before us, when looking at the autobiographical, self-analytic *Narrative of the Life of Frederick Douglass, an American Slave.* Allow and excuse a long recitation of the recording of this primal scene, its transferential resistance before and down:

> I have often been awakened at the dawn of day by the most heart-rending shrieks of an own aunt of mine, whom he used to tie up to a joist, and whip upon her naked back till she was literally covered with blood. No words, no tears, no prayers, from his gory victim, seemed to move his iron heart from its bloody purpose. The louder she screamed, the harder he whipped; and where the blood ran fastest, there he whipped longest. He would whip her to make her scream, and whip her to make her hush; and not until overcome by fatigue, would he cease to swing the blood-clotted cowskin. I remember the first time I ever witnessed this horrible exhibition. I was quite a child, but I well remember it. I never shall forget it whilst I remember anything. It was the first of a long series of such outrages, of which I was doomed to be a witness and a participant. It struck me with awful force. It was the blood-stained gate, the entrance to the hell of slavery, through which I was about to pass. It was a most terrible spectacle. I wish I could commit to paper the feelings with which I beheld it.
>
> . . . Aunt Hester had not only disobeyed his orders in going out, but had been found in company with Lloyd's Ned; which circumstance, I found, from what he said while whipping her, was the chief offense. Had he been a man of pure morals himself, he might have been thought interested in protecting the innocence of my aunt; but those who knew him will not suspect him of any such virtue. Before he commenced whipping Aunt Hester, he took her into the kitchen, and stripped her from neck to waist, leaving her neck, shoulders, and back,

entirely naked. He then told her to cross her hands, calling her at the same time a d—d b—h. After crossing her hands, he tied them with strong rope, and led her to a stool under a large hook in the joist, put in for the purpose. He made her get upon the stool, and tied her hands to the hook. She now stood fair for his infernal purpose. Her arms were stretched up at their full length, so that she stood upon the ends of her toes. He then said to her, "Now, you d—d b—h, I'll learn you how to disobey my orders!" and after rolling up his sleeves, he commenced to lay on the heavy cowskin, and soon the warm, red blood (amid heart-rending shrieks from her, and horrid oaths from him) came dripping to the floor. I was so terrified and horror-stricken at the sight, that I hid myself in a closet, and dared not venture out till long after the bloody transaction was over. I expected it would be my turn next. It was all new to me. I had never seen anything like it before.[9]

The slaves selected to go to the Great House Farm, for the monthly allowance for themselves and their fellow slaves, were peculiarly enthusiastic. While on their way, they would make the dense old woods, for miles around, reverberate with their wild songs, revealing at once the highest joy and the deepest sadness. They would compose and sing as they went along, consulting neither time nor tune. The thought that came up, came out—if not in the word, in the sound;—and as frequently in the one as in the other. They would sometimes sing the most pathetic sentiment in the most rapturous tone, and the most rapturous sentiment in the most pathetic tone. Into all of their songs they would manage to weave something of the Great House Farm. Especially would they do this, when leaving home. They would sing most exultingly the following words:—

"I am going away to the Great House Farm!
Oh, yea! O, yea! O!"

This they would sing, as a chorus, to words which to many would seem unmeaning jargon, but which, nevertheless, were full of meaning to themselves. I have sometimes thought that the mere hearing of those songs would do more to impress some minds with the horrible character of slavery, than the reading of whole volumes of philosophy on the subject could do.

I did not, when a slave, understand the deep meaning of those rude and incoherent songs. I was myself within the circle; so that I neither saw nor heard as those without might see and hear. They told a tale of woe which was then altogether beyond my feeble comprehension; they were tones loud, long, and deep; they breathed the prayer and complaint of souls boiling over with the bitterest anguish. Every tone was a testimony against slavery, and a prayer to God for deliverance from chains. The hearing of those wild notes always depressed my spirit, and filled me with ineffable sadness. I have frequently found myself in tears while hearing them. The mere recurrence to those songs, even now, afflicts me; and while I am writing these lines, an expression of feeling has already found its way down my cheek. To those songs I trace my first glimmering conception of the dehumanizing character of slavery. I can never get rid of that conception. Those songs still follow me, to deepen my hatred of slavery, and quicken my sympathy for my brethren in bonds. If any one wishes to be impressed with the soul-killing effects of slavery, let him go to Colonel Lloyd's plantation, and, on allowance-day, place himself in the deep pine woods, and there let him in silence analyze the sounds that shall pass through the chambers of his soul,—and if he is not thus impressed, it will only be because "there is no flesh in his obdurate heart."[10]

There has been much extended meditation on Douglass's narration and description of the savage beating of "an own aunt of mine," Hester, by his master (his owner who is also, perhaps, his father); this beating is "the blood-stained gate" through which Douglass entered into slavery, into the knowledge of slavery and of himself as a slave and into the knowledge of knowing what such scenes give and hide; it is also, by way of Aunt Hester's "heart-rending shrieks" which come in response to the violence of the master's cutting blows (BOOM! the sound that means something in excess of meaning, something Duke Ellington meant and didn't mean when he said "A Drum Is a Woman," meaning of and in excess of the double identifications that exist at the convergence of race, sex, and ownership, where "It's a Man's World") and "horrid oaths," the opening to a rich and powerful counterdiscursive tradition in black musico-critical and -theoretical discourse in which a certain interpretative/performative circle or, better yet, sphere, is imagined and disallowed, invoked, and critiqued. This showing, given in a looking that is only operative or generative when it is cut and augmented by a sound and sounding and sounded listening, becomes possible when you begin to think what and how a psychoanalytic frame *should* let you show but quickly or slowly come to notice a warp, an offset, a nonmeeting, an asymptote across which there is no bridge, where the bridge is cut or walks away. Aunt Hester, intermittent presence of the Mother who is not Douglass's mother, one of a chain of substitution(s), won't stay. Douglass's father, whose identity is suspected but never established, is coded as a sort of nonmysterious but persistently invasive absence; but his mother, in her appearances and disappearances and reappearances, fades in and out, simulates, modulates, remains, in a way the father doesn't, as the radical absence of a *problem*. The origin is displaced, evades, or is evaded. The (im)possibility of the natal occasion is established, then, but, in the tradition Douglass founds, the tradition he (re)sounds, this displacement is augmented, abounded by a *before,* a future always implicated in that redistanced origin. That future is freedom. The free sounding of Aunt Hester that shows up in the Music and that is also always discourse about the Music, James Brown, scream, and boom.

Please note: the fact that the frame does not quite fit does not allow some simple opposition of an apolitical psychoanalytic discourse and an essentially politicized black literary-musical discourse. Rather, these discourses are before one another, each enabling the other by way of a disabling and irreducible incommensurability not unlike and correspondent to that which separates and interinanimates idealist and materialist discourses on desire. The discourse on desire that is sounded in Douglass, funking up the transfer between its others, is articulated in the sounded discourse on sound/music; both are given in Hester's scream. This incommensurability is not the function of some originary and irreducible difference but is, rather, the locus of the ensemble that this discursive field implies and manifests; this incommensurability, this appositional difference or "dynamic universality" (as Anthony Braxton has termed it)[11] means that the *in-between* is not given here as such; that the bridge is not a bridge and more + one (that's not a one and more); that resistance is not resistance and more, that hybridity, and hybridity's assumed connection to resistance, is impossible and exceeded. If the process through which hybridity is articulated is inoperative here, and if this is not some impossible Afro-Euro-American encounter, then in this asymptote lies both a danger and a saving power precisely in that the illusion of hybridity is disallowed and, along with it, the presupposition of the originary difference of the two categories and the originary absence of the whole. The asymptote holds the hope of another descent, a hyperbolic before, a universality without reserve.

Aunt Hester's beating is a primal scene for Douglass and for the tradition of black literary discourse on music that his text "founds" in that it both literalizes and intensifies the metaphoricity of the psychoanalytic understanding of the primal scene (as an act of coitus between the father and mother that the child understands "as an aggression by the father in a sadomasochistic relationship"; as that which "gives rise to sexual excitation in the child while at the same time providing a basis for castration anxiety" and as that which is interpreted, "within the framework of an infantile sexual theory, as anal coitus").[12] All this is bound up with a double and doubling/splitting identification, with both the father and the mother, both of whom exist at the level of uncertainty, absence, or substitution. Aunt Hester's resistance to the master, sounded in her scream, is also doubled here: think of the transference embedded in Douglass's reading of the music and in subsequent readings—from W. E. B. Du Bois to Jean Toomer to Margaret Walker to Toni Morrison—of the music in the tradition he founds; these readings can be thought of as resistant, too, to the extent that we think resistance as that which "in the words and actions of the analysand . . . obstructs his gaining access to his unconscious."[13] This primal scene is an originary rupture or trauma, one that is determined/elaborated as identification and in interpretation. It is repressed and repaired, but at the cost of a failure to hear the echo of Hester in the slave song. Nevertheless, that echo reverberates and returns, as the repressed is wont to do. It does not return at the level of an abreactive crying, that expression of feeling which, among other things, places Douglass firmly in the tradition of sentimentality to which the slave narrative ambivalently adheres given the demand that the genre reveal the slave as both man of feeling and man of reason. No, it comes back another way as neither interpretation, nor reading, nor writing, but sounding, improvisation, what Cecil Taylor calls self-analysis.

The question of self-analysis is an important one. Freud, at first, advocates self-analysis, saying, in effect, it's fine for the ones who aren't too weird, too far gone, who are capable of entering a discourse and answering its imperatives. Later, he distances himself from self-analysis in the interest of precisely that space that an other/analyst provides. That distance is crucial because it marks the intersubjectivity that allows for that enabling/disabling resistance, the therapeutically indispensable transference. The fact that psychoanalysis, founded in part on Freud's own self-analysis, has, at its heart or conception, the lack or absence of the motive force of transference is interesting. Is psychoanalysis fatally flawed given that its birth comes about precisely in and through that self-analysis—an analytic mode that incurs a deficit of resistance by way of a broken line and an infinite curve but that might sound good, point expands to boom or hole and boom and hole—which is finally understood as a fundamental manifestation of the resistance to psychoanalysis? How do we deal with this strange interinanimation of resistance and enablement, interruption and possibility? Note that Douglass's self-analysis—which is correspondent to a certain self-analysis in the music and in the interpretative problem the music poses and in the (more than black, bourgeois, lumpen, proletarian) public sphere that is formed precisely by the border that problem marks—constitutes a form of resistance to external, objective, or scientific interpretative frameworks—in this case, psychoanalysis. Nevertheless, there is a transference going on. More later.

For now I'm thinking about slave narrative as analysis, self-analysis, repetition with a difference scream + one. This means I have to think about resistance in Douglass. And of course we can now see more clearly the double nature of resistance—political and prepsychoanalytic—in the narrative. Something resists—echoes or resounds Hester's sounded resistance. Something resists the reader-father-aggressor-master-analyst. It is precisely that unheard, unworded sound of Hester's shriek that, though it is repressed, though Douglass resists it, returns in his narrative. It returns *in his description* as what he would describe in the slave songs, returns as the echo of these songs and what they echo. What is the nature of that echo in Douglass? It is that which is a little off, that which operates as something before and more than the repetition with a difference and more boom. It corresponds to neither time nor tune, this unnotated sound(ing), this self-analytic improvisation. A demand is placed on Douglass by the reader and all that the reader doubles in transference, in his attempt to pierce, enter, play, violate the circle. But there's a new analytic before that demand, another "bone-deep listening"[14] that allows one to hear the thought that unworded sound carries, thereby tapping what is motivated and nonarbitrary about the signifier's relation to the signified (or, more radically, breaking down the psyche's adherence to the signifier's law), thereby tapping into that gap that happily separates voice and speech (in "our" language). Even Aunt Hester's words, her notes, were bent; even the sound of the "H," hard aspiration/plantation peculiarity, remains in place when, in revision, Hester becomes Esther and shriek (not muted but mut[at]ing) turns to meaningful plea.[15]

He repeatedly tells the reader that he'll never forget that scene of which he was a witness and in which he was a participant. But he does forget something. And what he forgets is repeated. He forgets his own ambivalence, and it is repeated. He forgets his sounding of Aunt Hester's scream, and it is repeated. Here, we've got to work out the relation between transference, interpretation, and their (im)possibility in self-analysis. What I'm trying to say is that the embedded reperepetition, resonance, echo of Aunt Hester's scream in Douglass's writing is the ultimate mark of the tradition he "founds." Where is this repetitionam+osb? What repressed material is repeated in the experience of his narration, his self-analysis (more on this in a bit)? I've just intimated that Douglass's narrative is an example of self-analysis; what I'd rather say, hopefully more precisely, is that there is a strange and unbridgeable and generative distance between analysis and self-analysis in Douglass that needs to be sounded and that is improvised. Who is the analyst for Douglass, the subject who is supposed to know, the one to whom this talking book is addressed in the interest of the abolition of the speaker/writer? (This is important because the presence of the analyst/abolitionist [and please note that I depend especially in the brief time and short space allotted, on your own elaborations of the asymmetries you must be aware of] will be what allows us to talk about the phenomena of resistance and/as transference in self-analysis, Dear Reader.) Dear Reader.

Constantly figured into the text, s/he's the one who sits at the location of a displacement, a transference, that is played out in the second passage. That figurative reader, like the image of an analyst constructed from some strange coupling of introjection and projection, takes on the ambivalent feelings and identifications of Douglass for and with Captain Anthony, the master, the father, the (failed) moral educator/immoral aggressor in Douglass's primal scene. The reader is the one who is presumed to be outside the circle, the one whose distance is supposed to allow a certain analytic objectivity, the one who exhibits mastery, the one who makes demands, the one who demands or evokes precisely that sound that he will not hear. Douglass identifies with that position; but his identification is a double one, one that prompts and is a function of an ego-splitting ambivalence that plays itself out both in the primal scene and in and as its repetitionnnnnnnn. Indeed, this double identification is precisely that which is acted out in Douglass's own interpretation and in his ambivalence toward interpretation, an ambivalence marked by the description of a jargon meaningful only to the singers, as if the sounds they made were augmented by the arcane critical theory of an exclusive interpretative community, one whose interpretation is embedded in its performance; as if on the way to the Great House Farm a public sphere is being formed that Douglass's divided and abundant description— its contextualization within a more classically determined and constructed public sphere, an audience engaged with the inscriptions of and on his body, bound within the heliocentric economy of a publicity formed by ocular exclusions and protocols of Dear Reading—divides and abounds.

So that Aunt Hester's sound is resisted. So that Aunt Hester's sound is resistant. Interpretation is resisted. Interpretation is resistant (bound up with the identification with the master that, paradoxically, allows Douglass to forget and resist Aunt Hester's resistant sound, the sound that resists interpretation and resists slavery: the sound that resists mastery). We arrive, then, at the interpretation of resistance and the resistance to interpretation and would move on after what's embedded in the acted-out rrrrepetition of a reductive or incomplete verbal or scriptural recollection wherein occurs a transference so powerful that the analyst fades into another, deeper analysis. And, at the same time that the ripetition of repressive recollection and interpretation takes place, there is also more of that which is disremembered and misinterpreted, a rep that is a resonance or echo, a sounding through of what otherwise blocks sound. That which blocks the sound—the taking on of certain whack conventions of misinterpretation and nonhearing that the master initiates—is something that could be both an intellectual and an affective ambivalence and is overwhelmed by the resonant endurance, the int-irruption, of that sound even in the words that would have silenced it. This happens in Douglass and it happens in the tradition he founds. It is the inoperative silencing of the racial/sexual other, in the scream boom that animates and marks the musical and musico-critical organization of the universally dynamic public sphere.[16] And, a century later, the Godfather also leaves the analyst babbling in the ambivalent echo of that scream and boom. His description falters (saturated by a transference neither controls, each psychotic to the other, each on the other side of the other's limit, each, nevertheless, intelligently felt by the other in extracommunicative refrain, sounded listening, descent) until he's taken out the way resistant Aunt Hester took Douglass out to the site of that public sphere that is still emerging, dark to itself, at the long and ongoingly exploded meeting place of slavery, as a specific regime of property, and pleasure.

2

The Black Public Sphere Collective prompts some interesting questions: What about "the possibility of a black public sphere articulated around the circulation and possession of Black things,"[17] an articulation that means that rather than being defined by resistance (either to modernity or to modernity's retrogressive contradictions, e.g., American slavery and its legacies), "the Black public sphere puts engagement, competition and exchange in the place of resistance and uses performativity to capture audiences, Black and White, for things fashioned through Black experience[?]"[18] *What about this opposition of a performative, culturalist consumptionism to a non- or even presecular asceticism that is driven by a politico-religious devotion to a resistance of diminishing returns if not infinitely deferred gratification?* Here, one hears an appeal to a depoliticization of the public sphere, to a notion of black public sphere that would be shaped not by a broader definition of resistance—one articulated along lines generated by Scott, one that would seek to undermine the interpretative framework that devalued unorganized, individual, unsystematic forms of resistance as either trivial or as not really resistance at all— but by a submergence of the very idea of resistance. What about the idea of a black public sphere that "can be studied from inside and from outside"[19] as if it had not always already offered the most devastating improvisations of this particular inside and outside and of insides and outsides in general? What does it mean to formulate an idea of the black public sphere that rests on the opposition of resistance and aesthetics, resistance and institution building, but nevertheless is imagined in relation to some notion of "the good life" and to some notion of a struggle—not only, though vaguely not only, with futurity and tradition—to come into existence? What, finally, and in light of the discussion of all that is held in and erupts from Aunt Hester's scream and the master's boom and Douglass's scream and boom toward the Godfather's screamBOOM, about the notions that: "sexuality becomes a medium in which Black struggles to define the good life for Black people are displayed and played out"; that "the effects of this in the dominant political public sphere are to turn Black life into spectacles of violence and exaggerated sexualized performance"; that "resistance politics as usual shuns crossing over and selling out, which is why rhetorics of Black freedom have traditionally used languages of inclusive feeling—dignity, fairness—to describe a desired relation to the law and material life"; but that "in many emerging sites of pleasure, struggle and discourse, the Black public sphere wants to sell everything as long as it is paid in full"?[20] Does this understanding of the play of desire—political, economic, and sexual—in the black public sphere allow for a description of that sphere which, in the end, is prescriptive as well in that it outlines a trajectory that moves from an understanding of resistance, beyond "fairness" (if not freedom) and "dignity," to that consumptive ethics, aesthetics, and politics that would emerge in a field that is, on the one hand "not . . . neo-conservative . . . , for such a discourse sees Black culture as a pathology," but is, on the other hand, not bound up in a discourse of conversion, revolution, resistance and is somewhere on the explicitly capitalist other side of that field wherein arguments currently rage—or, more precisely, fizzle—between those who would advocate socialism and those who, for pragmatic reasons, now call for radical democracy? Because all these positions hold the danger of a refusal to see "Black culture as an *asset*,"[21] why not celebrate an emergent hip-hop bourgeois black public sphere that is defined and to be more definitively articulated and shaped, by an intense, hyperlibidinal, supersecular, culturalist free-market ideology?

I've tried to point to some reasons why the premises that underlie the prophetic description of this emergent black public sphere are, at the very least, problematic. In the Godfather's work, getting paid, the victory that reward signifies, is not just some anticonversionist valorization of the already existing forms and protocols of publicity, not even just some entrance into "the American-style world of consumer identity with such an intensity of self-pleasure that White people feel compelled to worry about the cultural effects of capitalism."[22] Although what such publicity bears is definitely good to him (good enough that he wants to kiss himself) and although white people might very well be scared, the Godfather constantly signals that such enjoyment holds for, moves toward, represents by way of both negation and anticipation an utterly worldly, utterly material, but utterly new publicity, a site of free association against which the so-called liberty of the already existing market seems merely gross effigy and simulacrum, merely the image of the image of Aunt Hester's desire, the desire that must still animate the already existing black public sphere and the black public sphere of the future, both of which are audible—screamingBOOMING andmore+onnnnnne—in the music of the Godfather. But in excess of any last word, you should let him take you out too, out and way out, as Amiri Baraka would say, toward something essential, an ongoing performance/audition, a transferential explosion, the before of the communist ensemble, where performance and interpretation never mix and always collide, where the tightness of the band and the pants reveal the radicality of getting paid in full, where we begin the resistant, improvisational, self-analytic, organizational work that will allow us—the black, lumpen, proletarian, universal public sphere—to kiss the good life hello.

Notes

1. Cecil Taylor, "Sound Structure of Subculture becoming Major Breath/Naked Fire Gesture: Liner Notes for *Unit Structures*" (New York: Blue Note CDP 7 84237 2, 1987).

2. Arjun Appadurai, Lauren Berlant, Carol A. Breckenridge, and Manthia Diawara, "Editorial Comment: On Thinking the Black Public Sphere," *Public Culture* 15 (1994): xi.

3. Karl Marx, *Capital,* vol. 1, trans. Samuel Moore and Edward Aveling, (New York: International Publishers, 1967), 86.

4. I am thinking here of the formulation of the "sexual cut," in Nathaniel Mackey's *Bedouin Hornbook* (Lexington: Callaloo Fiction Series/University of Kentucky Press, 1986), 34. There it is described as "the feeling I've [N, the fictional author of the letters that comprise *Bedouin Hornbook*] gotten from the characteristic, almost clucking beat one hears in reggae, where the syncopation comes down like a blade, a 'broken' claim to connection. . . . The image I get is one of a rickety bridge (sometimes a rickety boat) arching finer than a hair to touch down on the sands at, say, Abidjan. . . . Some such flight (an insistent *previousness* evading each and every natal occasion) comes close to what I mean by 'cut'." Listening to Mackey, as indispensable as listening to the Godfather, you can start to imagine a field of such "'broken' claim[s] to connection," a whole animated by breaks, such that it works and moves as the structure of both bondage and freedom, tragic history and comic future.

5. This as percussionist Khalil El'Zabar would have it. I am thinking here of his Ritual Trio's *Renaissance of the Resistance* (Chicago: Delmark DE-466, 1994).

6. Félix Guattari, *Chaosmosis* (Bloomington: Indiana University Press, 1995), 7.

7. Ibid., 13.

8. James C. Scott, *Weapons of the Weak* (New Haven: Yale University Press, 1985), 292.

9. Frederick Douglass, *Narrative of the Life of Frederick Douglass, an American Slave*, ed. Houston A. Baker Jr. (London: Penguin Books, 1986), 51–52.

10. Ibid., 57–58.

11. Anthony Braxton and John Corbett, "Liner Notes" for Anthony Braxton, *Anthony Braxton Quartet (Victoriaville) 1992* (Victoriaville, Quebec: Les Éditions Victoriaville, Socan, 1993).

12. Jean Laplanche and Jean-Bertrand Pontalis, *The Language of Psycho-Analysis*, trans. Donald Nicholson-Smith (New York: Norton, 1973), 335.

13. Ibid., 394.

14. Nathaniel Mackey, unpublished excerpt from *From a Broken Bottle Traces of Perfume Still Emanate*, vol. 3.

15. I am here indebted to Stephanie Smith's "Heart Attacks: Frederick Douglass's Strategic Sentimentality," *Criticism* 34:2 (spring 1992): 193–216. I have a different take, however, on the recontextualizations and the changes that Douglass plays on "Aunt Hester." A detailed analysis of those changes, of the changes played on what I have called Douglass's primal scene and on its participants, is required but will have to be done elsewhere. See Frederick Douglass, *My Bondage and My Freedom*, ed. Philip S. Foner (New York: Dover Publications, 1969), 85–88, and Frederick Douglass, *Life and Times of Frederick Douglass* (New York: Collier, 1962), 47–49.

16. It is a silencing that Douglass enacts later in the text by way of an appeal to the fetish as mystical and mysterious ground of his own more conventionally enacted resistance to the slave breaker Edward Covey. The fetish, here, is exchanged between men, between a fellow slave, Sandy Jenkins, and himself, and would seem to exist wholly within the metaphysical economy of an alternatively suppressed and risen (male) spirit activated and deactivated by the tactile/visual object in which such spirit is held, out of which such spirit emerges. What I have desired to show is that another, sounded resistance already animates the object, that that resistance is already there as the object's secret, that the mystical veil that hides that secret must be stripped away in order to instantiate the material enactment of that secret, but that that material enactment, though held within the object, within the commodity, and therefore tied to the already existing relations of production out of which the commodity emerges, lies before us in other, freer modes of organization that we can only imagine by way of resistance, whose image we can only hear now when hearing is not enough. The animation of the object/fetish by a woman's resistant scream, its derivation of its character from that scream, and its being exchanged between men is a double operation whose parts have been described most notably by Kaja Silverman (in *The Acoustic Mirror: The Female Voice in Psychoanalysis and Cinema* [Bloomington: Indiana University Press, 1988]) and Eve Kosofsky Sedgwick (in *Between Men: English Literature and Male Homosocial Desire* [New York: Columbia University Press, 1985]). What remains, and what this essay can only weakly preface and call for is a much fuller understanding of how utopian resistance actually emerges from the connection and disconnection of acoustical mirroring and male homosociality.

17. Appadurai, Berlant, Breckenridge, and Diawara, "Editorial Comment," xii.

18. Ibid., xii.

19. Ibid., xiii.

20. Ibid.

21. Ibid.

22. Ibid.

Conclusion. Pushing through the Surface: Notes on Hybridity and Writing

Jennifer Natalya Fink

Past Presents

(do these images haunt?—
there is a child here
who does not exist
below the neck
she smiles softly at me
while looking over her shoulder
at the vivisector
and his tray of sterile instruments
her face rests against the glass

this is the one
I will return to life
so I imagine her face
about to surface
in a shallow rock pool
on a Bunnarong coastline—
only we know this)

—*Tony Birch, "The Anatomy Contraption"*

In the space carved out by Tony Birch's poem, the shadowy image of a human figure emerges. Placed dead center on the page, this spectral body—perhaps the body of the impossible, never-born child of whom the poem speaks—surfaces through the intervals between the inky words and the blank spaces of his text.

247

However postmodern, fragmented, urban, and transnational our lives may be, many of us are haunted by the murdered, transplanted, colonized, silenced, illiterate, illegible faces of our ancestors. The writers in this collection push these faces to the surface. They sketch in her eyes. Speak through her lips. Fill in the blanks gouged out by colonialist histories with smells, shawls, half-told stories, unwritten memories.

Whether using the language of theoretical exposition, as in Toby Miller's "Culture and the Global Economy," or employing the forms of English Romantic poetry, as in Meena Alexander's "Three Poems on the Poverty of History," each contributor rewrites familiar tropes, modes, and discourses, using colonialism's patterns and structures to write what lies beyond their scope. Fragments of voices, genres, and languages lost to "official" history push through the surface of these elegant poems, scholarly arguments, well-wrought essays. The incomplete past winds its way through the taught narratives of the present, erupting through the artificially seamless surface of Anglo-European discourse.

This is not a simplistic reclamation of a reified "native" past, but rather the inscription of the indescribable, the reconstruction of the erased. Nor are these invented histories any less accurate or factual than those found in "official" neo/post/colonial histories. The difference lies in the use to which these writers put various forms of discourse. The inventedness of all histories is foregrounded here, while at the same time, the real, lived effects of narration are underscored.

New questions emerge from this engagement with narratives of history and origin. Are there other lives than those already written? Can our own lives be recast, our presence reimagined through a new narration of the past? How can language serve as a conduit, a means of inventing our pasts to remake the present? What forms might such writings take?

> The past that we make, presumes us as pure invention might—
> our being here compels it: an eye cries out for an eye
> a throat for a throat, we muse on Rimbaud's lips caked with soil,
> his Parisian whites stiffening: Quick! are there other lives?
>
> —*Meena Alexander, "Translated Lives"*

The pasts remembered here are deeply personal and idiosyncratic. Yet, they also speak to the yearning for affiliation with a collective history beyond individual formations. These are highly politicized stories, infused with questions of cultural citizenship, national and postnational identity, bloodshed, longing, and genocide that have been allowed only to ghost the borders and margins of the *grand récit* of official histories. The problem of form, of how best to utilize the colonizing terms of language so as to describe and enact decolonization, is not a new one. In the pieces presented in this collection, however, some new strategies, new possibilities, emerge for writing hybridity.

Writing Hybridity: "As So Often, the Truth Does Not Lie in Between"

Many contemporary writers have argued that language, writing, and representation must be reoccupied in order to, as Ngugi Wa' Thiongo so succinctly states, "decolonize the mind."[1] Hybridity has been an extremely useful concept in this process. Theories of hybridity have offered a means to speak of the hyphenated, transiting, migrating nature of identity in postcolonial culture.[2] Hybridity resists the colonizing notion of singular identity, demonstrating that stories of original, "native," prelapsarian cultures are produced by the conquerors to dehumanize the conquered.

Yet, a yearning remains for the lost languages, colors, fabrics, textures of our individual and collective ancestors. Written out of history, misrepresented as prehistorical exotics or as downtrodden, faceless entities, the writers, artists, poets, and scholars in this collection redefine their own subjectivities through summoning to presence the tissues of otherwise forgotten lives.

The problem of writing lies at the heart of the problem of narrativizing and embodying hybridity. As Shani Mootoo suggests in the legend superimposed over her poster image, "It is a crime that I should have to use your language to tell you how I feel that you have taken mine from me." Rather than produce an anthology containing a dozen new theories of hybridity, we have instead attempted to present diverse performances of the *situation* of hybridity. This collection emerges from and responds to new hybrid states, particularly in relation to transnational, post–Cold War, and urban formations of statehood. What the writings in this collection demonstrate is that the in-between, interstitial position of hybridity garners its power through rearticulating and inventing particularized narratives of origin, place, displacement, arrival, culture, transit, identity. How are we to invent such narratives when the narrative tools at our disposal are always already the tools of colonization?

Although the interstitial, multiple condition of hybridity is often valorized by cultural theorists, this collection demonstrates how the situation of hybridity is often one that is compelled rather than chosen.[3] Each contributor moves beyond generalized formulations of the question of hybridity, instead teasing out the buried, obscured histories from which hybridity emerges. In the process of hybridization, cultural histories, origins, and fictions are too often erased and homogenized, the force of their specificity abstracted into new nationalistic formations. Hybridity can become simply another tool to dissolve difference, celebrate homogeneity, erase history. The task, then, may be not to celebrate hybridity as such, but rather to tease out the precise contours, lost languages, buried histories from which hybridity emerges. Or, as Ella Shohat argues in her essay on the destruction by Zionist nationalism of the Arabic cultural affiliations of Sephardic Jews, the most generative, hybrid act might be to reclaim and remember and invent specific cultural histories, rather than simply celebrate a hybrid, inchoate identity shorn of all but a nationalist rendering of its history. Or, as C. L. R. James wryly suggests, "The truth does *not* lie in between."[4] The hybrid truth of cultural experience may lie not in a comfortable middle ground between two cultural experiences, but in the irreconcilable distance between.

The writings in this collection insist on the traumatic unbridgeability of the gap between our present discourses and the longed-for, imagined past, and refuse to suture together the disquieting echos of the invented past against the equally invented present. Rather than creating new genres or styles that might seem to reflect a hybrid aesthetic, the contributors instead use familiar, recognizable forms such as the theoretical essay, poem, photo essay, and case study. Languages and practices that are literally illegible when rendered in these colonizing forms erupt through the surface of the text, and are often left untranslated. These uncommodified and unprocessed signs of histories, cultures, and identities create a break in the discursive flow, and refuse to be easily digested or homogenized into an easy, cozy "multicultural-ism." The fault lines between the present, colonized conditions of language and the desire for another language, prior and future to our own, is staged within a single piece of writing through the use of multiple, often discor-dant, forms.

Like the never-born child pushing to the surface in Tony Birch's poem, the collision of colonial forms with what these same modes of discourse have traditionally excluded exposes rather than covers over the contradictory sto-ries, longings, histories, and memories from which our postcolonial identi-ties may be rewoven. In juxtaposing rather than blending forms, a future-present is anticipated, invented, animated. The truth, once again, does not lie in the middle.

Colonization is too easily sanitized and rehabilitated by metadiscourses such as hybridity. To celebrate uncritically the condition of hybridity can re-sult in the promotion of what Fiona Foley aptly terms a "nouveau coloniza-tion" in her essay "A Blast from the Past." This use of hybridity may produce a recolonizing multiculturalism that homogenizes the complexity of cultural identities and erases the (already violently erased) historical specificity of narratives of origin. Instead, the essays in this collection consider the general question of hybridity through specific, historicized praxes that refuse to forget the dismembering of cultural autonomy wrought by colonization.

Precisely because we are all (differently and unevenly) embedded in postcolonial, postnational, post fill-in-the-blank cultural formations, we must necessarily reach back into the lost, fractured, silenced, mute past to seize the narrative terms by which we are constituted. The logic of writing at work here depends on a revaluing of this calling out to an often unknowable past. Threads of historical memory are danced with, invented, rewoven through contemporary forms of identity. This is not a reversion to a prelapsarian nativism; nor is it a simple acceptance of postmodern fragmentation, in which history, identity, and culture are all positioned in a state of monolithic ending.

Only by daring to revoice and invent the past can we hope to write a new future-present in which the terms of our longing and belonging will be opened up, rather than foreclosed. We rattle the buried bones, speak in long-dead tongues, press the unborn face to the surface, a half smile resting there.

The Poetics of Memory

The question of history reverberates throughout the writing in this collection. How can we write what has been erased? How do we invent the past anew? How do we dare wrap ourselves in those cultural memories always already only known through the lens of colonial history? Dare we do otherwise?

> If I were to do the white thing and pilgrimage there
> would my cousins, I wonder, gladly see Naan in me?
> and I, Naan in them?
> Do I dare wear a Topi?
>
> —*Shani Mootoo,* For Naan
> who made the incredible journey from Nepal to
> Trinidad to be a bride, and never,
> in all her years there, spoke a word of English.

"Do I dare wear a Topi?" wonders Shani Mootoo, echoing and rewriting T. S. Eliot's Prufrock and his peaches. Each essay, poem, image, and argument in this collection offers a similar dare to the reader, inciting her to refashion the terms by which identity is made and understood. Dare to wear the past so that the present might be redressed, written anew. Wrap yourself in past identities that never existed in the colonizing languages of the English, the French, the Spanish, yet now can only be spoken through their nouns, and their names. Write in as many genres as you know; invent ones you have lost.

Those of us who have repeatedly been posited as the barbaric Other to logocentric discourse cannot simply "write the body," as the French feminists of the 1970s suggested. The bodies we currently inhabit have already been inscribed as primitive, prehistoric, languageless. Instead of writing a pure, unsullied precolonial body, the authors in this collection each seize the colonized terms of discourse to refocus and refuse its distorting lens, infusing familiar structures of art and argument with a continual questioning of their unspoken, unknown, vanished stories and histories. They push against historical erasure, nativism, neocolonial multiculturalism, silence. And push again.

Notes

I would like to thank May Joseph, Fred Moten, Jon Keith Brunelle, and Theresa Senft for their thoughtful readings of this essay.

1. See Ngugi Wa' Thiongo's influential *Decolonising the Mind: The Politics of Language in African Literature* (London: James Curry, 1986).

2. By "theories of hybridity," I mean the work of Homi K. Bhabha, Robert Stam, Néstor García Canclini, Ella Shohat, Bruno Latour, Paul Gilroy, Gloria Anzaldúa, and numerous others.

3. Ella Shohat makes a similar point in "Notes on the Post-Colonial," *Social Text* 31–32 (winter 1992).

4. C. L. R James, *The Black Jacobins: Toussaint L'Ouverture and the San Domingo Revolution* (New York: Vintage Books, 1989), x. James speculates on the question of whether collective forces or exceptional individuals shape revolutions. "As so often," he incisively suggests, "the truth does not lie in between. Great men make history, but only such history as it is possible for them to make" (x). To paraphrase in the context of hybridity, individual cultural experience is hybridized, but only such hybridity is produced as is possible to be made. I thank Fred Moten for bringing this quote to my attention, and for our many animated conversations regarding the limits of hybridity theory for postcolonial writing.

Contributors

Meena Alexander is professor of English and women's studies at the Graduate Center, City University of New York. Her work has been widely anthologized and translated into several languages, including Malayalam, Arabic, German, and Italian. She is the author most recently of *The Shock of Arrival: Reflections on Postcolonial Experience,* the volume of poems *River and Bridge,* and the novel *Manhattan Music.*

Awam Amkpa is assistant professor of theater arts and film studies at Mount Holyoke College. He is the author of the forthcoming books *Homes and Border Crossings: Cinemas of the Black Atlantic* and *Overpowered but Not Tamed: Theatre and Textualities of Colonial and Postcolonial Cultures.* He is the writer and director of the following films: *Winds against Our Souls* (1993), a documentary on citizenship and subjectivity issues for blacks in England; *The Other Day We All Went to the Movies* (1997), a documentary on cinema audiences in West Africa; and *It's All about Downtown* (1998), a documentary on a community animation project by Wole Soyinka in Kingston, Jamaica.

Tony Birch has published both poetry and "nonfiction" dealing with the issues of identity, place, and history. He is centrally concerned with the loss of memory that pervades the national history project in Australia.

Barbara Browning is associate professor of performance studies at New York University. She is the author of *Samba: Resistance in Motion* and *Infectious Rhythm: Metaphors of Contagion and the Spread of African Culture.*

Manthia Diawara, professor of comparative literature and film, is the director of the Africana studies program and the Institute of Afro-American Affairs at New York University. He is the author of *In Search of Africa,* the director of *Rouch in Reverse,* and editor-in-chief of *Black Resistance.*

Jennifer Natalya Fink teaches drama at New York University and is visiting assistant professor in the Department of Art and Design Education at the Pratt Institute. She is the author of a collection of short stories, *13 Fugues,* and a novel, *The Mikveh Queen.* She is currently completing a study on the uses of sound in postcolonial poetry.

Fiona Foley is from the Wondunna clan of the Badtjala Nation. She was recently given a fellowship from the Australia Council to carry out research into Badtjala archival material. Foley resides at Hervey Bay in Queensland.

Sikivu Hutchinson is a doctoral candidate in performance studies at New York University. Her dissertation focuses on race and the decline of public transportation in Los Angeles.

May Joseph teaches performance studies at New York University. She is the author of *Nomadic Identities: The Performance of Citizenship* (Minnesota, 1999).

Deborah A. Kapchan is the director of the Center for Intercultural Studies in Folklore and Ethnomusicology and assistant professor of anthropology at the University of Texas at Austin. The essay in this book is expanded in the author's work *Gender on the Market: Moroccan Women and the Revoicing of Tradition.*

Toby Miller is associate professor of cinema studies at New York University. His books include *Technologies of Truth: Cultural Citizenship and the Popular Media* (Minnesota, 1998), *The Well-Tempered Self, Contemporary Australian Television, The Avengers,* and *Popular Culture and Everyday Life.* He is editor of the *Journal of Sport and Social Issues* and coeditor of *Social Text.*

Shani Mootoo is a videomaker and visual artist whose work has been exhibited internationally in group and solo shows. Besides writing poetry, she is the author of a collection of short stories, *Out on Main Street,* and a novel, *Cereus Blooms at Night.* Born in Ireland, brought up in Trinidad, she now divides her time between Vancouver, British Columbia, and Brooklyn, New York.

Fred Moten is assistant professor of performance studies at New York University. He has published articles and poetry in a variety of journals and anthologies.

José Esteban Muñoz teaches performance studies at New York University. He is the author of *Disidentifications: Queers of Color and the Performance of*

Politics (Minnesota, 1999), and his articles have appeared in the journals *Screen, Women & Performance, GLQ, TDR,* and *Social Text* as well as in anthologies. He is the coeditor of *Pop Out: Queer Warhol* and *Everynight Life: Culture and Dance in Latin/o America* and also of a special issue of the journal *Women and Performance* titled "Queer Acts."

Chon A. Noriega is associate professor in the UCLA Department of Film and Television. He is editor of *Urban Exile: The Collected Writings of Harry Gamboa Jr.* (Minnesota, 1998), *Chicanos and Film: Representation and Resistance* (Minnesota, 1992), and coeditor of *The Ethnic Eye: Latino Media Arts* (Minnesota, 1996). He is also curator and author of *From the West: Chicano Narrative Photography.*

Celeste Olalquiaga writes about popular culture. She is the author of *The Artificial Kingdom* and *Megalopolis: Contemporary Cultural Sensibilities* (Minnesota, 1992). She has won Rockefeller and Guggenheim awards.

Ella Shohat is professor of cultural studies and women's studies at the City University of New York. She is the author of *Israeli Cinema: East/West and the Politics of Representation* and the coauthor (with Robert Stam) of *Unthinking Eurocentrism: Multiculturalism and the Media,* which won the Katherine Kovacs Singer book award in 1994. Her work has appeared in numerous edited books and film, feminist, postcolonial, and cultural studies journals. She is the coeditor of *Dangerous Liaisons: Gender, Nation, and Postcolonial Perspectives* (Minnesota, 1997) and the editor of *Talking Visions: Multicultural Feminism in a Transnational Age,* a volume of essays and visuals.

Robert Stam is professor of cinema studies at New York University and acting director of the Center for the Study of Culture, Media, and History. He is the coauthor (with Ella Shohat) of *Unthinking Eurocentrism: Multiculturalism and the Media* and (with Randal Johnson) of *Brazilian Cinema.* His other books include *Subversive Pleasures, Reflexivity in Film and Literature, Bakhtin,* and *New Vocabularies in Film Semiotics* (with Bob Burgoyne and Sandy Flitterman-Lewis). He has won Guggenheim, Rockefeller, and Fulbright awards, and has taught and lived in Tunisia and Brazil. His most recent book is *Tropical Multiculturalism: A Comparative History of Race in Brazilian Cinema and Culture.*

Permissions

"Transplanted Lives," by Meena Alexander, was originally published in *The World* 50 (spring 1997). All poems copyright Meena Alexander, 1997.

"The Daughters of Gandhi: Africanness, Indianness, and Brazilianness in the Bahian Carnival," by Barbara Browning, is a fusion of sections of two chapters from her book *Samba: Resistance in Motion* (Bloomington: Indiana University Press, 1995).

"The Autoethnographic Performance: Reading Richard Fung's Queer Hybridity," by José Esteban Muñoz, was previously published in *Screen* 36, no. 2 (1995): 83–99; reprinted by permission of Oxford University Press.

Parts of "Taboo Memories and Diasporic Visions: Columbus, Palestine, and Arab-Jews," by Ella Shohat, appeared in preliminary form in *Middle East Report* 178 (September–October 1992) and *Third Text* 21 (winter 1992–93). An earlier version was included in *Cultural Identity and the Gravity of History: On the Work of Edward Said,* edited by Keith Ansell-Pearson, Benita Parry, and Judith Squires (New York: Lawrence and Wishart, 1997).

"From Pastiche to Macaroni," by Celeste Olalquiaga, was published in *Hybrid Cultures,* Exit Art Gallery, New York City, 1992.

"Afro-Kitsch," by Manthia Diawara, was published in *Black Popular Culture;* reprinted by permission of the author and Bay Press.

An earlier version of "Barricades of Ideas," by Chon A. Noriega, appeared in the exhibition catalog *Revelaciones/Revelations: Hispanic Art of Evanescence* (Ithaca, N.Y.: Hispanic American Studies Program, Cornell University, 1993).

A significantly different version of "Hybrid Genres, Performed Subjectivities: The Revoicing of Public Oratory in the Moroccan Marketplace," by Deborah A. Kapchan, appeared in her book *Gender on the Market: Moroccan Women and the Revoicing of Tradition* (Philadelphia: University of Pennsylvania Press, 1996).